I HEARD THE TURKKI CALL MY NAME

(with apologies to Margaret Craven)

BY MIKE TURKKI

◆ FriesenPress

One Printers Way
Altona, MB R0G 0B0
Canada

www.friesenpress.com

ISBN
978-1-03-916910-4 (Hardcover)
978-1-03-916909-8 (Paperback)
978-1-03-916911-1 (eBook)

1. BIOGRAPHY & AUTOBIOGRAPHY, PERSONAL MEMOIRS

Distributed to the trade by The Ingram Book Company

*To the boys of Ootsa Lake, for their friendship,
and my wife, for her unwavering support.*

These stories are true for the most part, but names and personal details have been changed to protect the innocent.

Table of Contents

Acknowledgments

Every writer owes a debt to the people who helped him tell his story.

I Heard the Turkki Call My Name would not have been possible without the support of my wife, Sashka, who provided the book's title and read it so many times that she can recite sections from memory. I also wish to thank beta readers Tenille Woskett, Carolyn Hainstock, Lynn Synotte, and Maria Sandberg—as well as eagle-eyed proofreader Sharon Marr—for helping make a mediocre tale somewhat better. They can take credit for the best parts of this book and deny responsibility for the worst ones.

Any errors that appear herein are mine.

British Columbia's
LAKES
DISTRICT

Palling

Decker Lake

Burns Lake

Tchesinkut Lake

Francois Lake

Colleymount

Clemretta

Francois Lake

Noralee

Tatalrose

Southbank

Danskin

Grassy Plains

Wistaria

Takysie Lake

Streatham

Ootsa Lake (Nechako Reservoir)

Ootsa Lake

Cheslatta

**Tweedsmuir
Provincial Park**

Marilla

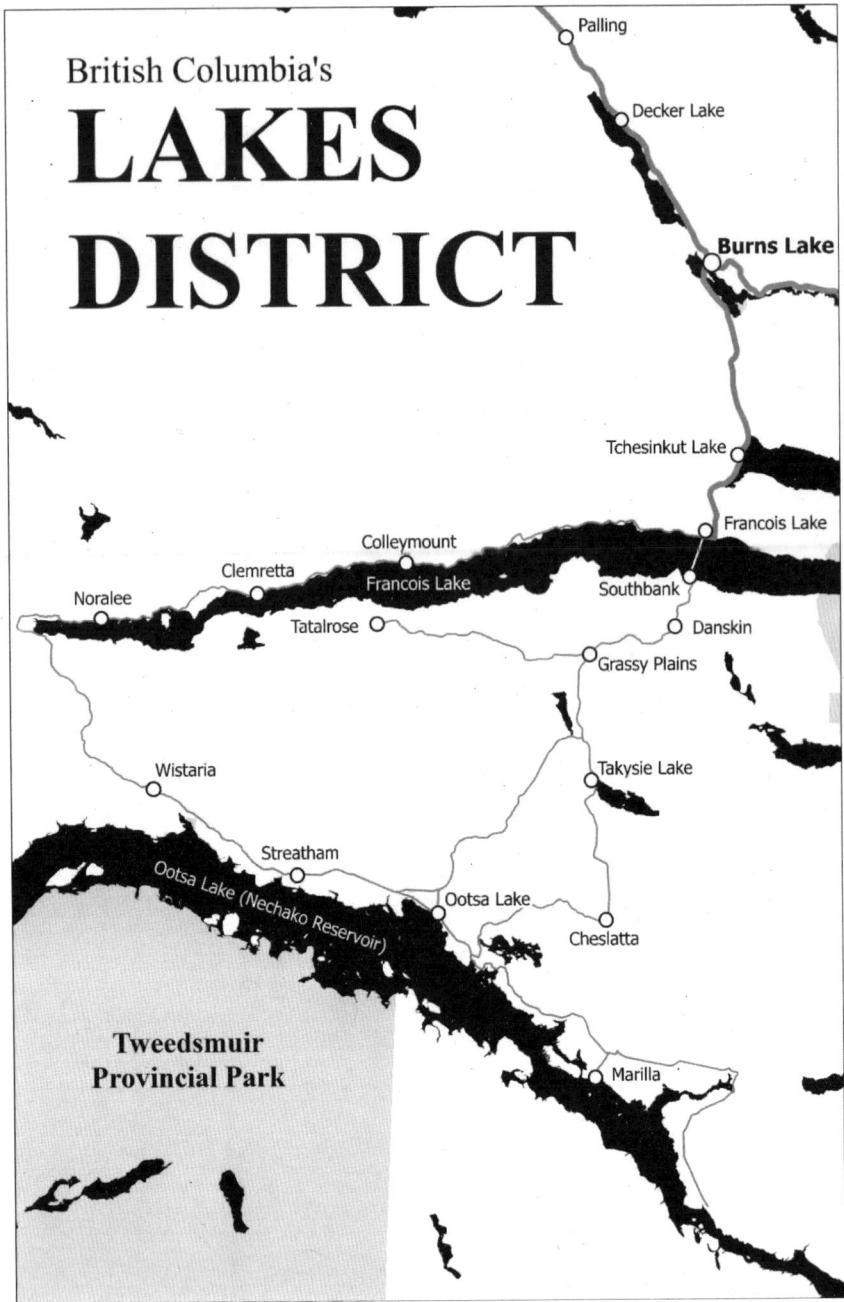

Map courtesy of Rowan Nagel, Regional District of Bulkley-Nechako.

Forward

Where the hell is Wistaria?

For the uninitiated, there is a region in the geographic centre of the province known as the Lakes District, in the middle of which is one of British Columbia's largest natural bodies of freshwater, Francois Lake. North of the lake is Yellowhead Highway 16 and the teeming metropolis of Burns Lake (population 1,659 at the time of writing this book); south lies a scattering of unincorporated hamlets with quirky names.

Wistaria is one of the most southerly communities in the Lakes District south of Francois Lake. Of course, the place is also north of something, but that something is mostly nothing, so most residents don't mention it. In BC, where the Lower Mainland is synonymous with culture and learning, people who live above the fiftieth parallel will do anything to say they live south of a known point.

Think of it as the geographic equivalent of a slapstick comedy.

Today, Francois Lake can be crossed by public ferry in twenty minutes, but in the early 1900s it was a formidable obstacle. Pioneers intending to homestead along the shores of Ootsa Lake either rode in from Bella Coola or walked east from Hazelton. Both routes were arduous, and their degree of difficulty dictated that trips to the outside world be made only when necessary.

The isolation moulded the people who moved there and changed the way they viewed life. Men and women who carved farms from the wilderness became self-sufficient out of necessity. They built their homes, cleared their fields, grew their food. A few courageous souls delivered their own babies. They learned to take difficulties in stride and accept the harsh realities of life far from the maddening crowd.

The hardship faced by these early settlers instilled in them a certain toughness, yet it did not make them cruel or insensitive. (Okay, there were exceptions.) Residents of Wistaria and other tiny communities along the north shore of Ootsa Lake shared the same lifestyle and goals, and because of it developed a rare kinship. Though they did not always get along—indeed, disputes were common—they learned to work together and shoulder each other's burdens. A homesteader in need of help always got it because his neighbours knew his misfortunes could easily be theirs. Samaritanism was everyone's insurance policy against disaster.

During the 1920s, highway improvements and the arrival of the first automobile made increased travel between Wistaria and nearby communities like Grassy Plains and Southbank possible. Yet this did not destroy the homesteaders' sense of community, only expanded it. Those who grew up along Ootsa Lake met others like themselves from neighbouring locales. They married, stayed in the area, and formed new family units and alliances. After several decades, they began to view themselves not just as residents of Ootsa Lake, Uncha, or Takysie but as members of a tribe distinct from those living north of Francois Lake.

They became Southsiders.

In 1952, the Aluminum Company of Canada flooded Ootsa and six other lakes to create the Nechako Reservoir. Eurocan Pulp & Paper, a Finnish company, established a modern logging operation in the area, and another wave of colonizers poured in. Yet through all these changes, the identity Southsiders shared remained intact, as did their sense of belonging.

Both were still strong when my family moved there in 1972.

THE BEGINNING PART

Moving Again

No matter how much you have read about Ootsa Lake, you are never quite prepared for it. Words cannot do it justice.

Driving south along Keefe's Landing Road from Grassy Plains, you catch tantalizing glimpses of dark blue water through jack pine forests, but it is not until your vehicle emerges from the timber atop Ootsa Hill that you get your first good look at the lake Alcan made.

Today, the lake the Indigenous people called "Ootsabunket" bears little resemblance to the modest body of water it was before Canada's largest aluminum producer dumped three million cubic metres of earth into the Grand Canyon of the Nechako. More than two hundred kilometres long and up to six kilometres wide, Alcan's miscreation is so large that ocean-going tugs and container ships loaded with brightly coloured boxes would not seem out of place. Only God and the company's pointy heads know how many litres of fresh water it holds. It snakes its way between the hills like a lazy serpent, head in the Coast Range, tail in the Interior Plateau, and the low-lying islands that dot its length like emerald scales are the tops of what were rocky bluffs in the halcyon days before the flood. Time and weather are eating away at these monuments to nature's resilience, and it will not be long before the islands, like the homesteads now lying deep beneath the waves, are swallowed by the reservoir.

But these are the observations of an old man, not a boy of eleven. When I first saw Ootsa through the front window of our overloaded panel van, the sight of all that water barely registered. My thoughts were elsewhere.

I was looking for a school with a baseball diamond.

It was late afternoon on a cloudless day in early September. The leaves on the aspen trees that marched toward the lake like a phalanx of tall, thirsty men remained green, but the adjacent hayfields were a carpet of golden stubble. Autumn was near, and we were on the road again.

This was our eighth move in two years. Our lives changed irrevocably in July 1970 when my mother and stepfather packed my sister Kelly and me, along with some camping gear and a lot of wishful thinking, into an ancient Pontiac and drove north from Vancouver. Mom said she and Olavi were looking for "something more," but she could never precisely communicate what they sought. If it was fame and fortune, their wandering had been for naught. My parents were itinerant farmworkers, and, like the impoverished Joad family in Steinbeck's *The Grapes of Wrath,* we never stayed anywhere long enough to put down roots. When one job ended, another farther north beckoned. We packed up and moved on.

My parents' search for meaning took us to some of the most remote settlements in British Columbia's interior. One winter, we inhabited a cabin so far back in the sticks that our employer forgot he hired us. By the time he remembered and plowed four feet of snow from the access road, we had been eating moose meat and rice for a month. Fifty years later, even the smell of Chinese food makes me nauseous.

It was a marvelous adventure at first, yet even an agoraphobic pre-teen like me could take only so much isolation. When Olavi walked away from his most recent temporary appointment, I secretly hoped his next would be in a more populated area. Not a big city like the one we had left two years earlier, but something between wilderness and a modest village. In my mind, the ideal community would be large enough to support Little League baseball and small enough to ensure I made the all-star team.

Which is why, even when presented with a sight as magnificent as Ootsa Lake, I was intent on finding a school with a ball field.

I had spotted one a half-hour earlier—a large, flat-roofed building eight miles south of Francois Lake—and it had given me hope. At last, I thought, my journey to baseball immortality could begin. Today, Buttville or whatever this place was called, tomorrow the Montreal Expos. Or maybe the Yankees, even though Mantle was gone, and the team hadn't won a World Series since '62.

"Is that my school?" I asked Mom, pointing to a drab structure on my left as we rumbled through Grassy Plains.

I had about a square foot of space in the van's back seat between two cardboard boxes full of housewares. I couldn't see much from there, but judging from the mountainous country ahead of us, there wouldn't be enough kids farther down the road to support another school.

I was wrong.

"No," Mom replied. "There's another closer to where we'll be living."

Her response wasn't music to my oversized ears. Nevertheless, I kept searching for the other school and hoping it would be as large as the one we had just left in a cloud of dust.

A half-hour later, as we motored down a long hill toward the largest body of water any of us had seen since turning our backs on the Pacific Ocean, I saw the noble institution that was to be my alma mater.

My heart sank. It was a dinky little flat-roofed school no larger than the last one I had attended in Nazko, a First Nation community seventy miles west of Quesnel. The place had two rooms at most and was incapable of holding more than sixty inmates. Above the single row of windows along the building's faded east wall were the words "O tsa Lake Elementary School." The missing letter, which I later learned was another 'O,' was nowhere to be seen, having presumably been deemed unnecessary by a juvenile offender.

The schoolyard was equally bleak. It was almost indistinguishable from the surrounding cow pasture, about two acres in size and enclosed by a rickety pole fence that cried for a coat of whitewash. There was no sign of a playing field, and the only green grass grew over what proved to be the septic field. One-third of the area was overgrown with weeds; another had already been reclaimed by the forest and was a jungle of scraggly poplar trees. There was no soccer pitch, no cinder running track, no gymnasium, and—worst of all—no ball field.

Seriously bummed out, I looked away. Mom sensed my disappointment.

"What's the matter?" she asked.

"That school is junk," I said. "It doesn't even have a backstop."

"What do you mean?" said my bearded stepfather from his position behind the steering wheel. "There was one in the back corner, near the big trees."

"That was a swing set. All I saw was a lot of dead grass. Looked like somebody's hayfield."

"Well, I'm sure they play baseball," Mom said, shifting my youngest sister to her other arm. Laina, less than a year old, responded by gurgling and spitting up her lunch.

On the other side of the seat, Kelly, four years my junior, hummed to herself and looked out the window. She appeared unconcerned by this latest development, probably because making the big leagues wasn't important to her.

The rest of the trip was made in silence. We passed a dozen homes in fourteen miles, most of them log structures set in small clearings surrounded by evergreens. This wasn't baseball country. Too many jack pines and hardly a flat spot anywhere. I was not a happy camper.

After passing the smaller school and heading west for twenty-five minutes, we came to a junction. Olavi slowed the van and turned right.

"Almost there," he said as if we were on our way to a birthday party.

The dirt road, barely wide enough for one vehicle, rose steadily into the hills. Our destination, according to Mom, lay two miles up it on the shore of a small lake.

Three hundred and twenty acres of timber and a few unproductive hayfields, the Bar M Ranch was owned by Mickey O'Brian, a farmer, logger, and opportunist who came to the Lakes District in 1912. When copper hit fifty cents a pound, Mickey took the advice of a friend and staked claims on an island of porphyry in the middle of Babine Lake. The properties were later optioned by a big mining company, which made Mickey and his wife Jude a lot of money. They used some of it to buy land in Wistaria.

The ranch was Mickey's hobby and retirement home, but his wife, who never adjusted to the "good life," tried to run the operation as though their next meal depended on it. They were both getting old by the 1970s and needed someone to help around the place, so Jude suggested they hire a caretaker. Mickey agreed but left the task of finding a suitable employee to Jude. I doubt he cared who got the job; he just wanted to be left alone to write poetry and read Karl Marx. Despite his wealth, he was a rabid Communist who preached revolution, social equality, and power to the people while at the same time paying his employees less than minimum wage. He was a walking contradiction, but as we soon discovered, a likable one.

Jude was cut from a different cloth. She had to search far beyond Ootsa Lake to find a hireling because all the locals who had worked for her vowed never to do so again. She paid little and expected a lot. A mutual acquaintance suggested my stepfather would be perfect for the caretaker's job, and Jude, clearly desperate, hired him after nothing more than a fifteen-minute telephone conversation with my mother. The old girl promised Olavi $150 a month and a share of ranch profits if he would cut hay, mend fences, and be at her beck and call. With no other prospects on the horizon, he accepted the offer.

The sun was sliding behind a veil of mature timber on the western horizon when my stepfather coaxed our labouring automobile through the ranch's ostentatious gateway. After turning left and bouncing through a meadow, we pulled to a stop outside our new home, a two-storey trapper's cabin overlooking the lake.

The calescence of fifty summers had greyed and split its log walls, and the peaked roof above them was bowed from the weight of countless snowfalls. Inside, a heavy iron wood stove dominated a small kitchen, its blackened chimney exiting through a cobwebbed hole in the ceiling. Rough shelves and a handmade counter lined one wall, while the opposite was bare except for a sizeable single-pane window and several eight-inch spikes hammered into the adjacent wood as makeshift coat hangers. The floor, originally of rough lumber, was worn smooth around the door and stove, and pitted everywhere else. Beyond the kitchen was another room and a narrow stairway leading to an attic that would have made the Seven Dwarves anxious.

We could tell that people had occupied the building over the years, yet judging from the accumulated dust and litter, its only recent inhabitants had been rodents.

"Well," said my mother after looking around, "might as well start unpacking."

The cabin was old and tired, like an elderly washerwoman who had spent too much of her life scrubbing other people's dirty laundry. Still, it was a palace compared to the other hovels we had inhabited since leaving Vancouver. The setting was idyllic too. A mere forty feet west lay the lake and a water-logged dock, both welcome sights to a boy whose primary chore for two years had been hauling water in five-gallon buckets from distant creeks. To the north, a mountain thrust its brooding countenance above the surrounding hills. South of the cabin and its detached woodshed, a stream tumbled out of a deep ravine before disappearing with a gurgle into a tangle of willows.

Although the place had been settled long ago, its natural beauty was unsullied. The lake remained clear, the creek continued to follow its natural course, grass and fireweed grew unchecked between the deciduous trees. There was, of course, the cabin and the woodshed, yet even these manmade structures did not seem out of place.

It looked like the other places we had lived but felt different, like a comfortable pair of sneakers.

While life on the Bar M Ranch never quite lived up to our expectations, that first night in the cabin was special. Fifty years later, the memories of that time and place, and how the haunting call of a loon echoed across the water at sunset, are still fresh in my mind. I know I am richer for having experienced them.

First Day

A vehicle was coming. It was a long way off, a mile or more, but we could hear the growl of its engine in the early morning stillness.

It was Monday, and the previous night's frost still clung like icing sugar to weeds in the nearby ditch. An hour earlier, Olavi had put on his cleanest dirty shirt, fired up the panel van, and ferried Kelly and me to Ootsa-Nadina Road so we could catch the school bus. Though we had only been waiting for ten minutes, it felt like a lifetime.

Kelly and I approached our first day of school differently. She appeared unconcerned about it, and her attitude irked me because I was worried. What would life at "O tsa Lake school" be like? Would it be like the last rural school we attended? Nazko Valley Elementary had been a nightmare, and the last thing I wanted to do was spend another year running from a bunch of Indigenous kids whose favourite pastime was beating up skinny white boys with weird last names.

I prayed the bus would never come. Maybe the vehicle we heard approaching was just another logging truck headed for some distant mill with a load of emasculated pines. Perhaps we had arrived at the junction too late, and the bus had already come and gone.

Better still, maybe our destination had burned down over the weekend.

"There it is."

Kelly's words, punctuated by frantic arm-waving, broke through my reverie. Rounding a curve in the road five hundred feet west was the bus. A cloud of dust billowed out behind it, so thick it looked like a smokescreen.

I looked to Olavi for a last-minute reprieve, but he was already driving away. At that moment, I would have done just about anything to avoid the fate that awaited me.

Boarding a school bus for the first time in unfamiliar country is a unique experience. The discomfort felt by new commuters is extreme. Imagine walking a narrow beam above a tank full of alligators, then multiply the associated sense of unease fourfold. Would I go through it again? Not on your life. I'd rather walk the plank.

I knew what the morning had in store for us. Nevertheless, when the bus screeched to a stop in front of me, I took a deep breath, lowered my head, and marched across the road. Kelly was hot on my heels.

The dirty bus doors slapped open, and I started up the steps like a prisoner on his way to the gallows. All conversation ceased. Heads swivelled in our direction. Eyes sized us up from head to toe. No one spoke. No one moved. Everyone stared.

Our footsteps echoed inside the bus as we walked down its narrow aisle. *Find an empty seat,* a voice screamed inside my head. Like a maze-trapped rat, I looked around for a corner in which to hide. There were none. Every berth had a staring kid in it. I paused, considered turning back, then started forward again.

And tripped.

Someone snickered behind me. That did it, face stinging with embarrassment, I took the seat immediately to my left. It was already occupied by a hipster who looked about my age, but there was enough room beside him for me. To heck with my sister. It was every kid for himself.

The doors slammed shut, and the bus jerked into motion. As it began to negotiate the steep climb away from O'Brian Road, conversation in the seats around me returned to normal. It appeared the first act of this tragedy was over.

I took a chance and looked at the guy sitting next to me. He was thin and dressed in the standard uniform of the '70s: faded denim jacket, dark T-shirt, weathered blue jeans. He wore aviator glasses, and his brown hair hung in oily strings to a spot well below his ears. His budding acne problem told me my initial assessment had been wrong. He was probably closer to twenty than twelve.

He was giving me the Big Guy Stare, that look of disdain older boys reserve for younger ones. Though I saw no immediate threat in his dark eyes, he was not thrilled to be sharing his seat with an underling. It looked like he might tell me to get lost, but then he decided to ignore me the way one does a harmless insect. Turning his head, he looked out the window at the trees flashing past.

I did the same.

The bus made six stops in the fourteen miles between our road and Ootsa Lake school. At most of them, two or three kids—boys dressed in jeans and white shirts, girls in bright cotton dresses or slacks—stood at the end of tree-lined driveways. There was one exception. Two miles east of Wistaria Hall, a long-time resident and guide named Tim Blakely had turned his hayfield into a trailer park. In front of his log farmhouse, beside a row of large green mailboxes, a dozen youngsters ranging in age from six to sixteen waited to board the bus. They were, in general, better dressed than most of the area's children because at least one of their parents worked for Eurocan Pulp & Paper's Andrew Bay logging operation in West Wistaria. Like Kelly and I, they came from somewhere else.

After what seemed like ages, the bus pulled up to the little school. The bus driver, an old guy with hair growing out of his ears, opened the doors, and the area's youth poured forth like spring freshet. I watched Kelly and the younger kids make a beeline for the playground, their coattails trailing behind like superhero capes.

I remained seated long after the first wave of kids had disembarked. Clutching my *Bonanza* lunch box, I waited for the other passengers, most of whom were older than me, to get off. They did not and instead continued their conversations about hot girls and fast cars and weekend pit parties, arms resting nonchalantly on seat tops, backs pressed up against the bus windows, legs extended into the aisle. Their indifference surprised me, but I assumed that at Ootsa Lake, cool kids showed contempt for the education system by staying away from it until the last minute.

I, too, waited. A minute went by, then two, and finally five. My anxiety, already nearing the top of the reservoir, crept a few inches higher.

"Hey, kid, aren't you supposed to get off here?"

It was the guy next to me. Surprised that he had deigned speak to me, I turned toward him. He was regarding me over the edge of his glasses, a hint of amusement on his pimpled face.

"I . . . guess so," I said and bolted from the seat as if my pants were on fire.

Experienced commuters later revealed that children in grades seven through ten attended classes in Grassy Plains. Each morning, after disgorging its cargo of pre-teens at Ootsa Lake, the Wistaria bus waited for a load of elder statesmen from Marilla before continuing its journey north. I would have ended up twenty-five miles from my destination if not for Zit Boy.

A rousing game of floor hockey was already in progress when I walked through the doors of Ootsa school for the first time. Boys of all ages, and even a few girls, had set up makeshift goals at either end of the institution's solitary hallway and were firing plastic pucks at each other with no regard for anyone's safety. After depositing my stuff in the room with the largest desks, I watched the game. It was not baseball, but it looked like fun.

"Okay if I play?" I asked a small curly-haired boy trying to stop a barrage launched from the opposite end of the hall. He swore as another puck whizzed by his shoulder and hit the wooden bench behind him with a resounding *thwack*.

"For Christ's sake, Diggs, take it easy. You're going to bloody kill me," he said to a tall kid who had already raised his stick in jubilation. When the admonishment had no effect, he turned to me and asked, "What do you want?"

I repeated my request.

"Hell, yeah," he said as he dug the puck from behind him. "You can play goal."

By the time a chubby girl with short hair started ringing the school's brass handbell to announce the start of classes, I had allowed four goals. That would have guaranteed us a loss on most days, but the curly-haired kid I'd replaced had scored twice and set up two more, giving us a 4-4 tie. After a brief conference at centre hallway, the team captains announced the game would continue at recess.

I followed a snaking line of children into the classroom. There was an empty desk in the middle of the first row near the windows, so I sat in it. Previous occupants had carved their initials deep into its hardwood top, adding a few messages for the damned who followed in their footsteps. According to my predecessor, a forgotten soldier named Bill was a homosexual, one of his male classmates collected women's underwear, and someone called Mac loved a girl (at least I hoped it was a girl) named Nancy. Another rising star had taken the time to chisel a lengthy judgment on long-haired urban interlopers. The words "Cityslikker hippies should be shot" occupied a prominent location below the inkwell, right next to a crude drawing of somebody's middle finger.

This did not bode well for me. I was a child of the '60s and wore my hair long. Mom had sheared it off in Nazko after hearing that head lice had invaded the area and were marching unimpeded toward our house, but that had been two years earlier, and my mousy locks were now a reasonable length.

If having long hair was an offense punishable by death at Ootsa Lake, our teacher was living on borrowed time. A jocular young man in his early twenties, he came from the teacher factory equipped with shoulder-length black hair and a Burt Reynolds moustache. His name was Mr. Baxter, and he seemed okay for a grown-up.

He joked with the class before introducing me.

"We have a new student today," he said. "Mike . . . Tur . . . Truk . . . Is it Turkey?"

"Close enough," I muttered, having long since stopped trying to say it with the proper trill. According to my Finnish stepfather, it meant "great bear" in his native tongue, but I never wholeheartedly believed him. Years later, my skepticism proved well-founded when I discovered a Finnish-English dictionary in a box of his possessions. The little book contained a multicoloured map of Europe, and the Mediterranean nation with the same name as North America's favourite holiday meal was also spelled "Turkki." So much for nobility of title.

I held my breath after being introduced. In Nazko, my derisible last name had earned me a world of hurt. The students there had gobbled like excited fowl when my name was read aloud during morning roll call, and the teacher had been too afraid of their fierceness to say anything. The bullying climaxed around Thanksgiving when a horde of boys armed with pocketknives chased me around the snow-covered playground.

"Come, Turkey-gobble, we want to eat you for dinner," they yelled in broken English, raising their weapons like bad guys in a John Wayne movie.

Much to my relief, my introduction did not produce even a giggle at Ootsa Lake. There were the usual stares and smirks, but no one made fun of me. This place, I decided, might not be too bad after all.

Baxter read the Lord's Prayer in record time and then got down to business. He had three grades and two dozen children in total. A quartet of Grade Four students was seated along the west side of the classroom next to the blackboard. In the middle were the Grade Fives. Me and the other sixth graders, the school's seniors, were given the privilege of sitting next to the fly-specked windows that dominated the east wall. The view was unremarkable, consisting of Ootsa Lake Road, some hayfields, and a prominent lump of basalt known as Bennett's Mountain.

The morning passed without incident. At recess, the hockey game resumed. We lost in overtime when the big kid named Diggs launched a fifteen-footer that careened off a wall before zipping past me into the goal. He and his three teammates celebrated like they had just won the Stanley Cup.

I apologized when the curly-haired boy who had let me play came to retrieve the puck. He wasn't in our class, so I didn't know his name.

"Shit, that's okay," he said. "No one ever stops those ricochets. Besides, we'll tie the series at lunchtime. This was only game one."

His affability set me at ease. "Do you guys ever play baseball?"

The question surprised him. "Once in a while, but we haven't since Brendan slipped on a cow pie rounding third and buggered up his ankle. Most of the time, we play hockey. It's more fun."

"I'm a pretty good base—" The school's bellringer began doing her thing again, cutting short the description of my athletic prowess. The boy I had been talking to ran off.

Rural schools don't have many students, so learning everyone's name takes about sixty seconds on a bad day. By lunch, I had figured out who the major players were.

The giant who scored the game-winning goal at recess ran the place. Though a Grade Six student like me, Diggory "Diggs" Cullen was a year older than the rest of us, having refused to attend school during his first year of eligibility. A bony farm boy from Wistaria who towered above the other students, he had brown eyes, a nose like an axe blade, and short-cropped hair the colour of river mud. His most dominant feature was his abnormally large incisors, which made him look like a huge rodent from the Pleistocene.

Diggs, I was told, did not have a father and had never been farther from home than Prince George, which he visited for one remarkable day with his Uncle Jem several years before my arrival. Having spent his life at Ootsa Lake, he harboured a deep-seated prejudice against outsiders, anyone with longer hair than his own, and all things not sanctioned by the area's old-timers. He loved hockey, hated dancing, and would fight anyone who disagreed with him.

No one wielded as much influence at Ootsa Lake school as Diggs. There were, however, other dominant males.

Ralph, otherwise known as "Carrot Top," was the class clown. A red-haired sixth grader of average height who lived in Marilla, he had freckles, Clark Kent glasses, and a devilish grin. One of his arms was always broken. During my year at Ootsa school, I remember only a few weeks when he was not wearing a cast. He was a fair left-winger when his brittle bones permitted him to participate in hockey but a better football player. During the brief period when we used the flat ground atop the school's septic field as a gridiron, he established himself as Ootsa's premier running back. Though he lacked Diggory's size and strength, he proved adept at avoiding tacklers. He would take the snap from centre and then follow the downfield blocking of Mr. Baxter for a big gain almost every time. His promising gridiron career was cut short that fall by three events: the school board's decision to ban tackle football after too many Ootsa Lake kids went home with sports-related injuries; the arrival of ten inches of fresh snow two days before Halloween; and the breaking of his right arm during an impromptu gymnastics exhibition.

Ralph learned the technique of open field running by necessity. He was a tease and spent a lot of his time racing away from children he had tormented.

Carrot Top had a talent for finding the physical characteristic or behavioural trait each student was most sensitive about. Having identified this soft underbelly, he would attack it mercilessly until the subject of his teasing either broke down or beat him senseless.

During Ralph's years at Ootsa school, Diggs—who did not appreciate criticism—was his favourite target. The irrepressible redhead would harass his tall classmate to the point of insanity.

"Diggs ever tell you why his teeth stick out?" Ralph asked me one day as we were eating lunch.

"No, not really. I figured they just grew that way. His cousin's are pretty much the same."

"That's bullshit," Ralph said, shaking his head and taking another bite of cheese sandwich. "Diggs wasn't born with that set of buckers."

Even then, I had a sixth sense for good stories. This one sounded like a winner, so I leaned forward expectantly.

Ralph chewed and swallowed before launching into it. "One day, I was teasing Diggs. I kept bugging him and bugging him, and finally, he got so mad he tore his clothes off like the Hulk and started chasing me. I ran under the volleyball net but was smart enough to duck. Not Diggs. He just kept running along." Ralph mimicked the older boy's frantic running style, arms pumping, head thrown back, mouth open like the hood scoop on a muscle car. "Diggs got his front teeth caught in the net. Yanked them half out of his head, and he landed flat on his back. That's why they stick out so far. And the stupid bugger wouldn't go to the dentist either. He just pushed those two chompers back into place with his finger and kept on trucking."

I knew the true test of manhood. "Did he cry?"

Ralph snorted. "Diggs cry? You've got to be kidding."

Ralph's secondary target was another Grade Six student named Brendan. Every class has its Brendan, an awkward, chubby kid who, while pleasant enough, is neither brilliant nor athletically gifted. Brendan came from a poor family that raised goats on a few acres of scrubland near the lake. The eldest of seven children and, like Diggs, a year older than everyone else in the class, Brendan had a speech impediment.

Ralph never let him forget it.

"Good mowning, Bwendan," Ralph would say as soon as the big boy got on the Marilla bus. "How 'ow you today, Bwwwendan? What's wong? Is dat smewwy goat's cheese in yow wunch? Yow sandwiches smew wike yow feet, Bwwwendan? If yow want, yow can have my socks for wunch today, Bwwwendan . . ."

Brendan was a good-natured kid who could take a lot of teasing. Every person has his breaking point, though, and Brendan had reached his.

It happened at Ootsa Lake school. Ralph, who sat in front of Brendan, had been tormenting the bigger boy all day about his appearance, intelligence, family, pets, lack of a girlfriend. Nothing was off-limits. Yet, to the redhead's amazement, his victim had neither cried nor retaliated.

Ralph had never encountered stoicism, and it discouraged him. After three hours and no visible reaction from Brendan, Ootsa's designated bully swallowed his disappointment and tried to do some schoolwork.

It was the moment Brendan had been waiting for. Rising from his seat, he walked to the pencil sharpener and honed his yellow Crownline HB to a fine point. He then returned to his desk, leaned forward, and drove the writing stick into his tormentor's lowered head.

"He just stood up and sunk his pencil in me," Ralph recalled, rubbing his scalp self-consciously at the memory. "And when it stuck, he snapped it off and sat down again. The pencil lead's still in there. Go ahead, feel it."

Ralph made a point of sitting behind Brendan after that. He also curbed his baiting of the bigger boy.

Ralph, Brendan, Diggs, and I were the only male students in Grade Six. There were three in Grade Five.

Eli was the quiet leader of the classroom's middle kids. A wiry youth with sharp, hawkish features and curly hair the colour of dirty straw, he spoke softly but carried a big fist. Like Diggs, Eli held fast to archaic beliefs concerning the acceptable length of hair (short), proper dress (real men did not wear bell-bottoms), and music (anything faster than a waltz was long-hair jive). Dancing, in his learned opinion, was for pansies.

Eli hung out with Kent, a suave boy whose carefully barbered hair framed a round, freckled face. Kent was accepted as one of the kingpins, but not because he was a great hockey player or a good fighter. Instead, his prowess in another important sport earned him a lofty position in the school hierarchy.

Kent was Ootsa Lake's acknowledged expert on girls. Although we were all well-versed in the birds and bees, his nearly encyclopedic knowledge of the subject was a constant source of wonder. And he wasn't all talk and no action. He seemed to have better luck with the opposite sex than most of us. If you wanted advice on matters relating to girls and women (the latter being any female over the age of sixteen), you went to Kent, who could have put himself through university had he charged consulting fees.

Abner, the youngest son of the area's wealthiest rancher, seldom missed a hockey game and was always involved in our misadventures at Ootsa Lake. His big ears, small eyes, and huge grin earned him the nickname "Chimp" early in school, a moniker he abhorred. He tolerated a certain amount of taunting but never allowed anyone to make a monkey out of him.

Abner's easygoing nature enabled him to find a kernel of humour in every experience. One morning at Ootsa school, I spotted him talking to Diggs at the back of the classroom. Abner was wearing a large toque pulled down nearly to his anthropoidal eyes, and at the end of his discussion, he lifted it.

The older boy examined Abner's forehead and then let out a shriek of laughter.

Curious, I walked over to them. "What's up?"

Diggs was laughing too hard to answer, so Abner told the story.

"I was out in the barn last night checking my horse's hooves," he explained. "Well, she kicked me right between the eyes and knocked me colder than a cucumber. I still got a headache.

"The funny thing is," he continued, "when I got up and looked in the mirror this morning, this was the first thing I saw." Breaking out in a giggle, he again pulled up his toque.

Visible in the middle of his forehead was the red, swollen outline of a horseshoe.

It did not take long for word to get around. Abner's forehead drew a crowd.

"Lucky you ain't dead or in the hospital," said one of the younger students. "My uncle got kicked by a horse when he was young, and Mom says he's been queer ever since."

Abner laughed about the incident. We didn't give it much thought either because we knew our simian classmate had lost his marbles years earlier.

Grade Four, the last group of students in Baxter's class, had four kids in it but just one of note.

Sean Alcott was the only fourth grader who rated membership in the big boys' club. A blond kid with freckles, wire-rimmed glasses, and a haircut the Beatles would have appreciated in 1964, he lived with his parents and older siblings on a small ranch west of Wistaria. His family had moved to the Southside from California a few years earlier and, like me, he was still adjusting to life in the bush. We had other things in common. We both had stepfathers, wore flared jeans, and knew the Moody Blues were not a strange emotional disorder running rampant in the world beyond Ootsa Lake. He was, like me, always looking for a girlfriend. At that age, neither of us knew what to do with a girl if we caught one, but it was inconsequential. The fun, Sean once said, was in the chase.

Sean was clever and, despite his angelic appearance, a rogue. Much to my delight, he was always willing to participate in ventures that challenged the authority of school and community leaders. At Ootsa, he and I formed a bond of friendship that lasted well into high school.

There was one other boy at Ootsa who ran with the big dogs. Though only in Grade Three at the time, Nicky Williams, the little con artist who so generously allowed me to play goal that first morning, was an acknowledged leader. A grandson of one of the area's original settlers, Nicky came from a single-parent home. His sisters and older brothers lived elsewhere, and while he visited them often, he spent the lion's share of his time on the family ranch with his father.

Nicky, a dark, handsome boy whose good looks earned him a lot of female attention even before he entered high school, possessed knowledge and wisdom beyond his years. Street-smart in a rural sense, he grew up with minimal parental supervision, a wild kid from a broken home where alcohol flowed freely. We envied his freedom, and I suspect that sometimes he may have envied our family lives. My favourite photograph of him, which seemed to epitomize his childhood, was a tattered snapshot taken when he was about four. It showed him seated atop the family's kitchen counter, a small boy with a reckless grin and a stubby bottle of Old Style beer.

Nicky was a survivor, not a problem child. Polite and well-behaved, he had more common sense than the rest of us. The scuttlebutt at Ootsa school was that he knew even more about sex than Kent, yet it was a subject he never discussed in detail. He also possessed an inner toughness we all came to appreciate.

Nicky didn't take shit from anybody. A year after Diggs and I entered high school, when Ootsa Lake school was embroiled in a prolonged conflict between Principal Hull and a very odd teacher named Richards, my sister came home with a story that was a testament to Nicky's courage.

In a blatant attempt to win the support of local parents, Hull began buying comic books for his students. Richards, an old school Englishman, tried to confiscate the "horrid publications" for "educational reasons." He would have succeeded had he not made one critical error in judgment.

The first comic books he tried to expropriate belonged to Nicky.

When the boy refused to hand over his comics, Richards tried to take them by force. It was a grave mistake. Nicky would not allow anyone to violate his rights. Positioning himself atop a desk, he fearlessly challenged the teacher to a fistfight.

Richards blinked first. The kids kept their comics.

Nicky was the first person I met at Ootsa Lake, and, in many ways, he is the one I remember with the most fondness. But on that day in early September 1972 when the sun hung in an azure sky and Ootsa Lake mirrored the pitted face of Mount Wells, he and all the others—Diggs, Ralph, Eli, Abner, Kent, and Sean—were just a bunch of new kids in a strange school.

Little did I know, their fears, hopes, and dreams would become as familiar to me as my own in the years ahead.

The Game of Our Lives

Hockey.

The word was magical to the boys of Ootsa Lake, and any sentence in which it was employed became a wizard's incantation. Even when thought, it had potency, conjuring visions of a three-inch black puck bulging lily-white twine and a solitary curved stick raised like a Canadian version of the exclamation mark.

For my friends and me, hockey derived its power not only from the godlike figures who played the game but also from our aspirations, which during the 1970s were entwined with it. We all wanted to be heroes like Paul Henderson, that humble Leaf who was mobbed by his teammates and lifted on the shoulders of a grateful nation after winning the Summit Series in '72, and we thought of little else. Because of this, hockey was sacred. Anything else could be blasphemed but not Canada's national pastime because doing so would have discredited the game and, by extension, us. More than fifty years later, even a mention of it can resurrect the feeling of sharp skates digging into hard ice on a frosty winter morning and the sound of a hardwood blade connecting solidly with six ounces of vulcanized rubber.

Hockey was king at Ootsa Lake, and we were its paladins. During the warmer months, we played the sport with plastic sticks and mangy tennis balls supplied by the school to ensure we didn't find less acceptable ways to amuse ourselves, but it was a pale shadow of the winter game.

There is nothing like playing hockey the way it was meant to be played, outdoors on natural ice with cold air nibbling your cheeks in defiance of the sun's brightness. At least once a week during the winter months at Ootsa Lake school, we'd walk to Bennett's Landing and play all afternoon as a substitute for gym class. Sometimes we'd save time by donning our skates at school and zooming down the frozen roadway, heavily-taped Sher-woods and Victoriavilles stuck between our spindly legs like rudders as we tried to avoid lumps of gravel deposited by government plow trucks. Upon arriving at our destination, we'd clear a rectangle of ice with long-handled shovels and elbow grease, then take our first hesitant strides toward immortality.

That was when the magic happened. Suddenly, we weren't awkward kids skating on a wind-blown stretch of frozen lake hundreds of miles from the nearest National Hockey League arena but legends of the game playing on a virgin sheet of alabaster ice inside the Montreal Forum or Boston Garden. At that moment, we became the players whose names we heard spoken with such reverence on the radio. The tall farm boy parked in front of the opposition goal like a parka-clad monolith wasn't Diggory Cullen but scoring sensation Phil Esposito, and the small kid crouched between two discarded toques was netminder Gerry Cheevers, not a nobody from Wistaria named Sean Alcott.

Skills development was an alchemic process too. We learned to skate, stickhandle, and shoot despite having no coaches. I had never played ice hockey before we moved to Wistaria. Yet during a prolonged game of shinny three months after our arrival, my left skate stepped over my right of its own volition at high speed, and I discovered the crossover turn. No one taught me this bit of magic, it just *happened*, and I was briefly a young Guy Lafleur.

I'm sure everyone who has played the game outdoors in Canada remem bers with crystalline clarity a moment when it transcended life. For me, it happened on a pond behind Wistaria Community Church. I remember taking a perfect pass from Diggs and speeding down my off wing. Only Nicky stood between me and the opposition's goal, but he was determined to break up the play and slid across in front of me. Though he wasn't a big kid, our makeshift rink was so narrow that he took up most of the available real estate.

My window of opportunity closed. Willow branches were tugging at my coat sleeve, and it looked as though I had no play. I almost gave up and passed back to Diggs, but at the last moment, just before Nicky sent me flying, I pushed the puck under his sprawling form and leaped over him. The puck found my stick on the other side, and I swooped in on Sean, who was guarding the enemy net. One dip of a shoulder, a slight nod of the head, and even he was beaten. My backhander slid unimpeded across the goal line.

It was a thing of grace and beauty.

I still cannot explain how I made that play. I've tried it a dozen times since with better skates and smoother ice yet have never pulled it off with the same finesse. It was as if those great Canadiens of the past—Morenz, Malone, Béliveau, the Rocket—put all their talents at my disposal for a few seconds, making it possible for me to do things with stick and puck that were far beyond the mediocre athletic abilities of an ungainly thirteen-year-old.

In recent years, I've thought a lot about the games we played on the ponds of Wistaria. What I remember most is the wondrous feeling of freedom that came with stepping onto the ice. Though we played with intensity, none of us felt any pressure to perform because it wasn't so much the score that mattered as the game itself. There was no crowd to boo, no parents to disappoint, no angry teammates to face when you missed an open net. We played for the sheer joy of it, not because peer pressure dictated that we should or because someone had bought us a spot on the team, and it allowed us to experience the game to its fullest.

But we were children, and our immaturity prevented us from seeing that this was hockey at its best. We thought the game would be better if we played for a real team, so we made one.

The Grassy Plains Cougars Hockey Club was the product of our ambitions and my introduction to organized sports. It was a less than satisfying experience. Winning became more important than having fun, which was unfortunate because the team was abysmal and lasted little more than a season before merging with a rival squad from Colleymount.

I played for a while after that, but the game was never the same for me. The coach gave my spot on Diggory's line to a kid with better hands and bigger biceps, and I found myself playing with boys I didn't know. Despite the urgings of the others, I began showing up for fewer games.

Eventually, I stopped going at all.

After a successful weekend series with their new teammates, my friends would sometimes ask why I no longer played. When they did, I'd shrug and change the subject. How could I tell them that the magic was gone for me?

A few years ago, in a fit of nostalgia, I bought new equipment and joined Burns Lake's commercial hockey league. Though I scored some goals and played on a team that won more games than it lost, everything seemed too rigid, too controlled. Unable to recapture the joy I had felt as a boy skating and stickhandling on the ponds of Wistaria, I turned my back on hockey a second time.

Today, Sean, Diggs, and Nicky have rediscovered their love of the game playing in a gentlemen's league. They take to the ice on Sundays and keep imploring me to join them, but I find an excuse for not showing up every week.

Yet sometimes, when the pressures of adulthood become too great, I dig out my old Bauers and drive to the Colleymount arena. The decaying rink gets few visitors these days, so I take to the ice alone, weaving figure-eights across the pitted surface and firing pucks into goal nets that are, like me, grey with age. Under the dim electric lights that hang from the ceiling of that great A-frame barn like stars in a midnight sky, I recapture some of the game's essence.

Suddenly, my burdens seem lighter, and I'm young again. It's magic.

When I stop to catch my breath during these solo games of shinny, I sometimes think I see a flicker of movement in the shadows beyond the boards. It doesn't bother me, though, because I know it's only the spirit of hockey searching for a better seat.

Wattle and Daub

Autumn comes swiftly to the Southside. Though September is often a heady reminder of sweet summers past, the landscape no longer holds the heat as it did a month earlier. Each evening, as the sun begins to fade behind the Coast Range like the embers of a dying fire, a chill rises from the region's thin, acidic soil. With the coming of darkness, it finds its way into the homes of Ootsa Lake residents, seeping through cracks around doors and windows, sliding silently down blacked stove pipes, slithering past the vents of unlit wood stoves. The nights grow progressively more inclement until one morning, as daylight slices through the pines, people wake to find their homes uncomfortably cold, and the ground outside covered with a thick coat of glittering frost.

That rime is the season's harbinger. Soon after, a hint of yellow appears in the aspen stands that line the north shore of Ootsa Lake. It is followed by dabs of red and orange, riotous tints splashed across the landscape as if by an unseen painter. Within days, the country is ablaze with colour, and it's fall.

At Ootsa Lake school, autumn was a time to build forts. During summer vacation, hay grew thick and unmolested in the schoolyard. By September, if the facility's wire gate and rickety pole fence held fast against the onslaughts of marauding cattle, the grass was tall and dry enough to be used as a building material.

The first forts, tiny structures of willow branches and grass, were built by the school's younger students for games of cowboys and other guys. The school's older girls had bit parts in this bizarre parody of colonization, serving as horses for both sides in the conflict.

While our committee of older boys had no interest in playing the game, we had other ideas. Our first hideouts were not much different from the teepee-like structures built by the younger kids. Yet over several weeks, they evolved from simple shelters to elaborate wattle-and-daub safe houses with peepholes and secret compartments. Twigs and straw were easy to come by, but mud for the forts had to be hauled in lard pails and lunch boxes from a nearby swamp. The school grounds soon looked like an African village occupied at various times of the day by a tribe of short people with dirty hands and faces.

We abandoned the round hut construction plan in favour of a modern wood frame design that utilized boards, plywood, and tin borrowed from neighbouring properties. By Thanksgiving, there wasn't a stick of wood or a blade of long grass within five hundred feet of Ootsa Lake school, and the lower limbs of all the trees had been trimmed to a height equal to that of one boy carrying another on his shoulders, but we didn't care. Some of the adjacent property owners did, though. One old-timer was baffled when the metal roof of his well house disappeared almost overnight, yet no one connected us to the surrounding devastation.

"Wow, what a fort," said Sean when we were done. "It's the best one I've ever seen, even better than the one my brothers built in California."

"Yeah," agreed Kent. "We ought to have an opening ceremony for it. Kind of like that thing they do when ships are launched."

"You mean a christening?" I asked.

"Yeah, that's what we ought to have," Kent said. "We should break a bottle of liquor over it."

A mischievous grin appeared on Diggory's thin face. "Sure. Except instead of busting the bottle on the fort, maybe we could sprinkle a little around and drink the rest."

The idea gained traction in a hurry because we were under the mistaken belief that alcohol made everything better. But we lacked suitable refreshments.

"I could probably sneak a beer from home," Nicky said after much discussion.

"Just one? What good is one beer among the eight of us? Can't you swipe a jug of your pop's dandelion wine?"

The young Williams boy shook his head. "My old man knows exactly how many he has in the pantry. Besides, he tried some last week and said it tasted terrible. Something about it not having sat long enough."

Sean laughed. "You mean it hasn't aged at least a week?"

Nicky gave him the finger.

"How about you, Diggs?" someone asked. "Your uncle takes a nip now and again, doesn't he?"

"Yeah, but the last time he brought a bottle to our house, Mum poured it down the drain."

It looked as though the fort would never get its grand opening. I was apologizing for my teetotalling parents when Ralph entered the discussion.

"Okay," he said, shaking his head. "If you jerks can't bring anything, I'll give it a try. But no promises. The last time my brother was caught in the liquor cabinet, he got his ass tanned."

Six of us were waiting for Ralph and Eli the following morning. We knew Carrot Top had struck pay dirt when we saw him get off the bus with a parcel under one arm. He cast an anxious look toward the school before striding across the playing field.

"You get some?" Diggs asked as soon as our redheaded classmate and his friend were within earshot.

"You bet your boots he did," said Eli with a rare show of emotion. "He brought two bottles."

"Cool!" exclaimed Diggs, stepping forward and reaching for the package under Ralph's arm.

Taking our cue from the big kid, we surrounded the two youths from Marilla.

"Far out! Ralph brought booze!"

"Let's crack it and have some."

Ralph shielded his precious cargo. "Back off," he said. "You trying to get us all in trouble?"

His words had a sobering effect. "Ralph's right," Eli agreed. "We'll all be in deep shit if the teachers find out."

Diggs suggested we retreat to the fort before sampling Ralph's merchandise. As soon as the plywood door closed behind us, we again gathered around our resourceful friend.

Taking one last look through a peephole in the fort's east wall, Ralph lay his package on the ground and unwrapped it. Inside were two squat bottles with long necks and brightly coloured labels. He picked them up.

"What the heck are those?" Abner asked.

Ralph shot the fifth grader a look of disgust. "This is expensive hooch. It's called liqueur, and it costs about twenty bucks a pop."

Abner was unimpressed. "There's not very much of it," he said, pointing toward one of the containers, "and the stuff in that one looks like swamp scum."

Ralph rolled his eyes before continuing. "This one is cream dee mint, and this is cream dee cocoa," he said, holding out the green bottle and then the brown one. "Most people drink it after supper, sort of like dessert."

"Then let's have dessert," said Nicky, reaching for the brown bottle. "I want the chocolate booze. You guys can drink the green junk."

"Hold your horses," said Ralph as he again clasped the bottles to his chest. "We don't want to go to class with booze breath. Let's wait until noon. Then we'll have a drink and eat our lunch. That should hide the smell."

The grumbling started before he had finished his spiel, but Ootsa school's twelve-year-old bootlegger would have none of it.

"We either do it my way, or I take the stuff home. You guys might get the strap if we get caught, but I'll probably get kicked out of school. And if that happens," he added in a hushed tone, drawing one hand quickly across his throat, "I'm dead."

Silence fell as everyone considered the matter. At length, there were murmurs of assent. No one wanted to see Ralph expelled, particularly if we found alcohol to our liking. He was, at that point, our only link in the supply chain.

"All right," Diggs said after a moment of reflection. "Let's stash them and come back later."

At noon, lunches in hand, we returned to the hideout. Our thin veneer of civility dissolved as soon as we were inside.

"It's party time!" Kent said as Ralph pulled the two bottles from their hiding place.

Ignoring the bedlam around him, Ralph opened the crème de menthe and raised it high.

"To the fort," he said with great solemnity.

"To the fort," we replied.

The green bottle began making its way around the group. At Nicky's insistence, the chocolate liqueur was also opened and passed from hand to hand.

"That's darned good stuff," Sean said after sampling the crème de cacao. "Tastes like chocolate syrup. I could drink a gallon of it."

"You could," said Ralph, "but you'd be smashed by the time you were done. This stuff is stronger than you think."

"Come off it. I can hardly taste the alcohol."

"It's delicious," said Nicky, who had poured a finger of each liqueur into Sean's Thermos cup and was sipping his way toward happiness. "If you mix the two with some milk, it tastes like a Peppermint Patty."

Sean heard him and grew concerned. "Make sure you wash that out before we go home today," he said. "If there's even a drop left behind, my mom will smell it. She's got a nose like a black bear."

We all laughed. Sean's parents were devout Christians who considered drinking coffee a sin.

Most members of the Ootsa Lake Boy's Club preferred the crème de cacao, but Ralph and Eli remained partial to the minty stuff. Demand soon outstripped supply, and it wasn't long before the rest of us were eyeing the crème de menthe with unabashed desire.

We were also getting a little giggly. Ralph was right: despite tasting like candy, the stuff had some kick to it.

"Pass the green junk over here, Woodpecker," said Diggs with a crooked grin. "Don't be such a pig with it."

Ralph recognized the early signs of intoxication. He gave the bigger boy a long, hard look and then said, "No way, you bucktoothed baboon. You've had enough."

Diggs didn't suffer teasing, and we waited for the explosion of violence that normally followed such a comment. But our friend, buoyed by liquid cheer, was feeling magnanimous.

"Might as well save some for later, I guess," he said with a shrug. "Chow time, guys." Reaching into his lunch bag, he pulled out several cheese sandwiches and laid waste to them in record time.

The field hockey game that followed was a riotous affair featuring wres-tling matches and a lot of raucous laughter. A couple of participants, having forgotten which team they played for, happily scored own goals. Others boasted that the pre-game festivities had improved their athletic prowess. Bobbing and weaving are so much easier when you're loaded.

Our antics drew a crowd. After watching for a while, Jules, Lizzi, and Esther—the school's self-proclaimed temperance league—confronted us.

"You guys have been drinking," they said.

Ralph's mouth opened, and he started stammering. "What? How? Where?"

Nicky came to his rescue. "We weren't drinking anything. Mind your own business, or I'll fart in your lunch boxes."

His threat sent the girls scurrying back to class. Nicky, everyone knew, had more gas than Imperial Oil.

Ootsa's alcoholics-in-training did their best to act normal that afternoon, but Hull called Baxter to the office toward the end of the day. We could tell by the expression on our teacher's face that something was up.

A minute later, Nicky poked his head into the classroom. "Pssst . . ." he whispered to Sean, who sat closest to the door.

"Nicky? What are you doing?"

"Shut up. I'm not supposed to be here," the black-haired kid whispered. "I was on my way back from the john when I heard Hull and Baxter talking. I think they're planning to raid the fort."

"Holy cow. I better tell someone."

As soon as Nicky disappeared, Sean walked over and whispered something in Ralph's ear. The redhead stiffened and got out of his seat. He was on his way out the door when Baxter returned.

"Where are you going?" the teacher asked.

"I . . . feel sick," Ralph said, covering his mouth with one hand. "I think . . . I'm about to . . ." He finished the sentence with a concerto of gagging sounds.

Baxter stepped aside, allowing Ralph to make a break for the bathroom. When the bell rang moments later, Sean briefed the rest of us. Scared, we pulled on our boots and ran for the fort.

Ralph met us near the entrance.

"Quick," I said. "We've got to stash the booze before the teachers get here."

Ootsa school's purveyor of fine liquor looked unperturbed. I was about to repeat my directive when Nicky ran up. His message was of such import that he hadn't bothered to put on shoes.

"Get out of the way," he said, hopping from one foot to another as hoar frost chewed his toes. "I think Hull's coming."

"Keep your gaunchies on," Ralph said. "Everything's under control."

We bombarded our bartender with questions.

"How'd you get out here so fast?" Diggs asked. "We thought you were going to barf."

"I was faking. I climbed out the bathroom window."

Diggs raised his furry eyebrows in appreciation. The school was built on a hillside, and the big boy knew from previous escape attempts that it was a long drop from the bathroom window to the ground. "Where's the booze?" he asked.

"Gone."

"What? You didn't drink the rest by yourself, did you?"

"Nope. I dumped it out and sunk the bottles in the swamp," Ralph replied, pointing toward the algae-covered puddle stinking in the northwest corner of the school grounds.

There were several loud groans.

"Jeez, the green bottle was more than half full. We could have drunk it later when the coast was clear."

Ralph shook his head. "I wasn't taking any chances, and I'm not bringing any more liquor to school."

Crestfallen, we trooped back to class. Dumping the liquor seemed like such a waste, especially when it turned out that Hull and Baxter had only been planning a field trip to Bennett's Mountain.

The incident ushered in a new era of Prohibition at Ootsa Lake school. Our fort, however, remained a hotbed of illicit activity for weeks.

Lighting Up

Today, it is estimated that only 1.5 Canadians in ten smoke tobacco. This means that on any given day, when eight astute people and someone like me gather around the water cooler at coffee break to discuss what the Kardashians ate for dinner the previous night, another person is going outside with a halfwit to light up. While I do not know the name of the cognitively impaired person in the latter group, and a case could be made that his cohort is also playing with less than a full deck, I bet they both discovered cigarettes in the 1970s.

If they started down this path to self-destruction earlier, I applaud their resilience. Most of their comrades are, like my mother, already dead from smoking-related ailments.

The number of Canadians who say "no" to tobacco has increased because most people now realize that using it is bad for them. This was not the case a half-century ago. Health Canada did not put warning labels on tobacco products until 1989, and the disgusting photographs that now cover seventy-five percent of each cigarette package were not required until 2012. Sure, we may have suspected that Uncle Herman's untimely demise from lung cancer was related to his penchant for Bubba's Special Selects, but we were not convinced of it. For millions like Uncle Herman, this element of doubt made consuming a product containing sixty-nine known carcinogens an acceptable risk.

How different was the public's attitude to tobacco fifty years ago? Consider this: we were a nation of smokers. More than half of all Canadians were puffing away during my formative years, and they were doing it everywhere—in bars, restaurants, hospital wards, even around highly combustible petroleum products. The result? Even non-smokers were sucking in a lot of stuff exhaled by their tobacco-loving brethren.

It's a wonder there are any of us from that era still alive.

Idiots and reprobates were not the only people using tobacco. I considered two of my three parents to be reasonably intelligent homo sapiens—the outlier, my biological father, had by some fluke escaped the extinction that claimed the other Neanderthals—yet they all smoked like chimneys.

"Smoking is bad for you," my parents said with the regularity of a metronome and then lit another cigarette.

While my sisters and I were discouraged from taking up the habit, our parents graciously allowed us to share their addiction in other ways. The two of them made second-hand smoke readily available throughout the house—during periods of familial stress, it sometimes hung in a cloud so thick that getting enough oxygen to sustain life was difficult—and they enlisted our assistance in preparing their drug of choice.

My parents could not afford tailor-mades. They instead bought tobacco by the can and rolled their cigarettes. This saved them money, which they used to purchase luxuries like food, clothing, and shelter. Or, as was often the case, more tobacco and rolling papers.

But hand-rolling your cigarettes is a slow and laborious process that yields mixed results. There is no uniformity to cigarettes fashioned in this manner; all are the same length, but their diameter can vary greatly depending on the amount of tobacco used and the fabricator's dexterity. My stepfather was better at it than my mother. After fiddling with the makings for five or ten minutes, she often forgot to lick the adhesive and found herself holding nothing more than a palmful of tobacco and a small sheet of paper suitable for use as a bookmark. On those rare occasions when she made something approximating a cigarette, the exercise often took so long that the tobacco dried out. Setting the coffin nail alight was like touching off a tube packed with saltpeter. She was drawing on her eyebrows long before it became fashionable.

There were other problems associated with this system of manufacture. When you are in a hurry and the need for nicotine has all your nerve endings sounding off while standing at attention, there is nothing more annoying, so I am told, than having to stop what you are doing and roll a cigarette.

According to long-time nicotine addicts, every second counts in situations like this, and the quicker you can get your fix, the better.

My parents solved their tobacco-related problems by purchasing a V-Master Deluxe Cigarette Maker from Simpsons-Sears. This handy device, which measured about twelve inches long and half as wide, consisted of a perforated metal bed covered with a thin rubber apron. By manipulating a roller that moved back and forth beneath the apron, one person was able to mass-produce footlong cigarettes that could then be cut into smaller lengths with a razor blade. The company even took the guesswork out of the chopping process. On the machine's underside was the equivalent of a mitre box, a grooved piece of wood notched at regular intervals. It was remarkable.

Rolling cigarettes was still a chore my parents hoped to avoid, so they took a page out of *Tom Sawyer*. The two of them acted as though the production of smoking materials was great fun and then refused to let us do it—for a while. Kelly and I got into a bidding war over the cigarette contract. I won, thus earning the exclusive right to provide Mom and Olavi with tailor-made smokes in perpetuity. It cost me a week's allowance, which I figured was a reasonable price to pay for a lifetime of entertainment.

And there were other benefits. I thought having the contract might allow me to add something special to my stepfather's cigarettes whenever his behaviour warranted it. The possibilities, which ranged from ground match heads (highly explosive) to dead bugs scavenged from the window ledge (possibly toxic), were intriguing. Kelly had some ideas too. She suggested we replace half the tobacco in Olavi's smokes with dynamite. None was available, but we did have a Red Devil left over from Halloween. With the aid of measuring calipers, I confirmed that a small firecracker could be concealed within a cigarette tube if the fuse was cut short and hidden with a plug of Macdonald's Export. The question was, would it do the job or only deafen the target and set his beard alight? It was an important consideration.

Unaware of our machinations, Olavi showed me how to work the V-Master, then surrendered his precious tobacco and a book of Vogue Extra Long Rolling Papers.

"Don't make a mess," he said.

I proceeded to do just that. My first efforts were no better than Mom's hand-rolled smokes, and Quality Control Officer Turkki rejected them after little more than a cursory inspection. But I got the hang of it after a while, and it was great fun. Everyone was happy; my parents had an endless supply of cigarettes, and I had a new hobby. At least it seemed that way until I came down with repetitive motion disorder from working the roller so much. Kelly took over the job and gave me half her allowance for three months' manufacturing rights. We both found the arrangement satisfactory. I had time to mend, and she got an opportunity for revenge. My only stipulation was that she not tell me what she was up to. If her plot to kill the Finnish Fuhrer went terribly wrong, I needed plausible deniability.

My experiences with the cigarette machine made for interesting discussions at Ootsa Lake school. Members of the boy's club were intrigued by the device because none of their parents had one. Most adults they knew either hand-rolled their cigarettes or bought them ready-made from the store.

Several classmates asked me to bring the V-Master to school for a demonstration, but I declined on the grounds that it was proprietary technology. To be honest, I was afraid of what might happen to me if the device went missing and my parents couldn't get their dose of nicotine. Ralph and Kent understood because they had already been caught bringing stuff to school without permission and had bruises on their backsides to prove it.

It was, however, only a matter of time before my friends decided to get into the cigarette business.

We were working on the interior of our latest fort when someone brought up the subject of smoking. Despite repeated warnings from our parents that the filthy habit would stunt our growth, we were all eager to try it.

Though Ralph, a hardcore survivalist, always carried wooden matches, we lacked tobacco and rolling papers. There was a supply of both in the school's tiny staff room, along with a few cigarillos in a package near the window and several cigarette butts in an ashtray, but theft was not an option. The risk of apprehension was too great, and the likely penalty (strapping) too horrid to contemplate. No one wanted to risk the wrath of Mr. Hull, the man who owned the smoking materials. Do not, my parents told me on numerous occasions, get between a smoker and his tobacco.

It appeared we would have to rule out smoking, at least for a day or two. Then Nicky came up with a workaround.

After asking us to keep watch for the teachers, he crawled under the school fence and made his way cautiously to a nearby stream. He returned several minutes later with an armload of something he called "wild celery."

Found along stream banks and marshes, these plants burst out of the northern soil almost as soon as the snow melts each spring, and often reach a height of up to eight feet before flowering in July. What makes them unique is their stem, which is hollow like a piece of bamboo. As much as an inch in diameter, wild celery stalks make excellent snorkels for shallow water diving and can even be fashioned into crude but serviceable spitball shooters of varying calibres.

And, as we soon learned, they could be smoked.

"Watch this," said Nicky, dropping the dried plant stems in a heap inside the fort. Cutting a six-inch section from one of the stalks, he began stuffing it with grasses and weeds of all descriptions. When the tube was full, he tamped its contents down with a slender piece of wood and placed the finished product between his lips.

"Anybody got a light?" he asked in his best tough-guy voice, the stogie dangling from one corner of his mouth.

Ralph was quick to oblige. After one or two preliminary puffs, Nicky took a long draw from his homemade cigarette and leaned back against one of the fort's grass walls.

"Not bad," he announced, stifling a cough and wiping his eyes. After looking critically at the smoking weed gripped between his left thumb and index finger, he added, "Kind of bitter, but okay. Anybody want a drag?"

The response was overwhelming, and Nicky's stogie was soon making its way around the semi-circle of boys. After several minutes of violent hacking, we all agreed it was excellent and began preparing smokes.

Experimentation was the name of the game. Everyone sought to create a cigarette that smelled like the ones smoked by our parents. Some tried different materials, substituting one type of grass for another, mixing this weed with that leaf in a vain search for the perfect blend. One concoction with a pleasant aroma, but a horrible taste, consisted of frost-bitten clover, finely chopped lawn grass, ground birch bark, and shredded toilet paper. The toilet paper kept the mess alight long enough for its creator to sample a puff.

After several minutes of violent coughing, Ralph announced that what he and everyone else needed was a menthol. His recipe included fireweed fluff, rose hips, and dried spruce needles. The smoke tasted bitter, like rags soaked in Pine-Sol, and the thing burned like a propane torch.

Kent made a half dozen small stogies and placed them in a du Maurier package he found discarded along the main road. He rolled the faded pack up in the arm of his T-shirt like James Dean and made a show of presenting it to the rest of us.

"Ciggy, anyone?" he asked every few minutes, opening the package and offering the stalks to everyone before selecting one. It was a novelty.

Much to our disappointment, no one could come up with a blend of weeds and grasses that smelled even a little like real tobacco when lit. Disgusted, we stopped making cigarettes and started fabricating monstrous Havana cigars. They kept getting bigger and longer until Nicky, who had slipped out unannounced, called for everyone's attention.

"Look at this, guys," he said.

Grasped in one hand was something that looked like a two-foot section of sewer line filled with muddy straw.

"Holy shit," said Diggs.

"You're not going to smoke that, are you?" asked Eli in disbelief. "It looks more like a hog leg than a cigarette."

"I bet you can't even get your mouth around it," said someone else.

The gauntlet had been dropped. We watched with horror as Nicky opened his mouth and began working one end of the dried stalk into it. After considerable twisting, during which he almost dislocated his jaw, he at last got the giant cheroot in place.

"Gammeealie," he said, supporting the sewer pipe with one hand.

"What did he say?"

"Ga-me-a-lie, fa crysays," Nicky repeated, motioning with his free hand.

Sean finally made sense of the gibberish. "He's saying, 'Give me a light.'"

Someone offered Nicky a lit stogie, and he placed its burning tip against the stuffed pipe protruding from his mouth. After several seconds of frantic puffing, our little Fidel Castro was rewarded. The end of the wild celery stalk caught fire, and two trails of smoke shot out his nostrils.

He also started to look a little green.

"Oh shit. He's either going to puke or pass out," somebody said, prompting everyone to move back a few feet.

With one last drag, Nicky jerked the smoking monstrosity from his mouth. Everyone cheered.

"Geez," he said, gasping for breath. "I need some air. Let me out."

Leaving the Havana behind, he crawled to the exit.

By this time, the fort's interior looked like the inside of an opium den. Acrid smoke hung at head level, swirling in great clouds whenever anyone raised a hand or shifted position. What transpired next should come as no surprise, because we were all goofy from lack of oxygen.

"Hey, you know what I heard," said Ralph in a hushed tone. Pausing for effect, he looked around the circle of faces before continuing. "I heard you can get high by smoking horse shit."

"You mean, like wacky-tobacky?" asked Abner.

"Yeah. Like pot," Ralph said, pushing up his black-framed glasses.

I was skeptical. "Oh, come off it. That's crazy."

"Maybe, maybe not. But that's what I heard, and it's from someone who would know, if you get my drift."

"What about cow crap?" a voice asked, obviously remembering the hundreds of flat black pies just beyond the schoolyard.

Ralph shook his head. "Nope, no good. From what I hear, only horse shit works."

"That doesn't make sense," I said. "Why would horse shit get you stoned but not cow shit? Shit is shit."

"Hey, don't ask me. All I know is what I hear," he said.

"Then why doesn't somebody try it?" asked a kid who encouraged others to do things he would not.

Snuffing out the last of our homemade cigars, we set off in pairs to comb the school grounds. Some adventurous souls, those most eager to test Ralph's theory, even disobeyed school rules and scoured nearby fields and animal trails.

We met back at the fort a short time later.

"Find any?"

"No. Did you?"

"Nope. Saw tonnes of cow pies but not a single horse bun. You know, maybe Ralph's right, and big kids have already gathered it up."

There were a few grunts of agreement. Then came a suggestion.

"How about these?" asked one kid, producing a handful of dark brown pellets the size and shape of almonds.

Everyone groaned. Ralph spoke for the assembly. "That's moose shit, you idiot."

"I know that," the kid said, "but maybe it'll work. A moose looks more like a horse than a cow."

"Then you smoke the damn things," said Diggs, "because I'm not putting my mouth anywhere near them."

The big boy's comment swayed public opinion. The search for hallucinogenic excrement was called off, and so was our quest for the perfect cigarette. Nicky threw the remaining wild celery stalks over the fence into No Man's Land, and we retired to the school for a game of floor hockey.

It was a fortuitous move because the plant Nicky introduced to us that day was not wild celery but *Heracleum lanatum michx.*, more commonly known as cow parsnip. Good old *Heracleum*, I now know, is a member of the *Apiaceae* or *Umbelliferae* family, a group of flowering plants to which *Conium maculatum* (poison hemlock) and several other lethal species belong. Many of the *Umbelliferae* family are indigenous to Northern BC, and though *Heracleum* is edible, it so closely resembles cousin *Conium* that botanists discourage foragers from touching anything that even resembles the plants. Some members of the *Umbelliferae* family are so toxic that according to the United States Department of Agriculture, children have died from blowing through whistles made from the hollow stems.

I shudder at the thought of what smoking the wrong stalk might have done to us.

The Tree House

A young boy acting alone will seldom do anything that might result in personal injury. Yet place him in the company of three or four friends, and there is a good chance he will lose all capacity for rational thought.

Disaster might be averted in such cases if even one member of the group retained his wits, but this rarely happens. They all troop toward misadventure with a smile on their face and a song in their heart.

As proof, I offer the following story, which involves eight boys, a grove of deciduous trees, and a pre-winter cold snap.

While plucking grass for our fort's new west wing, Diggs wandered to the edge of a stand of trees that had somehow been missed when the playing field was cleared years earlier. Growing weary of his task, the big boy stopped to stretch the kinks out of his lower back. Just as he was about to resume work, he spotted four large poplars standing a little apart from a dozen smaller ones. His gaze travelled up their wide, pale trunks to a point high above the ground and then came to an abrupt halt.

Dropping his handful of grass, he turned and swaggered back to us.

"What's wrong, Diggs? Forget what hay looks like?" Ralph asked.

Diggs glared at him. "No, I found something better. Come see."

We downed tools and followed our friend back to the grove.

There, in the space between four big poplars, some enterprising kid had started a tree house. He might have tried to build it alone and given up. Perhaps he had help but lost interest in the project. Whatever the reason, the fort was unfinished, just a crude rectangle of old planks nailed between the four largest trees. But it had potential, so we began hauling our building materials to the poplar grove.

The immediate problem was one of access. The tree fort's original owner had failed to leave a ladder, but this proved only a minor inconvenience. Nicky, the smallest kid present, stood on Diggory's shoulders and pounded our meagre supply of nails into the largest tree as footholds, then scampered to the top with a rope fabricated from surplus clothing. Arms crooked at shoulder height like a Muscle Beach bodybuilder, he grinned down at us from the platform as though he had just scaled Mount Everest.

With Nicky's climbing aid in place, work on the tree fort began in earnest. Over several days, using hammers, saws, and other tools smuggled from home, we added walls and a roof to it. Then came the hardest task of all.

Rather than add a second storey to the fort, we decided to build an elevated causeway between it and two smaller trees. This was accomplished using a couple of rails from the school fence and a roll of haywire from an adjacent farm. When the whitewashed poles were lashed in place, we spanned the gap between them with worn planks and started work on the roof. Despite being given strict orders not to cut live trees—teachers Hull and Baxter, like druids, seemed to feel the grove was sacred—four of us hacked down two fine specimens for roof supports while our noon hour supervisor was looking the other way. The makeshift rafters were trimmed with a hatchet, lifted into place, and then quickly covered with plywood.

We feigned ignorance when Hull and Baxter questioned us about the two fresh stumps.

"Honest, we didn't chop those trees down. They were already gone when school started. Someone must have cut them during the summer for firewood."

"I doubt that very much," said Mr. Hull.

Abner offered an alternative explanation. "Could have been beavers," he said, pointing to a shallow pond north of the poplar grove. "I think I saw one there the other day."

"That too seems unlikely," Baxter said with a frown.

No one could shed any light on the gap in the school fence either.

Finally, after stick and thatch walls were added, the tree fort was ready for occupation. It was an engineering marvel of which we were all proud, and one that would place us beyond the reach of adult authority for a significant portion of each school day. Diggs provided the pièce de résistance, a rope ladder he made one evening from several miles of binder twine and twenty pieces of kindling. Installed at the end of the causeway farthest from the main turret, the rope ladder became the fort's only access after Nicky removed the nails he had hammered into the poplar tree a week earlier.

With our fort at the lock-up stage, we began adding those little extras that make a tree house a home. We spent several days organizing our library, which consisted of two *Spiderman* comics and a dog-earned *National Geographic* containing several photographs of semi-nude African women. The paucity of reading material offended Kent, who subsequently donated more than a dozen pornographic magazines from his father's extensive personal collection. All were stacked on an orange crate that served as a coffee table in the fort's main tower.

Sprucing up the interior was easy. We each thumbed through the magazines and picked our favourite photographs, which were then hung with reverence on the thatch walls of the causeway. The plywood ceiling got special treatment in the form of a life-size poster of Miss April in her birthday suit.

By the time we were done, the place was a shrine to the feminine form. The effect was awe-inspiring, particularly on dark days when we lit a few candles to dispel the gloom. I remember staring up with the same sense of wonder that tourists exhibit upon entering the Sistine Chapel.

Still, the place lacked something. It wasn't until a cold front moved in that we realized what it was.

A heater.

Diggs put on his thinking cap. In retrospect, the fit must have been a bit snug because his solution led to misfortune.

Diggs found an empty five-gallon oil drum and a length of cast iron water pipe in an old generator shed near the teacherage. He lugged both up the rope ladder to the tree fort and, after prying off the drum's lid with the aid of Abner's pocketknife, lit a fire in the open container. When the flames reached a sufficient height, he replaced the lid and attached the pipe to its metal spout, which served as a chimney and carried away what little smoke the fire gave off.

When oxygen starvation threatened to put a damper on things a few minutes later, Diggs punched three air holes in the side of the drum with a six-inch spike.

"There you go, girls," he said when the system was operating to his satisfaction. "Now we got a stove."

Eli went outside to see if the fire could be detected from below. "Almost no smoke at all," he reported.

Every day thereafter, we chased away the unseasonable chill by lighting a fire in Diggory's furnace. One morning after the device was up to operating temperature, Sean, who had drawn guard duty, yelled a warning from his post near the fort's exit.

"Hull's coming," he said.

Peering through the fort's east window, I saw the principal, head down, striding across the playground. The warden was conducting a cell check.

"Shit, what do we do? The dirty magazines we can hide, but this?" Nicky asked, gesturing toward the sizzling oil drum.

"Don't sweat it," Diggs said. "Take down the stovepipe so he can't see the smoke from outside. That'll give me time to figure something out."

We weren't sure that was a good idea, but with no other options, we complied.

Nicky disassembled the stove while the rest of us tried to hide the girly magazines. Ignoring the chaos around him, Diggs sat down and started making a long rope from several pieces of leftover baler twine. His fingers were a blur, yet he had barely finished the job when Hull announced his presence.

"I'm coming up to check your tree house, boys. Kindly let the rope ladder down," came the teacher's stern request from below.

Sean, who had been staring through the hole in the floor at Hull, turned to us for instruction. Diggs, who had just finished tying his new rope to our stove's metal handle, just nodded.

"Just a minute, Mr. Hull," Sean said through the gap in the causeway. "I just need to make sure it's tied on good. Okay, here it comes."

We heard the ladder unravel and hit the ground with a thump.

Sean must have read Diggory's mind because he knew exactly what to do next. "That's right, sir," the younger boy said. "Foot on the bottom rung and come up slowly. Now the second, and the third . . ."

I heard a ripping sound and glanced over my shoulder. Diggs had torn the plastic off one window and was lowering the oil drum as Hull climbed the ladder. When the teacher's head appeared in the tunnel entrance, the big boy, his actions screened by the rest of us, tied the rope holding his fire pot to a nail and pulled the plastic window closed behind him. It was brilliant.

Hull wormed his way through the entrance hole and started crawling toward us. "This is quite the tree house you have here, boys, but I . . ." His words trailed away as he caught sight of Miss November 1970, whose portrait we had in our haste neglected to remove.

"Very impressive indeed," he reiterated, tearing his gaze away from the centrefold with difficulty. "You boys do good work."

Suddenly, his expression changed from one of admiration to consternation.

"Do I smell smoke?" he asked, sniffing the air like a hound. "You don't have a fire up here, do you?"

With the schoolyard a sea of dry grass and the nearest pumper truck ninety minutes away, lighting fires was verboten. We did our best to look shocked.

"A fire in a tree house, sir?" Sean answered with angelic grace. "This whole place is made of wood and straw. Where would we put it?"

Hull looked around but could find nothing amiss. Eyeing us with suspicion, he backed toward the exit, pausing when he reached the nude pin-up.

"Tsk, tsk," he said, taking another long look at the photo before tearing it off the wall. "We can't have any of this at Ootsa school."

Kent, standing beside me, whimpered and bit his knuckles. Miss November had been his nominee for Playmate of the Year. With voting scheduled to get underway later that afternoon, she was out of the running.

Hull reached the exit and prepared to leave. "Well, you boys have fun," he said, casting one last look around before starting down. "And be careful. We can't have you falling out of this place."

"Okay," we said.

As soon as Hull started his descent, Diggs reeled in the stove. The principal never saw a thing. By the time he reached the school, we had stoked the fire and were again basking in its warmth.

Hull may not have caught us, but he made regular visits to the tree house from that day onward. Each time, Diggs lowered the smoking can out the window. It was a foolproof system because the bearded principal had to take great care while climbing the rope ladder. But we grew tired of the exercise and decided to replace the stove with an open fireplace.

Building it was easy: we nailed a chunk of roofing tin to the fort's wooden floor and built our fire atop it. When an inspection was imminent, we opened the flies of our jeans and extinguished the flames by natural means. There was never a shortage of retardant, and the eight of us could reduce even the largest blaze to ashes long before the teacher arrived. We then covered the foul-smelling charcoal with whatever was available until our unwelcome guest left.

We thought the brazier lent an air of sophistication to the tree fort. Every day at dinner time, we retreated to the tower, built a fire, and toasted our lunches on willow sticks. Diggs acquired a taste for charbroiled peanut butter and jam sandwiches during this period.

Maybe it was fate. Perhaps we got careless. One day in mid-November, after eating our lunches and piddling on the fire, we threw a hemp doormat over the steaming embers and ran off to play hockey.

We were sitting in class when Baxter's wife, who lived with him in a teacherage a stone's throw from the school, burst in with the couple's eight-month-old daughter.

"There's a fire in the tree house," she said, cradling the half-naked infant in her arms. "For God's sake, Mel, do something!"

The classroom went as quiet as a morgue. Then Diggs, eyes wide, leaped from his desk and ran out of the classroom. We heard the school's big double doors crash open a half-second later as he exited the building. When the shock wore off, we followed him.

So did everyone else in the school.

The big kid's long strides put him far ahead of us. By the time we arrived on the scene, he had already scaled the rope ladder.

The fire was well-established. Clouds of black smoke billowed out of the main tower, and we could see a rosy glow through cracks in the floorboards. Running to the far side, I saw that most of the tower's east wall was already gone, and flames were licking eagerly at the tinder-dry roof.

That's when Diggs emerged from the covered tunnel. He stood unafraid at the tower's edge and stared at the raging inferno. The sight must have overwhelmed him because he did nothing for a few seconds. Then he looked around for something to throw on the fire and, finding nothing, did what seemed logical to him.

He pulled down his pants and trained a stream of urine on the flames.

"Hurry, Abner, whip her out and let fly," he hollered at the younger boy who had joined him atop the fort.

"No way," Abner said. "Everybody in the goddamn school's down below."

Diggs ignored Abner's comment and continued hosing down the place. I could tell, though, that he did not have the right tool for the job. Searching through our rubbish pile, I found the five-gallon can we had used for a stove and ran toward the swamp.

By the time I returned, Nicky had joined his compatriots atop the burning platform. Unlike Diggs, who was still determined to put the fire out, Nicky took a more pragmatic approach to the problem. He started digging through the thatch walls of the tunnel. A few seconds later, while the rest of us formed a bucket brigade, the first girly magazines started landing in the grass.

Sean stopped carrying water long enough to cheer. "Yay, Nicky," he said. "Save the library!"

Every kid in the school watched the spectacle unfold. As the pornography rained down and Diggory's bladder neared empty, members of the girl's temperance league gathered nearby to offer encouragement.

"Weenie roast!" said Jules, pointing at Diggs.

Hysterical laughter followed. "But he's following in the footsteps of great men," I heard Lizzi say. "Didn't one of the emperors piddle while Rome burned?"

"No, that was *fiddle*," corrected Esther. "But you're right about one thing: he'll be famous after this."

Even Angela, Brendan's demure sister, got into the act. "Diggory," she said in a sweet voice, "please be careful. You might need that little thing someday."

That's when Ootsa's patron saint of lost causes realized he had an audience. Face red with embarrassment, Diggs stuffed the portion of his anatomy that had drawn so much attention back into his underwear and pulled up his pants. The first bucket of water arrived in time to save him further disgrace, and he threw it on the fire. A grey cloud of smoke and steam enveloped him.

The bucket brigade proved far more effective in controlling the blaze than Diggory's urinary tract, and within minutes we had the situation under control. Taking a moment to catch my breath, I noticed the ground around us was littered with pornographic magazines, and around each clustered a little knot of primary students. One second grader was using a stick to turn the pages of *Playboy* while his classmates took in the peepshow.

Diggs, Abner, and Nicky, their faces streaked with soot, joined us on the ground when the conflagration was out. We waited as Hull and Baxter gathered up what remained of our library and tried to restore order.

"Shit, we're goners," Nicky murmured. "It'll be the belt for sure."

I tried to take the high road. "Well, at least we got the fire out before it burned down the school."

"I suppose," said Sean. "But wasn't it out when we went to play hockey?"

"Obviously not," said Kent. "Who was the last to leave? It was his job to check the fireplace."

No one took responsibility.

"What's done is done," said Eli when the accusations reached a crescendo. "Besides, we should have known better than to put a grass mat over hot coals. When you think about it, that was pretty dumb."

On that point, everyone agreed. We took a moment to consider our stupidity, and then Ralph spoke up.

"Hey, Diggs," he said with a broad grin, "how's it feel to know that every kid in the school saw your dink today?"

Diggs spat a glob of grey phlegm into the grass before answering. "Shut up, Woodpecker."

"Just be glad *your* pecker isn't made of wood, Pinocchio," the redhead replied, "otherwise, it might have gone up in smoke like the rest of the fort, the way you were waving it around up there." Fist clenched in front of his fly, eyes crossed, and tongue protruding from one corner of his mouth, he gave a pretty good imitation of the bigger boy's firefighting style.

Diggs was about to beat Ralph senseless when Hull and Baxter walked up. Everyone drew a deep breath, sure it would be his last.

For a moment, the two teachers said nothing. My angst grew, and I was about to start grovelling when Hull got the hearing underway.

"You boys are in big trouble," he said with undisguised menace.

We looked at the ground and hoped it would open beneath us. Hell would be better than Hull's cold fury, which we feared would translate into corporal punishment.

"Lighting a fire on school grounds is an offense worthy of strapping." The principal's statement made eight prepubescent Adam's apples go up and down as one. "But Mr. Baxter and I have decided that whipping you would serve no useful purpose. A month of detention will suffice, so clean up here and then report to me."

Behind him, Mr. Baxter was trying hard not to laugh.

There was a collective sigh of relief as the teachers walked away. We would live to build another day.

Our optimism proved unfounded. Two weeks later, forting was outlawed at Ootsa Lake school, probably because my mother thought the fire noteworthy and wrote a four-paragraph story about it for the local newspaper. Her lurid report sparked an emergency meeting of the school board, which, after fifteen minutes of heated debate, voted unanimously to prohibit the erection of unauthorized structures on school property. I've been told the ban remained in effect long after the eight of us moved on to the greener, less flammable playing fields of Grassy Plains.

The Bogeyman in
the Basement

Ootsa Lake school had a half basement, an unattractive, windowless cubbyhole beneath Mr. Hull's office and the southern portion of his classroom. Accessed by a set of rough-finished stairs at the end of the school's central hallway, it consisted of a narrow passage that opened into a small room lit by two naked sixty-watt bulbs. Three of the basement's four walls were rough concrete, while the other one was constructed of two-by-fours and knot-riddled laminate painted cadaver grey.

In the distant past, perhaps in response to parental requests for a cultural program, School District 55 had made a half-hearted attempt to convert the dank space into a theatre. A tiny stage and change room were added, and well-meaning trustees provided the school with enough folding chairs to accommodate thirty children. It wasn't the Orpheum, but we used it to perform such timeless classics as *The Night the Moose Ate My Homework*, and *Black Beauty Comes to Wistaria*. Sean and I once held our classmates spellbound for twelve minutes with a pantomime of Bill Cosby's *Chicken Heart*. I starred as young William, while my buddy, after playing both Cosby's mother and his father, donned a burlap sack and staggered around as the monster. The performance was so well-received that we held it over until Sean twisted his ankle during a matinee.

The theatre did not hold any surprises. What intrigued the Ootsa Lake Boy's Club was a door that led off the darkened corridor leading to it.

"What do you think is in there?" Sean asked one day after trying the door and finding it locked.

No one had an answer. It was a mystery begging to be solved, so we made inquiries.

"What's behind the locked door downstairs?" Nicky asked Principal Hull.

The bearded man, seated behind a scuffed hardwood desk surrounded by paperwork, didn't bother looking up. "Nothing you boys need to be concerned about."

"Can we go in there?" Kent asked.

"No."

"Why?" asked Diggs.

Mr. Hull let out a great sigh and dropped his ballpoint pen in frustration. "Because the storeroom is off limits to students." Softening his tone, he added, "Boys, there's nothing in there that would interest you, just school supplies and some old desks. Why don't you run along and play floor hockey or something?"

We retreated to the boys' washroom instead.

"He's hiding something," said Abner, who suffered from intermittent paranoia. "If there's nothing in there but school supplies, why keep it locked?"

"Gee, I don't know," said Ralph, making a goofy face. "Maybe because he's afraid we'll go in and set fire to the place like we did the tree fort?"

Ralph's parents had not taken news of the Great Fire well and still suspected their youngest son had something to do with two missing bottles of liqueur.

"Ah, come on," said Nicky. "Hull knows we're not dumb enough to start a fire down there." He hesitated a moment, then asked, "We're not, are we?"

Everyone laughed.

"Probably not," I offered without much conviction. "But it is strange the door is locked. There must be something more valuable in there than school stuff."

"Yeah," said Eli. "That's not a good enough reason to keep us out."

We pondered the problem for a moment. Then Kent put forward a theory.

"Maybe the door isn't locked to keep us out," he whispered, looking at each of us in turn, "but to keep something in."

Stunned, we looked at our friend. "What do you mean?"

"The school's well is down there," he said, leaning against the bathroom's solitary urinal, "and I heard my dad say they had to drill over three hundred feet before hitting water. Maybe they went so far that they broke into Hell and let something out. Something really bad."

Nicky picked up the narrative. ". . . and they have to keep it penned up in there, or it'll get out and kill us?"

His question went unanswered. None of us knew the exact distance to Hell.

"Ah, come on," Diggs said. "That's stupid."

"No, wait," Sean interjected. "That might not be as dumb as it sounds. The water here stinks like rotten eggs, right?" When we nodded, he continued. "Well, guess what? That's exactly what Hell is supposed to smell like."

His words gave us pause because if anyone knew something about Hell, it was Sean. He accompanied his parents to church every Sunday, and if they didn't teach about the place there, sitting through two hours of fire and brimstone was a reasonable substitute.

"Think the devil is in the basement?" someone asked.

"Well, I don't know about that," Sean said after adjusting his wire-rimmed glasses. "But don't you ever get a weird feeling when you're in the basement? When we were practicing *Chicken Heart*, I thought we were being watched. Made the hair on the back of my neck stand up."

"He did say something about that," I noted, though not entirely sure it was true.

Sean's revelation got us thinking. The basement could be a bit creepy at times.

"Well, if the devil's down there, he's bloody quiet," said Diggs. "I never hear nothing from the other side of that door."

Abner spoke for the first time in a while. "I have. It sounded like a moan."

"Maybe another kid went down there, and whatever's on the other side of the door has him and won't let him out," suggested Kent. "Remember that little jerk who was in Nicky's class for a couple of weeks and then stopped coming? Maybe his parents didn't move to Alaska like Mr. Hull said."

"I heard he drowned," Eli added. "Maybe it was in the well, and the teachers are keeping it hush-hush, so they don't lose their jobs."

"And the noise you heard," asked Nicky, "could that be the kid's ghost?"

"You're all full of shit," Diggs said with finality. He paused long enough to hawk up a big loogie and spit it into the sink. "But don't take my word for it. Go down there and have a look."

No one spoke for a moment. Then Ralph voiced his reservations. "Gee, I don't know. Hull did say it was off limits."

"You're just chicken, Woodpecker," Diggs said. To illustrate the point, he tucked his hands into his armpits, bobbed vigorously, and clucked.

Ralph took offense. "No more than you, Rabbit Mouth, but I don't want to get the strap."

Sean interceded. "I'm in."

"Me too."

"So am I."

Ralph, outnumbered, gave up the fight. "Okay. But don't say I didn't warn you."

We left the bathroom and trooped down the corridor. Kent stopped us before we got to the stairs. "If we all head down there now, Hull will know something's up. Is he still in his office?"

Nicky peeked around the corner and then nodded.

"Shit. How are we going to get past him?"

Ralph gave us a wink. "Why don't I go outside and pretend I've busted my arm again? That'll get his attention."

Diggs gave the idea some thought. "Yeah, that'll work. Get out there. Nicky, when he's ready, you come back in and tell Hull."

Ralph, happy to be a bystander in our latest illicit activity, ran down the hall and out the big double doors. Nicky followed him, and Sean—improvising wonderfully—led us to the school's equipment locker.

"Okay, let's play," he said far louder than necessary. "Me, Diggs, and Kent will take on Mike, Abner, and Eli for the Stanley Cup."

On cue, we started rummaging around for sticks. A second later, Nicky burst into the school.

"Mr. Hull! Mr. Hull!" he said, running toward us. "Come quick!"

We heard the principal's metal chair scrape against the floor tiles, and he emerged from his office a second later. "Nicholas, what on earth . . .?"

"You've gotta come quick," our friend said, tugging the teacher's sleeve. "Ralph fell off the backstop and hurt his arm bad. I think it might be broken."

"Good grief, not again," Hull said in a worried tone. Ralph had broken his arm twice the previous year, prompting complaints from several parents that their children were not being adequately supervised.

As soon as they were out of sight, we dropped our hockey sticks and shot down the basement stairs. Diggs slapped the light switch on his way by.

It was cool in the basement and as quiet as a mausoleum. Abner put one of his big ears against the storeroom door. "Don't hear nothing," he whispered with disappointment before jiggling the doorknob. "And it's still locked."

"No shit, Sherlock," someone said. "How are we going to get in?"

Eli pulled a bone-handled folding knife from his pocket and began prying at the door's locking mechanism. "If . . . I could just . . ."

There was a loud *snap*, followed by a rattle as something metallic hit the concrete floor.

"Shit," he muttered. "Broke my knife."

"Well, that's that," said Kent. Throwing his arms up, he turned toward the stairs.

Nicky met him on the way down. "We got a few minutes," the younger boy said before describing our classmate's antics on the playing field. "Ralph is rolling around on the ground, clutching his arm, and screaming like crazy. Hull keeps asking to see it, but every time he tries, Ralph screams louder. How we doing?"

We weren't doing at all. Diggs described Eli's failed attempt to jimmy the door.

"There's gotta be a way," Nicky said, kicking the door in frustration.

"What about through there?" asked Eli, pointing above our heads.

The wall, we noticed, extended only as far as the joists. There was a neat hole above the door, about twelve inches high and just as wide, where two steel water lines disappeared into the darkness.

"Jeez, that's not much room. You'd have to be awful skinny to get through there," Nicky said.

All eyes swung in his direction.

Nicky glanced up at the hole. Judging from the look on his handsome face, he was thinking about what might lurk beyond the door.

"Ah, come on . . ."

"You gotta do it, Nicky. You're the only one small enough."

He was about to refuse when we heard Principal Hull's footsteps on the linoleum floor above us. "Okay," Nicky said, shaking his head. "Gimme a boost and tell me if you hear anything."

Diggs braced himself against the door, and Nicky climbed his back like a monkey. Standing on the bigger boy's shoulders, the third grader grabbed one of the water lines and swung his legs into the gap between the joists. Then he rolled onto his stomach and started slithering feet first into the darkness. Soon only his head and shoulders were visible, and we could hear his feet seeking purchase on the inside.

"Shit," he said. "I can't find anything to stand on. What do I do?"

Diggs coached him through it. "Just slide back a little farther and hang on to the wall with your hands. Try to find the doorknob with your foot. You can stand on—"

Nicky disappeared into the darkness with a loud crash. There were several seconds of silence, followed by whimpering.

"You okay?" Sean asked.

"Yeah, but I think I got a broom handle up my butt," came a muffled reply from beyond the door. We could hear him fumbling around. "I can't see anything. Wait a minute . . . There it is!"

A block of light punched through the space between the ceiling joists, and the storeroom door opened a second later. Nicky, in some discomfort, stood to one side as we trooped in.

There was not a lot to see. The room wasn't much larger than a walk-in closet. Rough plywood shelving held reams of foolscap, cartons of chalk, and several cardboard boxes filled with poster paint. In front of us, stacked almost to the rafters, was an imposing wall of vintage oak-and-iron school desks in various stages of disassembly. A couple of decaying mops stood at attention beside a galvanized janitor's bucket. Everything was coated with a thick layer of dust.

"Doesn't look like anyone's been here for years," said Eli.

Kent agreed. "Nothing here worth looking at."

Sean was standing near the barricade of furniture. "Wait a minute," he said. Getting down on his hands and knees, he peered between the wrought iron legs of an ancient desk. "Hey, there's no wall back here, just some boards and dirt."

That's when we heard it. From beyond the closet came a dreadful moan. We ran.

"What the hell was that?" asked Abner. We were back in the washroom and panting from our sprint up the stairs.

"I don't know. But whatever it was, it came from behind those desks," said Sean as he brushed dirt from the knees of his corduroy pants.

"Should we go back and find out?"

"Screw that. I'm not going back down there."

"No, we better go and close the door," said Diggs with what sounded like regret. "If we leave it open, Hull will know we've been in there."

Though we hated to admit it, the big kid was right. Besides, none of us wanted to go down in history as the Kids Who Let the Thing Out of the Basement.

"Okay, let's close the door. Then we'll figure out what to do."

Creeping past Hull's office, we slunk partway down the basement stairs. Diggs tiptoed to the stockroom door, peered inside, and waved us down the rest of the way. "Nothing here, you pansies," he said before switching off the light. "I'll lock the door, and we'll go upstairs."

Seven of us gathered around Abner's desk to discuss our next move. After much debate, we agreed to make another foray into the storeroom the following day. Someone had to save the world.

"Better bring some flashlights," Eli said before boarding the bus. "It's going to be as black as a whippoorwill's ass in there."

The ride home that night was a subdued affair. I suspect we were contemplating the day's events and wondering what unholy terror lay in wait beneath Ootsa Lake school.

Every child has a demon that lurks at the edge of sleep and is fear in solid form. For me, it was the Wolf Man, that snarling creature brought to life in 1941 by Lon Chaney Jr. The lycanthrope terrified me. I cowered in my bed at night and avoided looking toward the window for fear that the Wolf Man would be there with his dead yellow eyes and menacing underbite.

When we drove away from Vancouver in 1970, I was sure I had given him the slip. Then, one snowy night as I lay half asleep in a cabin along the Baezaeko River, a long, mournful howl pierced the mid-winter silence, resurrecting that old familiar dread. Had he, against all odds, found me? My worst fears seemed confirmed when Olavi, after venturing outside with a flashlight, described with perverse delight the large black timber wolf he had seen sitting in the road less than fifty feet from our home.

Two years and several moves later, as Kelly and I walked home from the bus stop, I wondered if my old nemesis lurked in the basement of Ootsa Lake school. If so, I was determined to face him.

"Is this silver?" I asked my parents over dinner. We were seated around the kitchen table, and I was examining my knife with unusual interest.

"Don't talk with your mouth full," Olavi ordered, though his own maw was stuffed with pork hocks and boiled potatoes.

I ignored him. "Mom, is this silver?"

"No, it's stainless steel," said Mom.

"Do we have any?"

"Any what? You mean silverware?" Mom sighed and put down her fork. "We used to have quite a bit, but a person who shall remain nameless took most of it. Now we only have a partial set. Why?"

I lied. "Just curious. Can I try eating with it?"

Olavi paused long enough to wipe gravy from his beard. "No. Now eat."

Mom shot him a pained look before responding. "Not tonight, Mike."

"Aw, come on. If you let me, I'll do the dishes."

"I said not to . . . Oh, what the heck." Looking at the mess on her plate, she added, "This meal could use a little class."

Mom rose from her chair, walked to the kitchen counter, and returned with a small wooden box. Setting it down, she opened the lid.

Inside, nestled on worn red velvet, was an arsenal of cutlery.

"It doesn't look like silver," I said, picking up a spoon and examining it. The ornate utensil had a greenish tint.

"It is," Mom assured, "but it's tarnished. Turn it over and look at the handle.

I did. There, just visible, were the magic words: "Wm. Rogers - Sterling."

My lunch box was a little heavier than usual the next day, and it clanked when I set it down on the bus seat between Sean and me.

"What you got in there?" he asked.

I steered the conversation in another direction. "Bring a flashlight?"

"Yep," Sean answered, producing a shiny aluminum Eveready from a brown paper bag. "Works good too." He flicked it on and stared into the glowing lens. "Nicky couldn't find one, though."

The younger boy seated in front of me looked crestfallen. I tried to make him feel better by saying, "Don't worry. I couldn't bring one, either. My dad keeps it by his bed at night."

Nicky brightened. "I brought matches and a candle, though. Probably good to have them just in case the flashlight craps out."

That's when I noticed the odour. It was pungent and familiar yet not quite identifiable. For some reason, it conjured visions of meatballs smothered in spicy tomato sauce.

"What smells?"

No one said anything for a moment. Then Sean reached into his paper bag and pulled out a long string of white bulbs.

"Garlic," he said, "and I also brought these." Digging into the sack a second time, he produced a meat mallet and a small bundle of sharpened kindling.

We knew then what kept the Alcott boy awake at night.

I wanted to laugh but dared not. It is difficult to belittle someone's fears when you plan to ward off evil with a place setting of silverware.

Diggs, Kent, and Abner got on, and we started planning our expedition into the basement. By the time the bus ground to a halt outside Ootsa school, it was agreed the venture should be postponed until lunch hour.

"It'll give us more time," Diggs noted.

When Baxter dismissed our class at noon, we gobbled our lunches and ambled down the hallway. Ralph declined to join the crusade, but the fight he picked with Brendan created a convenient diversion.

We assembled outside the door to the storeroom. Diggs put aside the hockey stick he was carrying and helped Nicky clamber up the wall. Within seconds, the third grader had the door open.

Diggs shut the door and locked it after we all squeezed through. The click of the bolt sliding into place was loud in the stillness. "We gotta be quiet," he whispered, "or Hull will hear us."

"How we going to do that and move all those?" asked Kent, pointing to the wall of desks.

"Don't know. There sure are a lot of them. Must have been in here since Jesus wore diapers."

"They're old, but not that old," said Sean, who was on his knees inspecting the black iron leg of one monstrosity. "The writing here says it was made in 1922. But the good news is, I think we can crawl through."

We bent down for a better look. Sure enough, there was a kid-sized tunnel between two of the desks.

"Okay, let's do it," said Diggs. "Give me the flashlight, and I'll go first."

Sean relinquished his Eveready, and Diggs clicked it on before disappearing into the darkness. "Okay, I'm through. Who's next?" he asked a few seconds later.

One by one, we crawled through the narrow tunnel and gathered in a circle around our tall friend.

"You smell something?" asked Eli.

"That's Alcott," I said.

Diggs trained the flashlight on Sean in time to see him donning his herbal necklace. "Give me that," the younger boy said, snatching the flashlight.

"Why are you wearing those?" I asked with perverse delight, even though the answer was obvious.

"For the same reason that Diggs is packing a hockey stick, and you," Sean answered, pointing the flashlight in my direction, "are carrying that thing."

"It's a special knife," I said, looking down at the broad-bladed implement in my right hand.

"No, it's not," said Nicky with a chuckle. "It's pie shovel. What are you going to do if you meet something down here? Serve it dessert?"

Everybody laughed, and it helped ease the tension. Then we got down to the serious business of monster hunting.

"Shine the flashlight over here, Sean," Diggs said.

Beyond us, the grey dirt floor of the basement sloped gently upwards until there was no more than a yard between it and the ceiling. Cobwebs hung like lacy stalactites from the two-by-twelve joists, and there was mouse shit everywhere.

"It's a crawlspace," Sean said.

There was silence for a couple of seconds. Then, from somewhere in the darkness ahead came the haunting sound that had scared us the day before.

A tingle of fear crawled up my spine, and I held the Sterling pastry server higher. Beside me, an ornate silver crucifix suddenly appeared in Nicky's small hand.

"Holy shit," Kent said when the sound ebbed away. "Did you hear that?"

"Yeah, it sounded like it came from over there," Diggs noted, pointing his hockey stick to the left. "But let's clear this side of the school first."

We proceeded with great caution. Only the sound of our breathing disturbed the oppressive stillness. After ten minutes and no sign of anything supernatural, we started to feel more comfortable. But the light from our flashlight was also growing dimmer by the minute.

Sean sounded the alarm. "Not much juice left in this thing," he said.

Diggs took the flashlight a second time. After looking the implement over, he tried to extract a little more energy from its depleted batteries by banging them against his thigh.

"Hey, take it easy on the flashlight, man," Sean said. "Give it back."

"Fine," Diggs said as he returned the Eveready. "I don't need it anyway. I can almost see down here."

I doubted that was true. It was as dark as a root cellar on a moonless night.

With Diggs following Sean's waning flashlight beam and acting as a scout, our band of adventurers turned west toward where we had last heard the demonic moan. The dirt floor began to slope downward again, allowing us to stand upright.

About halfway across the crawlspace, we encountered an unfinished line of two-by-four framing. Now a little cocky, Diggs stepped through to the other side.

And started screaming.

"Oh shit, it's got Diggs!" Sean cried, fumbling for his stakes and mallet. He dropped the flashlight, and it rolled a few feet before coming to rest against a rock.

"Hold on, Diggory, I'm coming!" Abner yelled from behind me. Rising to his feet, the fifth grader managed two quick steps before tripping and falling headlong in the dust.

There was a crunch of breaking glass, and the flashlight went out.

The next few minutes were confusing. Yells and screams pierced the darkness. Sensing a rout, I turned and scuttled in the general direction of the storeroom. Something bumped me and, without thinking, I stabbed at it. The creature howled in pain, knocked me to the ground, and crawled atop my prone form.

Its fetid breath was hot on my face. Two bony hands landed on my chest and began clawing toward my neck. Crying out in alarm, I placed the dull edge of the pie server against one paw and sawed at it without effect.

This can't be happening, I thought as the thing's gnarled claws closed around my throat. *I'm only twelve. I haven't even had sex yet.*

Distraught, I turned my head away from the menace and prepared to die.

A light flared in the darkness, illuminating a scene that could have been an outtake from *Abbott & Costello Meet the Mummy.*

On the other side of the timber framing, Diggs rolled on the ground and swore as he batted madly at his face and hair. Abner, throwing caution to the wind, had tried to reach the bigger boy's side by crawling between a pair of upright two-by-fours, but had snagged his coat on an errant nail and was now hacking at it with a rusty hatchet.

Kent and Sean were locked in a passionate embrace. Their moment of intimacy ended when the Alcott boy hit his wrestling partner with a wooden mallet.

And in the middle of everything sat Nicky, a lit match clasped between thumb and forefinger.

He looked at the chaos around him and started to laugh. "You guys are retards," he said, transferring the flame to a stubby white candle.

The grip on my throat relaxed. I turned toward my assailant.

"Jesus," Eli said as he rolled off me. "It's just you."

"You almost killed me, you dork," I croaked. "And your breath stinks like rotten meat. What the hell were you doing?"

"What was I doing?" he replied. "First, you stabbed me. Then you tried to cut my hand off with that stupid pie thing." He rubbed his wrist self-consciously.

I looked down at the bent pastry shovel in my right hand. "Uh . . . sorry, I guess."

"That's nothing," said Kent, blinking and rubbing his head. "At least someone didn't try to cave your skull in with a hammer."

The flashlight was a write-off, so we regrouped around Nicky's candle. Diggs, it turned out, had run into a mess of spiders on his way through the framing.

"I could feel the suckers crawling on my face," he said with an involuntary shudder. "There were dozens of them. Must have been a nest."

His words were punctuated by an all-too-familiar moan from the west side of the crawlspace. Most of us cringed, but Diggs stood up and peered into the darkness.

"Come on, Thing," he said, brandishing his hockey stick in defiance. "I ain't scared."

When his challenge went unanswered, the big kid started toward the northwest corner of the school. Nicky followed with his candle, the rest of us close behind.

We could just make out the school's concrete foundation when the sound came again, louder and closer. The candle's tiny flame guttered.

Nicky figured it out. "Oh, for Christ's sake." Pushing past Diggs, he knelt and examined the concrete. "There's a crack in the cement here. I can feel cool air coming in. That noise is just the wind."

Almost on cue, the sigh came again, nearly snuffing Nicky's candle.

We were stupefied. "You mean there's no ghost?"

"No," the black-haired kid said before looking furtively into the darkness behind us. "At least not here."

"Well, we're down here now," Diggs said, turning around. "Might as well check out the rest of it."

We followed the foundation southward. Our group had not gone ten feet before Sean called a halt.

He and Nicky were staring at a circular hole in the ground. It was about eighteen inches in diameter and filled with muddy water.

My apprehension returned. "Think it's the well?"

Kent must have thought so because he grabbed Sean's arm. "Don't get too close. You might fall in and drown."

The younger boy looked at him, then stuck the toe of one shoe into the hole. "Doubt that," he said, smirking. "It's only four inches deep."

To prove the point, he stepped in with both feet. The water only came up to his ankles.

"Shit on a shingle," said Eli. He cast a scornful glance at Kent before adding, "So much for the well to Hell."

The freckled kid just shrugged.

We were all starting to feel foolish. The crawlspace, it seemed, was just an empty expanse of dirt and cobwebs.

"We wasted an entire lunch hour," said Diggs, looking wistfully at his hockey stick. "There's nothing down here."

We left the crawlspace after Sean wrung the Hell water out of his socks. Old Man Hull met us at the top of the stairs, but Nicky convinced him we had only been looking for Eli's broken pocketknife. The principal let us off with a warning, then patrolled the stairwell for a week in case his trust had been misplaced. He need not have because the supply room no longer interested us.

The Wolf Man's hold on me had also been broken. I never feared him after our expedition into the basement, convinced, like Diggs, that monsters did not exist. Years later, I learned that I couldn't have been more wrong. There is evil in the world, and it's harder to spot than the Wolf Man because it walks, talks, and looks like a human. Sometimes it even lives with us, just waiting for the right moment to pounce.

The boys who accompanied me into the crawlspace still live in the Lakes District. Our paths often cross around Halloween, and when they do, it reminds me of how we faced our childhood fears in the basement of Ootsa Lake school.

Do they remember the bogeyman in the basement? Probably not. The incident happened a long time ago. Yet sometimes, after I raise a hand to one of them in greeting, I think I see the ghost of a smile on his face.

THE MIDDLE PART

Real Dad

Kelly and I were the products of our mother's first marriage. It was an unhappy union defined by violence. For sixteen years, my mother endured episodic abuse separated by interludes of trepidation. I suspect she spent much of my early childhood recovering from a beating or waiting for one.

Like most women of her generation, she was expected to suffer mistreatment in silence. When she refused and finally locked my father out of the house in 1969, she got little support from family or friends. My Dublin-born maternal grandmother, herself a victim of spousal assault, made her feelings on the subject clear: marriage, she said in her soft brogue, was a sacred covenant between a man, a woman, and God. In her opinion, regular pummeling was just part of the package.

"If he hit you," Nana stated with conviction on more than one occasion, "you probably deserved it."

Mom's decision to date Olavi, a man she met on the bus, turned an embarrassing situation into a scandal. According to Nana, it also placed the fate of my mother's eternal soul in jeopardy.

"Take up with that man," Nana remonstrated, "and you'll go to Hell."

Nana's warnings went unheeded. My mother must have felt it was better to be damned in the next life than miserable in this one because I awoke one morning to find a strange man sleeping beside her.

"This is Olavi," she said as if the chubby Finlander's arrival was as normal as a sunrise and should be greeted with the same enthusiasm.

I was not happy. Neither was the man who had previously shared my mother's bed. After Nana informed my father of this development, he prowled the neighbourhood in his black-and-chrome Chevy Bel Air, glaring and shouting obscenities and making what Mom explained were rude gestures with his middle finger.

And there were threats too. Lots of them, most involving grievous bodily harm. Mom knew from experience they were not idle ones and began planning her escape.

When she and Olavi packed us into a second-hand Pontiac and fled Vancouver a few months later, I suspect they were looking for a fresh start. Yet if they'd hoped to leave the stigma of their relationship behind like outdated furniture, they were to be disappointed. As they soon discovered, people living in BC's hinterland took an even dimmer view of women who left their husbands and men who encouraged such behaviour.

This unique moral geography made full disclosure of our family's past hazardous. After losing one ranch job for perceived turpitude, my parents became historical revisionists by necessity, developing a new backstory in which Olavi figured as my biological father. It was a skillfully woven tapestry of fact and fiction that incorporated Mom's more benign memories of her first marriage with the realities of her second. Olavi learned the stories of my childhood. He left the narrative to my mother in social settings, smiling beatifically or shaking his head in bewilderment at appropriate junctures.

Kelly and I were expected to participate in this charade. Olavi was always to be addressed as "Dad," and we were never to mention our biological father in public. In-house references to him were also subtly discouraged. When we grew old and bold enough to pose questions about the man in part responsible for our existence, Mom's brusque replies made it clear he was a subject she preferred not to discuss.

We played along, though it meant denying our heritage and part of ourselves.

In truth, pretending my father didn't exist wasn't that difficult. "Real Dad," as I thought of him when I thought of him at all, had never been a big part of my life. It wasn't like we hung out together when he was around. I recall going to his workplace once—a cavernous establishment on Marine Drive that smelled of solvents and tired equipment—and roaming around while he spliced long strands of steel cable that hung from the ceiling like ferric gossamer. I sometimes sat beside him on the couch while he watched *All Star Wrestling*, and we occasionally went to the Pacific Coliseum for a

Canucks game when the team was still part of the Western Hockey League, but I do not remember any classic father-and-son moments. There were no games of catch in the backyard or piggyback rides at the beach. His presence was always more physical than emotional. We sometimes shared space but never a sense of companionship.

If Real Dad's absence did not leave a deep hole in my life, it was because he had never really been present in it. Three years after the Big Breakup, he was largely forgotten, a relic from my past that I was content to leave buried.

Yet time has a way of wearing away the strata of our lives, exposing like the bones of ancient saurians things long hidden. Nothing stays concealed forever.

It was late July at Rainbow Lake when it happened. With school out and nothing better to do, I played with my Matchbox toys in front of our cabin. A month of strong sunshine had dried the mud there to the consistency of concrete, making the construction of miniature roads difficult. Birds chattered in nearby willows, and a light wind blew off the sloping meadow to the east, bringing the scent of baked earth and wildflowers.

Rusty, our scarred Labrador retriever, was dozing in a patch of shade near the woodshed. Without warning, he sat up and looked expectantly toward the road.

I followed his gaze. A blue crew cab truck pulling a travel trailer drove past our gate and stopped. After a moment's hesitation, it backed up and turned down the rutted driveway toward our house.

Rusty, who took his job as watchdog seriously, started barking.

"Someone's here," I announced.

My parents emerged from the cabin. "Who is it?" Mom asked, balancing my sister Laina on one hip.

"I don't know," I said.

"Looks like a tourist," said Olavi, shading his eyes against the sun's glare. "Must be lost."

Visitors from afar were a rarity, those who arrived with recreation vehicles even more uncommon. Road conditions south of Francois Lake tended to discourage travel. Few out-of-towners got beyond Takysie Lake, which was okay with the area's permanent residents.

The pickup idled down the hill toward us, its attendant trailer swaying from side to side like a waddling duck. The tandem pulled up about twenty feet from our house. The truck's engine died with a snarl and then sat ticking in the heat.

The driver's door opened, and out stepped Real Dad.

He was just as I remembered: thickset, muscular, a few inches under six feet in height with a swarthy complexion and black hair out of a Brylcreem commercial. His face, dominated by a pronounced brow ridge, had a coarse unfinished quality to it, like the work of a potter who, finding himself at the end of a busy day with five or six mismatched pieces of argil and just as many minutes, decides to try his hand at sculpting. The resulting bust, hastily created, was identifiable as human yet somehow lacked humanity.

My father stretched, looked around, and turned toward me. Even at ten paces, he emanated energy. There was a feral power in the way he moved, a ponderous self-awareness that reminded me of Beltane, the great Hereford bull that Buford Atkinson loosed on the open range each spring. Like that creature, my father had an enormous appetite for destruction.

A broad smile of recognition creased his face. "Hello," he said, starting across the yard. His voice was in complete contrast to his build, high pitched and almost feminine.

Something like hope fluttered within me. While I had not missed this man, was it possible he had missed me? Two years was a long time to be without something. An equal length of time had passed since we'd owned a television, and I still pined for Saturday morning cartoons.

Did he want to be my dad after all? I wasn't sure I needed a father, but that didn't mean I didn't want one, someone who would take an interest in my affairs and spend time with me. It was possible, right? "People can change," Mom always said, though never in the context of her first husband. Perhaps he had become a better version of himself. Why else would he drive all this way from Vancouver?

Something momentous was about to happen. Excited, I dropped the toy truck in my hand and clambered to my feet. My father was close now, right in front of me. I could see the irregular scar on his chin from a previous car accident, smell the sharp tang of his aftershave. He was still grinning, and there was a spring in his step.

Would he hug me or—knowing that, at twelve, I was almost grown up—just shake my hand? I decided either would be acceptable, given that my friends were not around to witness any mushy stuff that might follow.

I stepped toward him. "Dad," I whispered, searching his face for signs of affection.

Real Dad placed a calloused hand on my shoulder, but instead of drawing me close, he used it to push me aside. He walked within a foot of my mother and put both hands on his knobby hips.

"Goddamn, Pat, it's good to see you," he said with enthusiasm, giving her the once-over. "You look great, just great."

In that instant, I knew this man had not driven six hundred miles to see me.

It was like a punch in the gut. The air whooshed out of my lungs, and my vision blurred. I felt dizzy. Sounds were muted. The adults were talking, but their voices were indistinct as if coming from a distance.

What had I done wrong? Had I been too eager? Should I have called him "Sir" or "Father" instead of "Dad?" Maybe it was my clothes. After all, I'd been sitting in the dirt all morning and looked like Pig-Pen's poorer cousin.

The squeak of a truck door opening stemmed the internal flood of questions. I watched as three children and a plump woman in a green polyester dress piled out of the pickup.

My father turned at the sound. "I'm so excited I forgot my manners." With a self-conscious giggle, he beckoned to the quartet and said, "Come here and meet these nice people."

"Pat, this is my wife Shirley," he continued, throwing an arm around the woman as soon as she drew near, "and these are my boys David, Jason, and Robert. Say 'hello,' boys." He gestured toward the rest of his party like a tinker displaying his wares.

The four of them muttered a greeting.

Olavi was nonplussed. Mom looked shell-shocked.

"Well, here we are," said Real Dad. Disengaging from the woman, he rubbed both hands together. "Let's go inside and have some coffee. You can get coffee up here in the sticks, can't you?"

He laughed at his cleverness and headed for the house. The three boys tried to follow, but he stopped them cold. "You stay here and get to know these kids," he said, pointing vaguely in the direction of Kelly and me. "You're all related, so act like it."

"Just don't pet the dog," the woman called Shirley said before going inside. "It might have fleas."

The grown-ups disappeared into the cabin, leaving the five of us alone. Kelly saw an opportunity and lit out for parts unknown. Rusty, sensing that his services were no longer required, followed her, leaving me to face the boys alone.

They were immaculately dressed in bright calico shirts and new blue jeans. The eldest, Robert, was about my height but slightly heavier, with short hair slicked back like Real Dad's. The youngest was a chubby monkey with wet lips. David, the middle kid, had a thin face, blond hair, and freckles; judging from the way he kept sniffing and rubbing his carriage bolt nose, he suffered from hay fever.

I hated them.

We faced each other like gunfighters at the OK Corral. I didn't like the odds but wasn't going down without a fight.

The one called Robert made the first move. "Who are you?" he asked.

"I'm your dad's real son."

I don't know why I said it. There had been no derision in his voice, only mild curiosity. But I was hurting and wanted to pass the feeling on.

Robert looked as though he had been slapped. He took a step forward. "Yeah? Well, he's ours now."

David joined the conversation. "And he loves us and not you," he added. "And he wouldn't make us live in a shithole like this." He nodded toward the ramshackle trapper's cabin that my family had called home for the past year.

It felt as though someone had rubbed crushed glass in my eyes. My hands bunched into fists. Should I hit the bigger kid first or take out the smaller ones? Maybe kick Robert in the nuts and then turn my attention to David, I decided. There was a good chance that Jason would run for Mommy and Daddy as soon as the other two went down.

A yodel prevented our family reunion from taking an interesting turn. I looked beyond my dad's new kids to see a familiar figure trotting down the hill.

Diggs joined our little circle. He was clad in worn denim and a T-shirt that had once been white but was now the colour of autumn storm clouds. His cheap tennis shoes, frayed laces knotted in several places where they had broken, were powdered with fine dust. He carried a fishing pole and scuffed green plastic tackle box in one hand and a five-pound Maple Leaf lard pail in the other.

"Hey, Mike," he said in greeting.

"Hey," I replied. "What's up?"

"I came over to ask if you would go fishing with me, but I see," he looked toward the trio of strangers, "you got company."

Robert looked at the newcomer and repeated his earlier question. "Who are you?"

"This is Diggs," I said, grateful for the distraction because I wasn't much of a fighter. "He's my friend from down the road. He's really tough."

Diggs, unaccustomed to compliments, smiled and did a little shuffle of pleasure.

I could see the Three Stooges eying up my friend's worn clothing. If it didn't impress them, his size did. The Wistaria farm boy was head and shoulders taller than the rest of us, all bone and lean muscle and sharp angles under a disorderly thatch of brown hair.

I almost dared them to say something derogatory. Diggs could have kicked their collective asses without breaking a sweat.

Instead, David asked, "What's in the bucket?"

My friend, oblivious to the tension around him, put down his fishing tackle. "My lunch," he said, removing the lard pail's rusty lid and withdrawing a sandwich wrapped in waxed paper.

Jason leaned forward and peered into the receptacle. "What's all that other stuff?"

"Dirt with worms in it," said Diggs. Turning to me, he added, "Found some really big ones under the shit in the chicken coop. The fish will go crazy for them."

"You carry your lunch in a worm pail?" Robert asked in disbelief.

"Sure," said Diggs, unwrapping his sandwich and taking a massive bite of it. "Want to see them?"

All three crowded forward. My friend held the sandwich in his mouth while he stirred the dirt with one long finger. "Look at the size of this mother," he said, holding up a choice specimen about six inches long. It writhed and shed bits of black loam.

"That one's a good size," agreed Jason.

"It's not that big," said Robert, stepping back. "We get them bigger in Vancouver. Dad says they're called dew worms. He digs them out of the back-yard the night before we go fishing."

Real Dad takes these jerks fishing? He never took me fishing.

Diggs looked skeptical. He returned the worm to Death Row and closed the lid. After wiping his fingers in the grass, he retrieved the sandwich and continued munching. "I've found bigger ones," he said around a mouthful of peanut butter and jam. "These are summer worms. They're bigger in the fall."

"Yeah, they are," I agreed, though I had never known worms to vary in size depending on the season. It just seemed important to back up my friend. "They're much bigger just before winter. That one will probably be a foot long after eating crap for a few more months."

Silence followed. I wasn't sure Jason, David, and Robert bought the worm story.

Diggs finished his sandwich. "You got something to drink? I'm drier than a popcorn fart."

I wanted to avoid Real Dad at all costs lest some embarrassing questions be asked. "Let's go down to the lake. There's nice cold stuff there."

We walked to the beach. Diggs found the ladle on our dock and helped himself to water. "Anyone else want some?" he asked, offering the utensil around.

"You drink water right out of the lake?" asked David. "Shouldn't you, like, boil it or something first?"

Diggs looked at me and raised one eyebrow. "Why?" he asked with genuine surprise. "This lake is clean. And the shitter is way over there." The Wistaria boy gestured toward our outhouse seventy-five feet away to empha-size the point.

"I'll have a drink," said Jason. He accepted the ladle and took a long draught before his brothers could react. "That's good. Nice and cold."

Robert was poking around the shoreline. He reached down and picked up a rock. "Watch this," he said.

He threw the missile with a flick of his wrist. It bounced across the water's surface several times before sinking out of sight twenty feet away.

"Six skips," he said, hoisting his pride like a flag. "Bet you can't beat that."

"No sweat." Selecting a flat rock, I took a running start and hurled it toward the lake. It touched down several times before disappearing, but not nearly enough.

"Only four skips," Robert said. "I win."

"I was just warming up. You wait and see."

Everyone got into the act. Rocks flew like shrapnel, and the lake—which had been a sheet of burnished steel in the midday sun—was soon covered in ripples.

"Did you see that?" said David after a good throw. "Eight skips!"

Diggs pushed his way to the water's edge, a rock the size and shape of a dinner plate clutched in one dirty hand.

"Out of the way, gomers," he said, elbowing Robert and me aside.

The big kid crouched low and studied the lake. When the wavelets from previous tosses faded, he wound up and launched the projectile sidearm like a young Kent Tekulve.

It was a perfect throw. We watched in awe as the rock struck the water ten feet away and skipped gaily onward for another forty, creating a chain of bright splashes before sinking out of sight.

". . . nineteen, twenty, twenty-one," Diggs counted with satisfaction. "That's how you do it."

No one challenged him. Score one for the hicks from the sticks.

Kelly showed up with a message. "Mom said to come get you. We're going somewhere."

Diggs retrieved his fishing gear, and we returned to the cabin.

The adults were milling around Real Dad's new pickup while he extolled its many virtues. My parents had no idea what to do with our unexpected guests.

Mom saw us, and her face lit up. "When did you get here, Diggory?" she asked.

"A bit ago," he said. "Came to see if Mike could go fishing."

"Dad, he skipped a rock twenty-one times," said David. My father, in the middle of assuring Olavi that the travel trailer cost more than he made in a year, did not respond.

"That's a great idea," Mom replied. "Why don't we go to Mumford Lake?"

No one had any objections, so Olavi scrounged up some more fishing rods while Real Dad disconnected his precious Chevrolet from the travel trailer. "You sit in the front with me, Pat," he said, winking at my mother. "We've got lots to talk about. Ollie and Shirl can sit together."

Mom didn't take the bait. She sidestepped him and climbed into the back seat.

The smile disappeared from my father's face. "Go on, get in. We haven't got all goddamn day," he said to the rest of us, and we scrambled into the truck box.

The truck growled up the hill and onto the main road. My parents, seated in the cab, were having an animated conversation with our guests, but I heard none of it. After about a mile and a half, Olavi pointed to an old logging road on the left, and the truck eased in that direction.

We crawled along in low gear. Leafy willows reached for us from the roadside. My father was able to steer wide of these hazards at first, but soon the track was so overgrown that he made us climb out and hold the branches aside so his pickup wouldn't get scratched.

The truck rounded a corner five minutes later and eased to a halt. Before us lay what Olavi referred to as the La Brea Tar Pit, an epic mudhole that stretched at least fifteen yards down the trail. My stepfather had attacked it the previous fall with Mickey O'Brian's bulldozer, but his efforts to drain the hazard had only deepened it.

Truck doors opened, and the adults got out. They walked to the edge of the quagmire for a closer look.

"Better go that way," said Olavi, pointing to some enterprising fisherman's detour through the nearby poplars.

My father glanced at the makeshift trail and snorted. "I don't know what you're thinking, Ollie. That way looks worse to me. All deep ruts and tree roots."

Olavi put forward a second alternative. "We could leave the truck here and walk. It's only twenty minutes to the lake."

Real Dad swatted at the mosquitos whining around his head. "With all these bugs? I'd be bled dry in a minute. Besides, it doesn't look like much."

"Go around," said Mom. "Olavi almost got the Cat stuck last year."

"Please, honey, listen to these people," pleaded Shirley. "They know this country. If they say it's bad, it's bad."

Real Dad would have none of it. "Don't you tell me what to do," he said, poking a finger at his wife. "What do you know? You couldn't drive a wheelbarrow. This truck is the best four-wheel-drive General Motors makes, not like that bucket of scrap Pat and Ollie get around in. We'll make it."

He strode back to the Chevy, climbed in, and slammed the door. Gears ground, and we heard a *clunk* from the pickup's transfer case. "Robert, turn the hubs for me," he ordered.

Diggs shot me a look of bewilderment as the city kids bailed out of the truck. "He's not going to try to get through, is he?"

I shrugged. "Looks like it."

"Jesus," said Diggs, standing up, "I'm getting out. So should you." With that, he grabbed his fishing tackle and tumbled over the side. I snatched the other rods and followed.

We lined the track as my father backed up to take a run at the mudhole.

Mom tried once more to prevent disaster. "Don't be stupid, Donald," she said. "Just park the truck here. We can walk. The fresh air will do us good."

Real Dad gave her a long, hard stare, revved the engine several times to emphasize his masculinity, and popped the clutch. The truck shot forward, all four tires clawing at the dirt.

The La Brea Tar Pit was deceptive. It looked shallow, even from a yard away, no more than eight or ten inches deep. Yet as many unsuspecting motorists had discovered over the years, what appeared to be the bottom was suspended sludge. Beneath it lay a thick layer of primordial ooze.

Real Dad's four-by-four hit the trap at thirty miles an hour, spraying slime and stagnant water in a wide arc. The truck made good headway for a second or two, and I thought it might prove us liars and reach the far side. Then the front end dropped into Olavi's excavation, and the unit started down like a submarine with full ballast tanks.

Forward progress slowed and then stopped. Real Dad kept the tires churning. The small-block engine screamed, and the vehicle shuddered as he slammed the transmission from forward to reverse time after time. Yet instead of working itself free, his late-model Chevrolet settled ever deeper into the muck. Its bright silver bumper disappeared under black goo. Dirty water reached the running boards and started up the doors. Steam rolled from the wheel wells and slithered through the mud-spattered grill. The submerged tailpipe burbled.

Perhaps ten seconds later, swamp juice reached some crucial electrical component, and the motor died with a cough.

Real Dad stared straight ahead with his hands clenched around the steering wheel. Then he bellowed like a gut-shot water buffalo and looked around for someone to blame.

Without a word, Olavi started back the way we had come.

"Where the hell is he going?" asked Real Dad. His tone was evil, and I looked around for someplace to hide, just as I had when I was little.

"To get the tractor and a long chain," said Mom. Then she turned and followed her husband.

It took two hours to drag Real Dad and his truck from the mudhole. Diggs and I made the most of our opportunity and slipped away to Mumford Lake.

We took Real Dad's boys with us out of pity. Diggs, displaying infinite patience, baited their hooks and showed the younger ones how to cast while I polled the raft around the lake barefoot like a character out of *The Adventures of Huckleberry Finn*. We all caught fish, fat rainbow trout with glistening sides and crimson mouths, but Diggs and I caught the biggest ones.

David and Jason drank from the lake without complaint. Robert stripped off his clothes and went swimming. We had fun without worrying about our bloodlines.

Late in the afternoon, Olavi came and got us on the tractor. On the way home, David, Robert, Jason, and I shared space on the warm green fenders while Diggs balanced like an acrobat on the three-point hitch.

As expected, the boys' father was in a fearsome mood. He glared at everyone and cuffed Jason for no reason, which prompted Shirley to gather her sons like a nervous hen protecting its brood.

I kept out of the way.

When Olavi took the tractor back, Real Dad pulled Mom aside for one last attempt at atonement. They had a heated conversation in the shadow of the woodshed. He put a hand on my mother's shoulder; she reacted as if burned and retreated to the cabin.

Real Dad stormed around for a while. Then he connected the truck and trailer, crammed his instant family inside, and left without saying goodbye.

We never saw him again. We heard, however, that the first thing he did upon returning to the Lower Mainland was raid my Aunt Betty's basement and make off with the stuff we had left there. In what I considered his final act of betrayal, Real Dad stole my toys and gave them to his sons.

Diggs and I had a sleepover at his house that night. We ate pan-fried fish with mashed potatoes and canned corn slathered in butter; dessert was half a package of chocolate chip cookies washed down with gallons of fresh cow's milk. When it grew dark, we commandeered his mother's double bed and talked of fishing and hockey and cute girls with breasts like watermelons.

Later, as we lay in companionable silence under a warm comforter, having exhausted these topics and several others, my friend asked the question I had long hoped to avoid.

"Who were those people today?"

I held my breath for a second before answering. "Just some dorks from before."

Portentous silence followed.

"Was that guy your dad?"

The room seemed to shrink around me. Mom had coached us on how to answer questions like this one. *Admit nothing,* she said. *Never tell anyone about your father. If you do, bad things will happen.*

I was about to utter one of her canned responses, say the man with the nice truck was my uncle, but the words tasted like bile and caught in my throat. Diggs was my best friend and lying to him didn't seem right. If I couldn't trust him, who could I trust?

"Yeah," I said, my voice a whisper. "But you can't tell anyone. Ever."

"I won't. So . . . those kids . . . were your brothers?"

"No!" I almost yelled the word. "They're hers, not his. They've got nothing to do with me. I'm his only son."

"Okay."

There was another anxious interlude.

"Do you miss him?"

"No," I said, and for the first time, I meant it. "He doesn't love me."

We said nothing for several minutes. When Diggs eventually broke the awkward stillness, the catch in his voice spoke of pain long concealed.

"Never knew my dad."

I felt his anguish yet did not know how to assuage it. "Sometimes," I said in the darkness, "it's better that you don't."

We never spoke of our fathers again.

Real Dad died in 2015 after a long battle with cancer. Before he did, he called Kelly to let her know he was on his way out.

He promised to call me but never got around to it. When word of his passing reached me a week later, I felt sadness. It was not the sharp-edged sorrow that had accompanied my mother's death nineteen years earlier, more a dull ache of regret, like the phantom pain of an old amputation. I mourned what might have been. My father's demise, and perhaps my obstinacy, had robbed us of any chance at reconciliation. There would be no belated apologies or words of contrition, no deathbed asseverations. The chasm between us would never be bridged.

In the years since, I have tried to tell myself Real Dad's misdeeds didn't matter and that any wounds he inflicted upon me were minor. I focus on the present more than the past. I try to be a better father than he was, as if doing so will transform his leaden neglect into emotional aurum by some alchemic process.

These strategies have given me some peace, and I consider myself a reasonably well-adjusted adult. Yet sometimes late at night, when personal demons slip their chains and shamble across the landscape of my mind, I hear the voice of a small boy asking, *What was wrong with me, Dad? Why didn't you love me?*

I have no answers for that child.

The Boxing Day Incident
or How Betty Crocker
Won the War

It was Christmas morning and judging from the jumble of parcels under the decorated evergreen in our living room, the bearded fat man had visited us during the night. Not Olavi, who had been a member of our household for four interminable years and was still asleep on the adjacent bed, but the world-famous philanthropist known as Santa Claus.

It was almost seven and not yet fully light. Kelly and I were surveying the field from a forward observation post on the stairs that led to our second-storey bedroom. We wanted to go down and check out Saint Nick's leavings but dared not wake our stepfather.

"What can you see?" Kelly asked me, peering into the gloom. "Is there an Easy-Bake Oven under the tree?"

"Can't tell," I said. "It's still too dark. Besides, Mom told you not to ask Santa for that because we don't have electricity."

My sister made a face. "I don't care. All I really want is the instant cake mixes that come with it."

Kelly loved cake or, to be more precise, cake batter. We both did. We made a batch and had an impromptu feast whenever our parents left the premises. We always washed our dishes after and disposed of the incriminating paper evidence by tossing it down the outhouse hole. Our larceny went unnoticed until Olavi glanced into the latrine one morning. It looked, he said, like a Duncan Hines truck had collided with a cattle liner. Nothing but excrement and superfluous packaging.

He put strict inventory control measures in place after making the discovery and limited our access to the pantry. We hadn't yet been able to crack the enhanced security, which explained Kelly's decision to ask Santa for an Easy-Bake Oven, a device that came with a quantity of Betty Crocker mixes. While I understood the logic behind her request, I thought petitioning Saint Nick for baking supplies made more sense.

"So, what are you going to do with the oven?" I asked her as we waited in the half-light for our parents to wake up.

Kelly gave me a sly look. "My friend Margie wants one. I'll sell it to her and then have lots of money for cake."

My eldest sister, I decided, was smart for a nine-year-old.

Another twenty minutes went by. Pale December sunlight crept into the attic through an upstairs window. Mom and Olavi, unaware of dawn's arrival, remained comatose on the ground floor. So did Laina, our baby sister, who slept in a crib nearby.

Kelly started to fidget. Unable to bear the suspense any longer, she said, "I'm going down there. I don't care if Mom and Dad get mad."

"No, wait," I said, restraining her with one arm. "I have an idea."

Without waiting for a response, I peeled off the heavy wool socks I wore 24/7 to ward off chilblains. Then, taking careful aim, I fired one toward Laina's crib.

My first shot went wide, the second one high. When I was out of ammunition, Kelly donated her footwear and went upstairs for more. The barrage continued when she returned, and we soon got the range. Salvo number eight zipped through the crib bars, bounced off the headboard, and hit my youngest sister in the forehead. She snorted, screwed up her face, and started crying.

Olavi groaned and rolled over. Mom rose like a zombie from the grave and looked around in confusion.

"Don't cry, Laina," Kelly yelled as she pounded down the stairs. "It's Christmas!"

Thirty seconds later, surrounded by a mountain of cardboard and crumpled wrapping paper, Kelly was adding water to her first mini-chef cake mix.

"Slow down, girl," Mom said. "I haven't even lit the wood stove yet."

"Oh," Kelly said with mock chagrin. "Guess I better eat this before it goes bad. Then I'll make another one."

While my eldest sister shovelled cake batter into her mouth like a stoker fueling a steam engine, and Laina played with the box Kelly's gift came in, I looked under the tree for a package with my name on it. There were several, but the largest one drew my attention.

I picked it up. It was too heavy to be a plastic ship model, and the contents sounded like peas in a milk carton when shaken.

Fearing it was a jigsaw puzzle from my unhinged but well-meaning grandmother, I put it down and reached for another box.

"Don't be too hasty," Olavi, now awake and puffing on a cigarette, said in a tone that was not unkind. "You might want to open that."

His words intrigued me, so I picked up the gift and unwrapped it.

Inside was a cardboard box, the lid of which featured an artist's rendering of a battleground as seen through a three-strand barbed wire fence. Silhouetted against a purple sky pierced by jagged thunderbolts were several pieces of military hardware, their blunt gun barrels pointed skyward at a squadron of prop-driven fighter planes. Soldiers were visible here and there; some rushed toward a concrete pillbox, while others stood at attention around one of the big cannons. A few, draped over an artillery carriage in the foreground, appeared to be either dying or pushing the fieldpiece into battle.

At the bottom of the box, printed in a typeface derived from old German gothic, was a single, red-letter word. While I wasn't sure of the pronunciation, I knew what the word meant, and it sent a jolt of excitement through me.

"Blitzkrieg," Olavi said as if I couldn't read. "The Realistic Game of Lightning Warfare."

On the birthday of the Prince of Peace, Santa Claus gave me a war game.

Today, the irony of the act is obvious, but it was lost on me at the time. I thought the gift was perfect.

Young boys are fascinated by mankind's propensity for collective violence, which probably explains why it remains part of the human condition. I was no different, and by eighth grade, war had become my obsession. I thought about it, dreamed about it, studied it with monk-like dedication. Most of the books I read were military histories, with a smattering of war novels by gritty authors like Alistair MacLean and Douglas Reeman thrown in for good measure. To hell with the adventures of Frank and Joe Hardy. I was more interested in Sun Tzu's *The Art of War.*

While I was familiar with every major conflict since Cain slew Abel, my specialty was the Second World War. I knew all the participants and could tell you what happened in most battles, complete with names, dates, and casualty rates. I considered myself the Gwynne Dyer of Grassy Plains school and took every opportunity to prove it.

"Actually, that's not right," I told my social studies teacher for the third time in as many minutes. "September 1, 1939, was the start of war in Europe. It didn't become a global conflict until the Japanese bombed Pearl Harbour on December 7, 1941, and brought America into it. And Chamberlain wasn't a complete knucklehead. Great Britain wasn't ready for war in 1938."

My antics were not well-received. School officials got another shock when they asked me what I wanted to be when I grew up. In their opinion, communicated to my parents by letter, "War-Hero-Turned-Benevolent-Dictator" was not an appropriate career choice for a thirteen-year-old boy.

Yet as the arrival of Blitzkrieg on Christmas Day proved, my fixation with all things military did not worry Mom and Olavi. They were just happy I wasn't doing drugs like my cousin Johnny.

"A war game!" I said when I saw what Santa had brought. "Cool!"

"Want me to play it with you?" Olavi asked casually. "It's a two-person game."

An offer like this, made by a father to his son, would have been eagerly accepted by most boys but not me. There were extenuating circumstances in my case. Not long after his arrival, Olavi had taught me to play chess, apparently to prove that his intellect was superior to mine. He won every game and took great delight in uttering the word "checkmate." After two years and countless drubbings, my ego was so bruised that I ran whenever he reached for the chess set.

"I don't know," I told him, my wariness dropping like a shroud between us. "I think maybe I should play it myself a few times first."

"Okay," said Olavi with obvious disappointment. "But don't wait too long. I go back to work in a few days."

I took the game upstairs, opened it, and entered the world of military simulation.

In Blitzkrieg, two fictional nations, Great Blue and Big Red, fight for control of an area that bears more than a passing resemblance to pre-war

Europe. Gameplay consists of maneuvering small pasteboard counters representing infantry, armour, artillery, and aircraft across a giant map board. Battle occurs whenever the units of one country are positioned adjacent to those of another, and the roll of a die resolves it. To win, you must eliminate all the enemy units or capture most of your opponent's cities.

Playing both sides in a conflict, I soon learned, has its drawbacks. After stalemating myself four times in the attic, I felt confident enough to challenge my stepfather for global domination.

We commandeered the kitchen table and got down to business, with Olavi playing as Great Blue and me as Big Red. War was declared at 11 a.m. on Christmas Day.

By noon, it was over.

Olavi proved even more adept at Blitzkrieg than he was at chess. His units stormed through several neutral countries, circumvented my version of the Maginot Line, and paused just long enough to vaporise my First and Fifth army corps before crossing Big Red's border in a pasteboard wave. My subsequent withdrawal made Napoleon's retreat from Moscow look well-planned.

"Checkmate," Olavi said as the last remnants of my army succumbed to cannon fire. "Want to play again?"

"Maybe later," I said and went upstairs to lick my wounds.

Just before lunch, after consulting the works of Carl Von Clausewitz and several other long-dead military geniuses, I again took the field.

I intended to offer only token resistance for several rounds and then spring a trap that would leave Olavi reeling. My stepfather must have seen through the ruse because he changed his strategy. Instead of tearing through Blitzkrieg's equivalent of the Low Countries, he proceeded cautiously and set up a strong defensive position at the first sign of resistance.

Then he sat back and waited.

I am not a patient person. After two turns with no sign of movement, I climbed out of my Trojan horse and threw everything in Big Red's arsenal at Olavi's fortifications. He weathered the storm, counterattacked, and the rest was Blitzkrieg history.

"Checkmate," he repeated twenty minutes later as his armies occupied Big Red's last free city. "Another game?"

I said nothing and again retreated to my room.

What to do? I wanted to give my stepfather a serving of humble pie, but victory had so far eluded me. It wasn't a question of materiel; the two sides in the conflict had almost the same number of units. The difference was one of leadership. Great Blue won every war because Olavi was a better strategic thinker.

I needed to get him off his game. I was pondering the matter when Kelly came upstairs with another bowl of cake batter. This one, by the look of it, was chocolate fudge.

"Mmmm," she said as she licked the wooden spatula. "This is so nummy." Her feasting gave me an idea.

In 1943, having had enough British stoicism to last a lifetime, Adolf Hitler decided to assassinate Winston Churchill. Because Britain's prime minister had a fondness for sweets, the Fuhrer's henchmen decided to use a bomb disguised as a bar of chocolate. British intelligence discovered the diabolical plot before it could be put in motion, but some historians feel that "death by chocolate" might have changed the trajectory of the war.

Olavi, like Churchill, had a sweet tooth. He was also a glutton. Was this my chance to snatch victory from the jaws of defeat?

I didn't have any explosives, but I did have access to a medicine cabinet and a potential accomplice.

I briefed Kelly. When I was done, she had only one question.

"Will it kill him?"

"No," I said. "Only make him sick."

"Too bad," she said.

Olavi and I faced off across the Blitzkrieg board again on Boxing Day. Not long after he'd made his opening move, Kelly showed up with a plate of baking.

"Want a cookie?" she asked. "They're chocolate chip, and I made them specially for you."

One cookie was the size of a pancake and contained a lot more pieces of chocolate. My sister had etched a reasonable facsimile of a happy face on one side of it.

I held my breath.

Olavi didn't hesitate. As soon as the cookies were within reach, he took the biggest one.

Needing an alibi, I also accepted one of Kelly's offerings. Gnawed on it while Olavi ate his. Watched him take another.

When all the cookies were gone, the game resumed.

An hour went by, then two. The war was not going well for me. I was about to request a ceasefire when there was a loud report from my stepfather's side of the table. Not unlike a gunshot, it was followed by a lot of gurgling noises that sounded like water roiling in an iron drainpipe.

My stepfather stood up without warning, did an about-face, and headed for the latrine at a quickstep.

He returned ten minutes later, greatly diminished in both body and spirit, but had to excuse himself again soon after.

"What's wrong, Olavi?" my mother asked when he placed the game on pause for the seventh time.

"Something didn't agree with me," he answered on his way out the door. "Might have been the cookies." After a moment's hesitation, he looked in my direction and asked, "How do you feel?"

"Fine," I said. "But I only had one cookie. You ate six."

He had no comeback.

The most popular brand of chocolate-flavoured laxative promises gentle, dependable, overnight relief from constipation. As my stepfather learned on Boxing Day, the extra-strength stuff, when consumed in bulk, works a lot quicker and with more violence.

Olavi finished the game, but his heart wasn't in it. My tank divisions destroyed most of his army in an elaborate pincer movement and then steam-rolled over the rest of it.

"Checkmate," I said with unrestrained glee as my troops entered his capital city. "I win."

Olavi scowled, got up, and stormed off to the outhouse.

Kelly celebrated the victory by making another batch of cake batter, and I gave myself a silver medal made from foil laxative wrappers. I still have it.

As author Francis Edward Smedley once wrote, "all's fair in love and war."

Hindenburg

Most children believe their parents know the answer to all life's mysteries and are thus incapable of lying or making mistakes. I was no exception. If Mom and Olavi told prospective employers they could wrangle cattle and cut hay, it must be so. The fact that I'd never seen them do either was irrelevant, as it was assumed they had mastered these and other arcane skills in the shadowy years before my birth. Since leaving Vancouver, Olavi had regaled us with fantastic tales of travelling vast distances on homemade skis and shooting rabbits from the hip with a .30-30 lever-action rifle. Surely, a man capable of such superhuman feats could handle a few farm chores?

By the time Wistaria land baron Jude O'Brian seduced my parents with empty promises, reality had hit home with the force of a sledgehammer. My mother still seemed remarkable, but Olavi wasn't Superman. He couldn't run faster than a speeding bullet, had the power of a disabled locomotive, and the only time I'd seen him leap was when Mom, frustrated at having to raise three children on her own, placed several lit matches between his gnarled toes while he took one of his twice-daily naps.

And when it came to ranching, it was evident my stepfather was making it up as he went along.

To be fair, Jude didn't make things easy for him. After securing his services, she purchased fifty Herefords and had them bred by the largest Charolais bull in the country. Those poor heifers never knew what hit them. By the time calving season rolled around, they all looked like brown-and-white barrage balloons tethered to the ground by tiny hooves.

Olavi managed the situation as best he could. He was up all hours with the cows, most of which required assistance giving birth, but the calves were just too big. One was so large he had to pull it from the host with a tractor. Neither the cow nor its progeny survived.

His run of bad luck continued. By late February, calf mortality was a shocking fifty percent, and the ranch owner was nearly speechless with anger. Olavi, sensing his bonus slipping away, was more sullen than usual.

One member of the herd had my stepfather's undivided attention. Two or three years older than the other cows, she had a gentle, endearing nature. She allowed us to pet her and would even come when called. But she had been bred by the same bull and was so large that we nicknamed her Hindenburg.

I think Olavi felt that his efforts would not be in vain if he could save Hindenburg and her calf. Desperate for a break, he swallowed his pride and sought the advice of an expert: Jem Keighley, Diggory's uncle.

Jem, already on the downside of fifty at the time, had grown up in Wistaria. A confirmed bachelor, he lived with his mother in a small house on the family homestead overlooking Ootsa Lake. Though not tall, he was a powerful man whose thick chest and muscular arms resulted from years of hard labour in an unforgiving country. Beneath the stained tractor cap he always wore was a dense matt of curly black hair cropped short for convenience, and his permanent five-o'clock shadow, shot through with flecks of grey, provided no protection against the sun or wind, which over the years had turned his round, lined face the colour of newly dug russet potatoes. He had a broad, full mouth that always seemed on the verge of breaking into a smile, but his deep-set brown eyes caught your attention. Unless he'd been drinking, they were kind, clear, and without guile, though within their limpid depths lurked a trace of sadness, the suggestion of a life lived to less than its fullest.

Jem's wardrobe was limited to scarred work boots, coarse woolen trousers held up by grimy red suspenders, and an ashen sweater over a long-sleeved Stanfield's undershirt. In winter, he traded his cap for a toque and added a thick coat to the outfit. It was rumoured he wore long johns year-round.

Though Jem didn't have much schooling, he knew a lot about cattle. Like his sister Mona, he was generous to a fault, so it was not surprising that he agreed to give the greenhorn at O'Brian Ranch some lessons in animal husbandry.

Olavi and I were feeding cattle in the outer corral when Diggs and Jem arrived one Saturday morning in early March. It was clear and only a few degrees below freezing, the kind of day that suggests spring may be just around the corner.

After parking his corroded pickup near the barn, Jem climbed out, stuffed both calloused hands deep into his pockets, and ambled toward us. Though I had never seen him ride a horse, he walked with a cowboy's bowlegged gait.

We met them at the corral's entrance.

"Hear you got a cow that's slow to calve," Jem said as he eased around the gate.

Olavi nodded.

We ushered our guests into Hindenburg's stall. Jem walked over to our favourite heifer and gave her an appraising look. After a few seconds, he knelt and ran a hand under her belly.

"When she due?"

"Well, Jude says she was bred at the same time as the others, and they've all calved," Olavi answered. "This one's the last of the lot."

Jem grunted. "She's carrying a big one."

"They all were," Olavi muttered, his bitterness evident. "She lay down this morning, and I thought she was going into labour, but then she got up again. Since then, she's been up and down a few more times and walking the fence line in between. What do you think?"

"Water's broke?"

"Yup."

Jem stood up with effort. "Well, let's take a look. Got a halter and some udder salve?"

Olavi sent Diggs and me searching for some petroleum jelly while he fashioned a halter from one of the farm's old lassoes. Jem had already shed his coat and rolled up one sleeve of his sweater by the time we returned.

Taking the Vaseline jar from us, he began spreading a thick layer of goop over his exposed forearm.

"Better hold her still," he said to Olavi, who went around and held Hindenburg's head.

Diggs and I retreated to a nearby haybale.

"What's he going to do?" I asked my friend.

"He's going to check the calf."

I was in the process of seeking clarification when Jem walked over, lifted Hindenburg's tail, and without ceremony inserted his hand into her behind. The old cow mooed plaintively.

"Holy shit," I whispered, "your uncle's cramming his hand up our cow's crack."

Diggs just smiled, but I watched spellbound as Jem eased his right arm into Hindenburg. First, his wrist disappeared, then his elbow; when all had been said and done, he was up to his armpit in Hereford.

"Well, the calf's pointed the right way," he announced from his station behind the animal. "I can feel the nose. One foot may be backward, but I'll see if I can fix it."

Jem continued to explore Hindenburg's insides as he might a length of blackened stove pipe. When his right arm tired, he withdrew it and inserted his left. After perhaps five minutes of pushing, pulling, and prodding, he grunted again and pulled out his arm.

"Not sure I got that foot right," he said, turning to Olavi, "but she'll probably calve anyway."

"Any idea when?"

Jem shrugged. "Soon." Scooping up a handful of hay, he cleaned off both arms before pulling down his sweater sleeves. "Later this morning, this afternoon at the latest. Wouldn't let her go far."

Because there was no water trough in the barn, Olavi released Hindenburg to an adjacent round pen.

"Anything else I should do?" he asked as Jem prepared to leave.

The old farmer took off his toque, scratched behind one reddened ear, and looked thoughtful. "No, nothing but waiting now," he said after a moment. "Just keep an eye on her."

Having rendered judgment, he replaced his woolen cap, motioned to Diggs, and headed out into the sunshine.

We waved as the two of them drove away.

They passed Jude on their way out. The old biddy was stomping up the frozen road toward us, granddaughter Dana in tow.

"Here comes trouble," said Olavi.

"Turkki," Jude barked as soon as she was within hailing distance. When feeling charitable, she sometimes referred to my stepfather as "Ollie," but those days were few and far between. Two weeks earlier, as the farm's losses mounted, she had started addressing him by his last name—and always with a note of distaste.

"Yes?"

"I need to talk to you. Come with me." She strode past him, never once making eye contact. "Dana, you stay here."

Olavi followed her like an obedient slave, leaving Dana and me alone in the outer corral.

We eyed each other like players over a chessboard.

Dana was my age but seemed older. A bright, slender girl with shoulder-length blonde hair and jade-green eyes, she had led a nomadic life with her mother Tilley, Jude's eldest daughter, before they put down semi-permanent roots in a fashionable section of Victoria. Dana made the pilgrimage to O'Brian Ranch two or three times a year at her mother's insistence. Judging from her moodiness during these fortnight exiles, she came only under duress.

Tilley was touted as a recovering hippie, but Dana resisted rehabilitation. Fiercely independent, she knew all the latest slang, played Black Sabbath and Cream endlessly on her grandmother's expensive stereo, and showed zero interest in gardening.

What bothered Jude most was that her "maturing" granddaughter wore makeup but not a bra and used the "F" word in place of most adjectives and adverbs.

I found these qualities endearing. To me, Dana was racy, sophisticated, and the most exciting thing to arrive at Ootsa Lake since the curved hockey stick. The rumour that she carried a switchblade to fend off unwanted suitors only added to the allure.

I was madly in love with the girl. My previous attempts to impress her had failed miserably, but as Olavi and Jude disappeared into the barn, I vowed to try again.

Jude's granddaughter had arrived a week earlier wearing faded designer bell-bottoms, a tie-dyed T-shirt, and stylish Adidas sneakers. Jude had lent her an insulated leather jacket, but she still looked cold and uncomfortable.

I took a deep breath. "Nice jacket."

Dana stared at me as though I'd just crawled from beneath one of the hundreds of frozen cow pies that dotted the barnyard. "Yours too," she said, nodding toward my torn and dirty chores coat. "And your shit-kicker boots are also something else."

I felt my face redden but forged ahead. "Diggs was just here. You know Diggs, right?"

"That inbred hillbilly Cullen kid? Yeah, I know him. So what?"

Drawing Dana into a civil conversation was proving more difficult than anticipated.

"Nothing," I said. "They were here to help with one of our cows."

"You mean *my grandma's cows*," she said, a challenge in her eyes. "Big deal."

Silence hung like a lead curtain between us. I looked at the ground, kicked a chunk of frozen snow, and pondered my next move. Fresh out of ideas, I went for shock value.

"Diggs' Uncle Jem stuck his arm up Hindenburg's hoo-haw."

"Ew," Dana replied. "That's so disgusting. But I bet you liked watching, didn't you?"

Jude and Olavi emerged from the barn in time to save me further embarrassment.

"I don't care, Turkki. I need you to go to town," Dana's grandmother said, her voice hard. "You can take the red Ford. I've already filled it with gas."

Olavi tried to reason with her. "But that cow could go into labour at any time. I don't want to lose her or the calf."

Jude turned and gave him a withering stare. "At this point, does it really matter?" she asked, raising one white eyebrow.

With that, Countess O'Brian gathered Dana and headed toward the gate. "Your boy and my granddaughter can watch the cow," she said over her shoulder. "If you leave now, you can be back by six. Stop by the house before you go. I have a list."

Olavi was still brooding when he loaded Mom and my two sisters into the cab of Jude's four-wheel-drive pickup. "Keep an eye on Hindenburg," he said. "If you run into problems, get Mrs. O'Brian to call Jem."

I hung out at home for an hour, stoked the stove, and then walked to the O'Brians' elaborate log home. It was nothing like the knocked-together trapper's cabin we lived in. Designed by Mickey and constructed with love by a famous log builder, the nine-room structure contained a library, twin fireplaces made of rock from a profitable copper mine, three bathrooms with running water, and an indoor sauna.

Jude answered the door. "You here to see the old cow?" she asked, giving me the once-over.

I wanted to laugh at the double entendre but thought better of it and just nodded. In my experience, the less said to Jude O'Brian, the better.

"Dana, young Turkki is here to check on the cow," she said over her shoulder.

The girl appeared in the foyer and snatched her borrowed jacket from a peg on the wall.

"I'm only going because Grandma says I have to," she said to me as soon as the door closed behind us.

We trudged up the snowy track to the barn in silence. By this time, I was happy to avoid conflict.

Hindenburg was lying in the round pen. As we approached, I saw her massive belly convulse.

"Shit," I said, scaling the pole fence and dropping into the corral.

Dana, curious, followed. "What's wrong?"

"She's calving. Jem was right."

"What do we do?"

Fighting panic, I tried to remember everything I had seen or heard about cattle in the past two years. It wasn't much.

"Well," I said, trying to sound authoritative, "nothing right now. We'll just watch her for a while."

Petting the Hereford's scruffy head, I circled her and took a long look at the end where the action was to occur. I could see what looked like a gaping wound below her tail. When another convulsion stretched her abdomen as taut as a bass drum, a tiny hoof appeared in it.

Dana and I climbed the weathered log fence and sat on its top rail.

"Should I get my grandma?" she asked.

The thought of Jude rushing around the barnyard bellowing orders didn't appeal to me. "No. Let's just see what happens."

We sat without speaking. Every so often, Hindenburg would moo and give a mighty push.

After twenty minutes of this, Dana started to get antsy. "Nothing's happening," she said. "Why's it taking so long?"

I shrugged. "It just does. Cows aren't like pop machines. You don't just plug in a quarter, and a calf drops out."

Dana was quiet as she considered this information. "I suppose you're right. Mother said she was in labour twenty-eight hours with me." After another moment, she turned to me. "We're not going to have to sit here that long, are we?"

"No. It usually happens in a couple of hours."

Just then, Hindenburg gave another mighty heave, and one hoof was again visible beneath her tail. "There, did you see the calf's foot?" I asked.

"Yeah, but it went back inside again."

"Sometimes it does, but eventually both feet come out, and then you'll see the calf's nose."

Dana groaned. We sat for another couple of minutes. "My ass is getting sore," she said. "Want to play in the barn?"

Her invitation, coming after so many caustic rebuffs, surprised me. I wanted to shout "yes," but the tug of responsibility made me say, "I better not."

"Why?" Dana asked, pointing to Hindenburg. "That old thing isn't going anywhere. We can check on her every so often."

It was tempting. "Geez, I don't know . . ."

Dana sensed my indecision and jumped on it. "Aw, come on. Grandma says you got a rope swing in there. It'll be fun." She punctuated the statement by giving me a playful shove.

It was the shove that got to me. Though hardly an act of intimacy, it was still physical contact. Maybe Dana didn't hate me half as much as she pretended to. Still, given her earlier petulance, I was cautious.

"Okay, but only for a while."

"Right on!" she said, swinging both legs over the fence rail and jumping to the ground. "Last one inside is a rotten egg."

Hindenburg's plight forgotten for the moment, we raced each other to the old log barn. The ninety-foot structure was divided into three equal sections. The middle contained a half-dozen unoccupied stalls of varying dimensions, while the north and south ends held hundreds of haybales stacked in compact tiers. A large rectangular opening in each gable helped illuminate the place, which smelled of dried cow dung and old straw and packrats running in the rafters.

I don't know how long we played there, chasing each other across broad plateaus of cured hay and swinging without fear over the chasm between stacks. It may have been only minutes, but it could have been an hour because we grew too warm and had to discard our coats. When we finally collapsed, tired and laughing, atop two bales warmed by a broad shaft of late winter sunshine, tendrils of vapour rose like gossamer from our sweating bodies and mingled with dust motes that sparkled in the light.

"See, I told you it would be fun," said Dana as she plucked hay from her hair with one hand. "Way better than watching that old cow heave and groan."

I jerked upright. "Oh, crap."

"What?"

"The cow," I said in a panic. "We forgot about the cow. If something's happened to her, my dad will kill me."

I didn't wait for Dana to follow. Grabbing my coat, I tumbled down the haystack and ran out of the barn.

Hindenburg was sprawled on her left side near the fence. The cow's breathing was laboured, and her brown body was damp with sweat despite the chill. As I approached, her distended abdomen was wracked by a convulsion of such intensity that her legs stiffened.

Ice crunched beneath my boots. "Easy girl," I said, kneeling beside the old cow. At the sound of my voice, she mooed and tried to lift her head.

"She's not looking very good," Dana observed. She had followed me out of the barn and was peering between the fence rails.

Without a word, I rose and walked around to Hindenburg's flank. One tiny white hoof was visible in the orifice below her tail.

We watched for several minutes. Despite her best efforts, Hindenburg got no closer to birthing the calf. And she was getting tired. Her large brown eyes were glassy, and the air rushed out of her as if pushed by tired bellows. Her contractions were of greater concern; instead of increasing, they came with less frequency and intensity. There was also a thin trickle of blood dribbling out of her behind, which I figured couldn't be good.

"Something's wrong, isn't it?" Dana asked.

"The calf's too big," I said without looking up. "It won't come out."

Dana thought this though.

"Is she going to die?"

I didn't want to answer the question. It scared me.

"What do we do? I mean, couldn't we push on her stomach or something?"

"I don't think so," I said. "Pushing on her stomach might hurt the calf."

Hindenburg's body tensed yet again as we watched, but the tiny hoof barely moved.

Dana bit her lip. "It's like something's stuck in there," she said when the contraction eased. "Maybe we could try . . . stretching her . . . you know . . ." Her words trailed away.

I gave the idea some thought. "We could try pulling the calf if the other leg . . ."

The other leg. That's when I knew the problem—and maybe how to solve it.

I turned and headed for the barn.

"Come back," Dana said. "You can't just take off."

"I'm not," I said without looking back. "I'm getting the Vaseline."

I was gone no more than a minute. Pulling off my coat and peeling back a shirt sleeve, I opened the squat blue jar and scooped out a baseball-sized glob of petroleum jelly. It was thick, cold, and very greasy.

I pushed the jar into Dana's hands.

"What are you doing?" she asked.

"The calf's leg is stuck backward," I replied as I slathered grey goop over my left hand and forearm. Its texture, as much as its temperature, raised a trail of goosebumps. "We have to pull it forward."

Dana looked at my arm, then Hindenburg's butt, then my arm again. A look of horror spread across her face. "Tell me you're not going to . . ."

I didn't answer, just dipped into the Vaseline jar for a second helping of slime.

"Oh fuck, you can't. It's gross, and you don't know what you're doing."

She was right, of course: I didn't know what I was doing. I'd only seen the procedure done for the first time that morning and had no idea what lay beyond a cow's tail other than a tube followed by some guts and other stuff that later connected to another tube through which food entered. And yes, poking around inside that bovine mystery was repugnant. Yet if I didn't find and straighten that other foreleg, the calf it belonged to would never be born. Both Hindenburg and her baby would die.

That knowledge, combined with the realization of what Olavi would do to me if they didn't survive, was even more frightening than exploring the old cow's innards.

"I've got to do it. There's no other way."

Dana stood beside me. Her lips were a thin hard line, her body stiff with tension. "I'll go tell Grandma, and she can call Jem. He'll know what to do."

"I know what to do," I said, my tone harsh. "Even if your grandma can reach Jem, it'll take him an hour to get here. By then, it'll be too late." I pointed to where Hindenburg lay in the icy barnyard, neck extended and mouth open. "Look at her, Dana. She's so tired she can't even lift her head."

The city girl stared at the beleaguered cow. When she again looked at me, compassion had replaced the anger in her eyes. "Okay. What can I do to help?"

I thought it over while applying a final lump of Vaseline to my wrist. "Maybe you could rub her head and talk to her. She likes that, and it might help keep her calm."

Dana walked over, squatted on her haunches, and gave Hindenburg's fuzzy head a tentative pet. I saw the girl's lips moving as she whispered indistinct reassurances.

My preparations complete, I took a deep breath and walked toward Hindenburg's hindquarters. Kneeling in a puddle of steaming amniotic fluid, I looked at the wet red gash beneath her tail. The knowledge of what I was about to attempt horrified me. I didn't want to stick my hand in there. Hindenburg was a friend. Poking around in her privates seemed wrong.

I hesitated. The old cow heaved and groaned again in anguish.

Like it or not, it had to be done.

I took a deep breath, placed my right hand on Hindenburg's rump, and guided my left hand toward the target area. An instant before my cold, Vaseline-smeared fingers met warm flesh, I looked away so as not to see the act.

My fingers reached the spot. I made a blade of them as I'd seen old Jem do and tentatively pushed forward—first an inch, then more. It was like sliding your hand into a rubber bag full of warm snot. The air was thick with the smell of blood and body fluids.

My stomach heaved, but I closed my eyes and pushed deeper. My fingers encountered a tiny cloven hoof, rubbery to the touch, and I forced them to follow it until they encountered something smooth and soft. There was a dime-sized indentation on each side of it above a tight crease, and I realized that I had found the calf's muzzle.

"You okay? You look a little sick," Dana said.

I opened my eyes to see the girl watching me. She looked concerned and amused at the same time. "Yeah, I guess. I can feel the calf's nose."

"Having any fun?"

Her words sailed over me. Leaning over Hindenburg's rump, I eased my arm in further, blindly following the line of the calf's neck until it met the right shoulder.

"Shoot. I can't quite reach the leg," I said after maybe thirty seconds of fruitless prodding.

"Can't you get in a bit . . . more?" Dana asked with distaste.

"Maybe."

Another contraction wracked the cow's body as she tried to expel the calf. My forearm felt like an anaconda was squeezing it. I waited for the moment to pass, then changed position and plunged my arm deeper. My fingers traced their way along the shoulder, found the bent foreleg, and closed around it.

"Got it," I said with my cheek resting on the old cow's hindquarter. Her coarse brown hair stank of sweat and stale urine.

Using Hindenburg's rump for leverage, I tugged on the trapped leg. It moved slightly before hitting something solid and unyielding. I pulled harder; the old cow lowed and made a half-hearted effort to rise.

I'm hurting her. I released the leg, and Hindenburg's body relaxed. For the first time, I became aware of a pulsing, slow and regular, against my constricted arm and realized with wonder that it was the old cow's heartbeat.

In my mind's eye, I tried to picture what my hand was feeling. "I can't seem to straighten the leg," I said to Dana in frustration. "There's not enough room in there. It's still stuck."

Dana, now sitting nonchalantly on Hindenburg's shoulder, looked thoughtful. "Maybe the calf's too far out already. Could you push it back in and try again?"

Pushing the calf backward seemed counterproductive, but I was out of ideas. "I guess so."

I withdrew my arm until my fingers traced the outline of the calf's chest beneath its outstretched neck. After Hindenburg gave another monumental heave, I made a fist and pushed as hard as possible. The calf moved a fraction, but not enough. I tried again without success.

"Is it working?" Dana asked.

"No," I said, grimacing from the effort, "but I think it might if I had your help."

The city girl looked at me in alarm, then shook her head. "Uh-uh. There's no way I'm sticking my hand in there."

"You wouldn't have to stick your hand inside. Maybe just push against my arm when I tell you."

She got off the cow with reluctance and took up station behind me. I felt her place a hand on my shoulder blade. It felt warm through my thin shirt.

"Here okay?" she asked.

"Yeah, that's about right. I'll tell you when to push."

I waited for another labour pain to pass. When it did, I grabbed the old cow's bony hip with my right hand for leverage and said, "Okay, now!"

Dana leaned into my shoulder blade, and I shoved hard against the calf's chest. Nothing happened for a second or two, and then I felt the calf ease back inside the womb an inch. My hand shot past the obstruction, found the trapped leg, and pulled it upward. The appendage caught briefly, then slipped into the birth canal.

Relieved, I withdrew my arm. It came out of Hindenburg with a sucking sound, followed by a trickle of fluid and more fresh blood.

"That's so gross," Dana said. She turned away and gagged. "Fuck, I think I'm going to be sick."

"Yeah, it's nasty," I said, stepping back to inspect my handiwork, "but the leg's straight now."

Sensing that something inside her had changed, Hindenburg pushed with renewed effort. It was enough to force the calf's front hooves and part of its nose out of the bloody opening.

"It's working," I told Dana. "But she's tired. We'll have to pull the calf."

I spied some baler twine draped over one of the corral's weathered fence posts. Dana watched with interest as I knotted two pieces together, then made loops at each end and slipped them over the calf's exposed hoofs.

"Here," I said, stepping back a pace and handing Dana a section of the rope. She immediately started pulling, which was the wrong thing to do.

"Wait," I said.

We braced our feet against frozen cow pies in the corral until Hindenburg's stomach cramped again. I gave the signal, and we strained against the coarse twine. It dug painfully into our fingers, but the calf's head, brown with a white blaze, began to emerge.

We repeated the process in time with the next contraction. The calf slid out of Hindenburg in a rush, followed by a torrent of bloody afterbirth.

I knelt and examined the wet creature. Its eyes were lifeless, its brown body flat and unmoving.

My heart sank. The calf was dead.

And then it wasn't. The tiny body shuddered. Frothy bubbles rolled out of each pink nostril as the calf tried to draw its first breath.

"Quick, help me lift it," I said, grabbing one of the calf's back legs. Dana took the other, and we struggled to raise the animal's hind end.

We got three-quarters of the calf off the ground for a few seconds before dropping it with an awkward thump. I knelt and scooped pale liquid from the calf's mouth. It drew a shallow breath, coughed, and blinked.

I stepped back, marvelling as the calf struggled to right itself. Dana reached down and tried to help. At her touch, the calf bawled.

Hindenburg's head shot up at the sound, and her brown ears twitched. She mooed. When the calf responded with a soft bleat, the old cow heaved herself erect.

We backed away as Hindenburg stumbled toward her calf. When it cried out again, she came close, extended her thick neck, and sniffed the creature at her feet. There was a pause as she processed this olfactory information, then she gave the calf's head a tentative lick.

Dana and I sat on the fence and watched as Hindenburg cleaned the calf from head to toe, then stood protectively over it. After a time, the creature— a tiny reproduction of its mother—managed to stand. Tottering on spindly legs, it fumbled for Hindenburg's udder and, after a few false starts, found it and began to nurse. The old cow sighed with contentment.

At that moment, the late afternoon sunshine seemed warmer, the sky bluer, and the snow atop the ancient barn much whiter than before. I smiled.

Everything was going to be all right.

"We did it," I said, turning to Dana.

"We did, didn't we?" she replied. There was warmth in her eyes, and maybe a measure of respect that had not been there before.

I revelled in it and started to give her shoulder a comradely pat.

Dana's expression hardened. "Don't you dare put that on me," she said, stepping back and pointing to my outstretched hand. "If you do, I'll break it."

I looked down. My arm was covered with clotted blood and other vile substances.

"Oops. Sorry."

Dana sighed. "It's all right. Just don't touch me, okay?"

There was a moment of awkwardness, and the rapport between us faded. I tried to re-establish it.

"Funny how something that big can come out of something that small," I remarked, pointing toward Hindenburg's hind end.

Dana gave me a speculative look. "Yeah," she said with a knowing smile, "but what's even weirder is how it got in there in the first place."

Then she turned and walked away, leaving me to puzzle my way through the comment.

I stayed with Hindenburg and the calf for another hour before walking home, heating a basin of water on our wood stove, and washing the dried nastiness from my arm. When Olavi and Mom returned a few hours later, I told them what had happened.

My stepfather grunted and muttered something incoherent through his beard, but Mom listened with interest. In the weeks that followed, she made a point of telling the story to everyone she met.

Even Mona Cullen was impressed. "She said Diggory has never delivered a calf by himself," Mom told me one night soon after the incident.

Her words filled me with pride, but not as much as the sight of Hindenburg and her healthy baby, which we called Zeppelin.

The feeling lasted until Jude O'Brian announced she was selling the cows. A huge cattle liner, its grey sides streaked with the excrement of previous occupants, arrived in June. I watched through the fence as the surviving Herefords were loaded into it.

Jude made a point of supervising the exercise with a scowl planted on her wrinkled face. When Hindenburg and Zeppelin disappeared inside, the question eating at me could no longer be contained.

"Where are you sending them?"

The old lady looked down at me, her eyes as hard as two dark marbles.

"The slaughterhouse," she said in a flat and emotionless voice. "Where else would they go, you silly boy?"

Her answer made me want to cry.

Granny and the Television

Every light was on in Mona Cullen's log cabin. Squatting there in the darkness, its big picture window illuminating the surrounding field of drifted snow, the place looked like the top of a wave-battered lighthouse. But for our family and all other travellers that cold winter night, the light was an invitation rather than a warning.

Something was happening at Mona's house, and everyone in the country was headed there.

Seeing the lights, Olavi slowed our decrepit International Travelall and turned its blue snout up the icy driveway. Mona's backyard was filled with vehicles of every size and description. Finding parking space was difficult, but we wedged the old truck between Herb Eaton's rusty Volkswagen and someone's shiny new Ford.

The cabin's owner, a thin stick of a woman, greeted us. "Well, hello," she said, a smile cracking the weathered surface of her face. "Come in, and I'll fix you a cup of coffee. Diggs and Jem have just about got it hooked up."

A wave of heat and noise met us at the threshold. "Lots of company," my mother noted after glancing into the living room.

"Yes," our hostess said with a short, indulgent laugh. "I don't know where they're all coming from."

Mona pulled three worn chairs out from the kitchen table and motioned for us to sit. Then she moved to the counter with a sense of purpose and began washing an equal number of cracked mugs in a scarred plastic basin full of tepid water. Her hands, strong and calloused but as nimble as a girl's, were quick and efficient.

"I don't know, I just don't know," she reiterated, shaking her head in disbelief. The movement barely jostled her hair, which had the colour and malleability of old baling wire. "Such a commotion. Everyone wants to see it."

I left my parents behind to make polite conversation and entered the crowded living room. Smoke from home-rolled cigarettes hung in a thick blue cloud below the cobwebbed ceiling, and the sound of a dozen interwoven conversations greeted my ears. The best seats in the house, two threadbare mid-century sofas and a pair of mismatched recliners, one strategically placed beside the crackling wood furnace, were already occupied. Herb, a wizened bachelor with rheumy eyes and thick Buddy Holly spectacles balanced precariously on a pockmarked nose deformed by rhinitis, was leaning over the arm of one chair and engaging another man in bright conversation. Herb, as much a fixture at Mona's house as the worn furniture, was seeking advice from his neighbour on how to best winterize a Beetle.

Bob the Bus Driver was there too, stroking his greying handlebar mustache with one hand while telling Harvey Stapleton all the mischief children can get into during a forty-mile commute. Harvey, who didn't like young people much, nodded now and again and even shook his head from time to time, but I suspect he wasn't listening. He couldn't have been because he was woefully unprepared when he took over Bob's route three years later. We played the same practical jokes on him that we had on other rookie drivers.

If Harv was a little distracted that night, he wasn't alone. Everyone's attention was focused on two people huddled around something at the far end of the room.

My best friend Diggs was in the thick of it. He and his Uncle Jem were peering at what looked to be the back of a large wooden cabinet. Their hands held a snarled mess of electrical cords and frayed wires, some of which snaked across the cabin's blackened plywood floor before escaping through a half-open window.

At last satisfied, the two stepped back. The end of an extension cord in each hand, Diggs looked to Jem for guidance.

The older man ran a meaty paw through his curly black hair and said, "Okay, try her."

Diggs joined the cords without hesitation, filling the room with light and sound.

Television had come to Ootsa Lake.

The set was a dinosaur from the early 1960s, and the sound emanating from its orphan speaker was so loud that old Herb grimaced and covered his hairy ears with both hands. ". . . Savard being bothered at the blue line by Keon, but still gets the pass away. It's up the wing to Cournoyer. He turns the puck over, and here come the Leafs . . ."

"Right on," said Diggs. "*Hockey Night in Canada.*"

My friend backed away and looked for someplace to sit. The only unoccupied piece of furniture in the room was a coffee table, so he claimed it. Light from the TV's twenty-one-inch screen danced on his youthful features.

"Looks great," someone said of the grainy black-and-white picture. Almost on cue, the frame began to roll, and static invaded the room. "Therezzzzz a pazzzz in front . . . Itzzz loozzzz in the creazzzz . . . Mahovlizzzz . . . zzzzz . . . he . . . zzz."

"Oh no," Diggs said. Leaping from his seat, he twiddled a few knobs on the television's console, then tightened the elastic band that held its tuner in place. When these efforts failed to correct the problem, he swore and brought a fist down hard on the top of the set.

Much to his surprise, the picture and sound returned in time for bug-eyed Marty Feldman to introduce Imperial Oil's new hockey pool promotion.

Jem's slow laughter pierced the din. "You're quite the repairman, Diggory." With that, the older man reached over and twisted the set's volume control. Pandemonium became a dull roar.

Everyone began talking at once. Television, they agreed, was amazing.

"What's all the racket?" came a raspy voice from an adjoining bedroom. "Jem, have you got the radio on?"

It was Granny, matriarch of the Keighley clan. A short woman whose thick mane of white hair framed a face as wrinkled as a sun-dried raisin, she had to be at least eighty. Like many Ootsa Lake pioneers, she had come to the country at an early age and stayed too long. Years of isolation eroded her social skills until she could no longer deal with the unfamiliar. By the time my family arrived on the Southside, her world had become so small that she could survey all of it from her kitchen window. Not that she minded; according to her, it was enough to look at.

Granny had never seen a television until the night her grandson connected two electrical cords and created a miracle in his living room. Drawn by the hubbub, she shuffled to Jem's side.

"God, what's this?" she said, waving a bony finger at the flickering screen.

"It's a television, Granny," Diggs said, his voice loud in deference to the noise and her poor hearing. "You can watch things on it, like hockey."

"No." There was disbelief in Granny's voice, and she smiled as if someone had just told an early April Fools' joke.

Diggs, shrugging his shoulders, went back to watching the game.

Jem explained television in terms Granny could understand. "It's a new kind of radio, Mum. But on this one, you can also see what's happening."

"No," Granny said again, though with less suspicion. Father Time had stolen her teeth and most of her hearing, yet in a fit of generosity, had left her wits intact.

"Yup. Look."

Granny's head swivelled on her thin neck. At that moment, Dave Hodge was interviewing Montreal defenseman Serge Savard. The scene garnered no response from the old woman until the camera zoomed in for a close-up.

"My God, Jem," she said, recoiling as Savard's battle-scarred face filled the Electrohome's screen. "That's a big man, eh? With a head like that, he must be over eight feet tall." She paused, then added with disgust, "And so ugly."

What followed was a lengthy explanation of modern photography, not a bit of which Granny understood or cared about. After a while, she left the room to tell her daughter about the hideous French giant she had seen on the new radio that Diggs had brought home.

"Eight feet tall, maybe nine, Mona," we heard her yelling in the kitchen. "Huge. Must have big feet too."

Jem laughed and shook his head. "She'll never watch it."

He was wrong. Television brought the outside world to Granny, saving her the trouble and angst of travelling to it. Yet the world she saw on that small screen was very different from the one she had left behind sixty years earlier. Cars and planes were everywhere; almost no one took the train. Fashion had done an about-face, and men and women had nearly identical hairstyles. They even wore the same clothing, none of which Granny would have been caught dead in. And they were doing many things she considered scandalous.

While prime time programming often perplexed Granny, she accepted most of what the boob tube offered. But she remained skeptical of news reports.

Granny was the original conspiracy theorist. Not long after her introduction to television, CBC News broadcast a lengthy update on the Apollo 17 mission.

Granny watched the report in silence from her seat beside the wood stove. Her eyes never left the screen until a talking head announced that man had landed on the moon again and had returned to earth safely. Then she snorted and heaved herself out of the chair.

"Ach, what bullshit," she said to those present, waving her hand and shambling toward the kitchen. "Those men didn't land on the moon. It's just a story made up by the government."

No one could tell her otherwise, and they stopped trying after a while. It was easier to let Granny cling to her outdated beliefs. She didn't want to join modern society anyway.

Granny continued to watch television and became such a fan of soap operas that she badgered Jem into buying a TV for their house. But the world beyond Ootsa Lake and the technology that brought it to her remained a freak show.

I sometimes wonder how Granny would have reacted if her first exposure to television had come during Neil Armstrong's famous moonwalk.

"Good Lord, Jem," I can almost hear her say at the sight of Armstrong in a spacesuit. "Look at that monster. A hideous thing it is, and what a head. Must be ten, twelve feet tall. Probably has big feet too."

For Granny, life might never have been the same.

Neotoma Cinerea

In 1974, I found a paperback entitled *Willard* at the Burns Lake Public Library. A cursory review of the back cover suggested the book was about a man and his pet rat. It sounded like something Jack London would write, so I tucked it under my arm and headed for the checkout counter.

My parents had already left the building when I handed *Willard* and my borrower's card to the librarian, a tall woman with frizzy red hair and the mottled complexion of a person who has seen too much sun.

She turned the book over and gave me a searching look.

"How old are you?" she asked.

"Almost fourteen," I replied.

"This is an *adult* book," she stated, emphasizing the adjective.

The statement seemed irrelevant, so I said nothing.

She took my silence for incomprehension. "You know what this book is about, don't you?"

This was starting to feel like an interrogation. Impatient, I said, "Yeah. It's about a guy and some rats."

One of her auburn eyebrows rose at my tone. "Young man, are you sure you want to read this?"

A dissonant rumble from the parking lot indicated that Olavi had fired up our International Travelall, a hoary vehicle with a bad clutch and no muffler. "Yes," I repeated. "Um, can you hurry? My parents are leaving."

The librarian opened her mouth to continue, but a strident honk from the Travelall intervened. Making a small noise of disapproval, she opened the book and gave its lending sheet a resounding whack with her date stamp.

"Due back October 28," she said with finality. "Enjoy."

Willard, I soon realized, was no *White Fang*. It was terrifying, and while I was tempted to abandon it several times on the way home, I could not. Later that night, in my eight-by-twelve room in the attic, I continued reading the book by the light of a guttering candle, reluctantly putting it down after Olavi threatened me with grievous bodily harm. I took it up again the following day after hauling water and chopping wood and finished it later in the afternoon.

Willard was my first foray into the genre of horror fiction. It both fascinated and frightened me, perhaps because, on some level, I identified with the title character, a social misfit more at home with animals than people. Although my sense of humour gave me an in with the cool kids, I suffered periodic bouts of agoraphobia, during which I escaped into the woods with our faithful dog and hid at the first sign of another human.

The book weighed on my mind for days, particularly the disturbing final scene in which the protagonist cowers in his bedroom while hordes of angry vermin, led by a diabolical black rat named Ben, try to gnaw their way through to him. Could such a thing happen? More to the point, was there any chance of it occurring at Ootsa Lake?

I consulted Grassy school's well-thumbed set of encyclopedias for answers to these and other troubling questions. The thick tomes yielded a great deal of information about rats. While much of it was grim—*Rattus rattus*, I discovered, was in part responsible for the Black Death—it was a relief to learn the vile creatures were not native to Northern British Columbia.

Willard went back to the library, and I discovered C. S. Forester's magnificent Hornblower series. Ben and his beady-eyed collaborators were all but forgotten.

That changed a month later. Our household had turned in for the night, and the cabin was dark and still except for the intermittent crackle of the wood furnace downstairs. Sleep had so far eluded me; the stove pipe that emerged through the floor near my bed was pumping out a fearsome amount of heat, making the attic uncomfortably warm. To pass the time until it cooled, I fantasized about Hornblower and the Napoleonic wars. In my mind's eye, I was standing on the quarterdeck of a sleek frigate as she knifed her way through the North Atlantic not far from the rocky shores of Portugal. A midshipman in the topmast had just sighted a heavily laden

Spanish merchantman, hull low in the water as she struggled toward Cadiz, when there came a rustle from overhead.

"Avast," I thought, annoyed at the interruption. "What is that infernal noise in the rigging?"

It came again, more clearly this time, and then I recognized it as the pitter-patter of tiny paws on asphalt roofing. The sound progressed up one side of the steep, peaked roof and down the other, then, without pause, moved along the eves toward the far corner of the cabin until it was no longer audible.

I listened hard in the darkness for several minutes, wondering what manner of creature had made the noise. It sounded larger than a mouse. A squirrel, perhaps? There were plenty of them in the pine forest a short walk from the cabin, and they sometimes frequented the woodshed for the sole purpose of dementing our dog. Yet to my knowledge, squirrels were not nocturnal, so it had to be something else. A weasel? Maybe. Then again . . .

I grew tired of these speculations after a while. They were immaterial because whatever had disturbed my daydream by running across the roof had fled into the night and was probably miles away now. Again, my thoughts turned to Hornblower, the North Atlantic, and that sailing ship full of gold.

In time, the temperature upstairs became bearable. As sleep came upon me, random, unrelated thoughts slipped unbidden into my Napoleonic fantasy. I boarded the Spanish treasure ship and found it crewed by members of the 1973 Boston Bruins, its hold filled not with bullion but thousands of new hockey pucks bearing the scarred likeness of team captain John Bucyk.

My mind was trying to reconcile these incongruities when it became aware of a strange sound. At first, the noise seemed a product of my imagination, possibly part of the dream, yet it persisted. Vaguely worrisome, it at length forced its way through to some primitive section of my brain and set off alarm bells.

Something was trying to gnaw its way into my room.

I awoke with a start. From the corner of the attic behind my toy box, where the cabin's rafters met its log walls, came the unmistakable sound of sharp teeth worrying old wood. Determined but not desperate, it had a sinister quality, as if the masticator had a clear plan and was confident of success. He made no effort to conceal his activities or intentions, taking only a brief respite when a tennis shoe was tossed in his direction.

All this suggested a certain intelligence and malice of forethought that disturbed me. It also evoked images of Willard's last stand against Ben and the army of rats, which did nothing to ease my anxiety. Heart hammering against my bony rib cage, I lay in the dark and silently hoped that whatever sought ingress would lose heart and scamper off. But it did not. The terrible chewing, so very loud in the darkness, continued.

After twenty minutes, I could take the assault no longer. Striking a match, I lit the stub of a candle beside my bed and shuffled toward the noise. Sure enough, it was coming from behind my toy box. I picked up the discarded tennis shoe and rapped its rubber sole against the wall several times.

"Take off," I yelled, stamping one bare foot for emphasis.

"What the hell is going on up there?" Olavi asked from below.

"Something is chewing in the wall."

"Go back to bed."

I dropped the tennis shoe and stayed put. "But it's trying to get inside."

"I said, 'Get back into bed.' It won't hurt you."

"Says you," I muttered, bending down to pull my toy box from the corner. The insolence was meant for my ears only, but Olavi must have heard it. The man had ears like a rabbit. "Do I have to come up there?" he asked with menace. I heard the bedsprings squeak as his weight shifted.

"No," I responded, retreating to my bed. Silence followed, then I added in frustration, "But I can't sleep. It's really loud."

"All right, that's it. I'm coming up there."

Mom intervened. "It's okay. He's back in bed," she assured my stepfather before addressing me. "Michael, it's twenty past eleven. What you hear is probably just a mouse. Go to sleep."

With no allies on the first floor, I extinguished the candle and slipped back into bed.

Our family settled itself. Night walked like a polite house guest from room to room, leaving in its wake familiar nocturnal noises. From downstairs came the sound of gentle snoring; at the other end of the attic, Kelly mumbled something incoherent and then giggled in her sleep. The metal chimney beside me ticked as it cooled, and outside, far in the distance, a great horned owl hooted.

I was just dozing off when the chewing started again.

Sleep fled. Sometime toward dawn, exhaustion overcame fear, and I passed out. What seemed like seconds later, Mom was shaking me awake.

"Time for school," she said, her features barely discernable in the pre-dawn darkness. "Didn't you hear me calling?"

I groaned. "I'm so tired. Can I stay home?"

"No. You've already missed more school than all your classmates combined."

It was true. I had set a modern record for truancy the previous year by missing an average of one day a week and was already on a pace to eclipse the achievement. Wasn't sick most of the time, just bored. Still got passing grades, so I figured attendance was optional.

"But I hardly got any sleep, and I've got double PE today."

Mom held firm. "It's Friday. You can catch up on your sleep this weekend," she said, giving me another shake. "Come on, the oatmeal's getting cold."

She left. I pulled on my clothes and staggered downstairs past the prostrate form of my stepfather. Why didn't he have to get up? My head felt like a pumpkin with the seeds scooped out.

Mom ladled several blobs of oatmeal into a bowl and set it on the table in front of me.

I stared at it. The mush looked worse than usual this morning, like wallpaper paste mixed with coarse sawdust. I hoped it didn't come from the bottom of the bag where the weevils liked to hang out.

"Do I have to eat this? It looks gross."

"It's good for you. Now hurry up and eat. The bus will be here in twenty minutes."

On a hunch, I picked up my spoon and dropped it business end first into the bowl from a moderate height. The utensil pierced the mush and remained upright for several seconds before listing to port like a mouldering tombstone. My stomach rolled.

Kelly, seated across from me, laughed. "Mike's oatmeal's so thick his spoon stands up by itself."

"Oh, for God's sake," Mom said. She rushed over, pulled out the spoon, and used it to draw a happy face in my breakfast. "Put some milk and brown sugar on it," she said, pushing both toward me. "It'll be fine."

It wasn't, but I ate the glutinous mess anyway.

We barely made the bus, running the last hundred yards in the grey half-light to where it crouched by the side of the road like a giant yellow-and-black toad. To my surprise, school proved a welcome distraction that allowed me to forget, at least for a while, the terrible events of the previous night. But upon returning home, I found myself reliving the attempted home invasion. I tried to remain upbeat and, by bedtime, had even convinced myself there was a good chance the perpetrator wouldn't return.

My optimism proved baseless. Tunnelling resumed as soon as the lights in the cabin had been extinguished. I moaned and pulled the blankets over my head.

Agonizing hours later, the chewing ceased. Everything went quiet.

I poked my head out of the covers and listened. For a few seconds, nothing, then a sound like tearing paper, followed by the tiptoeing of tiny, clawed feet across rough pine. There was another pause, some scrambling, and something shifted in my toy box.

The thing was in my room.

My right hand slid from beneath the blankets and groped beside the bed for something approximating a missile. It closed around an old bread bag full of quartz and I flung it toward the corner of the attic without thinking.

The bag landed with a bang and exploded, scattering pebbles across the room like shrapnel. Rusty barked, my baby sister started crying, and Kelly voiced objections from her end of the attic.

"Jesus Bloody Christ," Olavi said. "What the hell was that?"

"Something's in my room. It was in my toy box. I threw a thing at it."

He growled, an ominous sound, and I heard him get out of bed.

"What did I tell you last night?" he asked from below. The flashlight came on as he mounted the stairs.

An even greater terror gripped me. "It was a bag of rocks. It was an accident. I'm sorry."

Mom said something indistinct, but Olavi kept coming.

I panicked. "I won't do it again. I'll be good. Honest. Please don't . . . Dad."

I heard him pause and held my breath. After what seemed like ages, he spoke. "All right. But it damn well better not happen again."

The air came out of me in a rush as he started back down the stairs. "It won't. I promise," I said, my voice just above a whisper.

The flashlight flicked off. Laina whimpered a few more times, then fell silent. Quiet returned.

Kelly's voice drifted over the divider between us. "I won't do it again," she said, mimicking my desperate snivelling. "I'll be good, I promise. Please don't, *Daddy.*"

"Oh, shut up," I replied.

Rising early, I discovered, is easier if you don't go to sleep. As soon as the scampering stopped and it was light enough upstairs to see, I surveyed the crime scene. The floor was a minefield of coarse gravel, and my playthings looked like they had been through a cement mixer, but nothing was missing. Relieved, I stole the six-volt Coleman lantern from beneath my parents' bed and used it to search the dark recess behind my toy box. Sleep might again be possible if I could find the entry hole and plug it with something harder than wood—a marble, or perhaps the lid from a can of baked beans.

I couldn't find it but did come across the animal's spoor, several hard, black pellets the size and shape of charred Rice Krispies. Because they were proof of the invader's existence, I gathered up a few and trundled downstairs in my pajamas to show the doubters.

Mom was up by this time and banging around the kitchen, but Olavi was still dead to the world. Clad in boxer shorts and a grey T-shirt, he lay spread-eagled on the bed in all his corpulent glory, mouth open and snoring. Vulnerable. I eyed the compact little turds in my hand and considered dropping one into his gaping maw, then decided against it. No clear avenue of escape, the likelihood of violent retribution high. Sighing, I placed the chunky flashlight on the floor beside him and continued to the kitchen.

Mom was stuffing kindling into the cookstove. I waited until she turned around.

"See what I found behind my toy box?" I said, shoving the palm full of micro-turds into her face.

She recoiled but recovered quickly. Grabbing my wrist, she hauled me toward the wood box. "Get rid of them. Now."

I complied. "Told you something was in my room. You didn't believe me."

"I believed you," she said, filling our blackened coffee pot with water. "But I said it was just a mouse."

I wasn't buying the mouse theory. "Come on, Mom. Ever seen mouse crap that big?"

She went back to the wood box for a second look. "Okay," she said after a brief examination of the evidence, "so it's a packrat."

Mom kept talking, but everything after "rat" sounded like the unintelligible squawking of Charlie Brown's teacher. A mental slideshow began playing in my head. It was filled with nightmarish images, pictures of sharp-snouted creatures with glinting eyes and needle-like teeth, apocalyptic oil-on-canvas renderings of the Black Death, graphic photos of bite marks on slum babies, and, at last, those terrible scenes from *Willard*.

A tsunami of horror swept over me, leaving cold, hard fear in its wake. It must have shown on my face because my mother stopped jabbering.

"Are you all right?" Her voice came to me from the bottom of a deep well, dragging me back to reality.

"A rat," I said. "You said it's a rat. They're . . . bad."

Mom bent down and looked into my eyes. "I said a '*packrat*,'" she added, giving my shoulder a reassuring touch. "It's not a wharf rat like the ones in Vancouver. It won't hurt you. Here, look at this."

She showed me a children's book she had illustrated for a local woman. *The Packrat Story* was filled with pen-and-ink drawings of a small creature with bright eyes, big ears, and a long fluffy tail. The rodent appeared to be smiling in a few sketches. According to the author, it did nothing more harmful than steal shiny objects, emit a foul odour, and chew leather belts.

I didn't believe a word of it. Even the creature's Latin name, *Neotoma cinerea,* sounded malignant.

"See?" Mom said at the end of her presentation. "You don't need to be scared."

"Right," I said. "Now, how do I kill it?"

When Olavi got up a half-hour later, Mom told him my story and asked where I might procure a rat trap. Clearly in a foul mood, he poured himself a coffee and took his customary seat at the head of the kitchen table before answering.

"Maybe in the equipment shed," he said, scowling into his cup.

Thinking the discussion over, I got up and moved past him. I was reaching for my coat, which hung from a rusty spike by the door, when he spoke again.

"Where do you think you're going?"

I froze. "To look for a trap?"

"Did I say you could go? Sit down."

I took a seat opposite him and as far away as possible.

"You woke everybody up again last night," he said while pretending to study his coffee. "What have you got to say?"

I glanced at Mom, but she avoided me and busied herself making breakfast. "Sorry?" I said with a degree of uncertainty.

Olavi was looking at me now, his gaze baleful. "Is that all?" he asked. Pointing toward Laina, who watched the proceedings from the end of her crib, he added, "It took nearly an hour to get your sister back to sleep."

Which, of course, was a lie. Laina had settled down within minutes, and her biological father had gone back to sawing logs soon after. I had been the one awake an hour after the rock-slinging incident, alone and afraid, while a creature with evil intent ran amok in the attic and crapped behind my toy box.

My anger flared. I wanted to scream at him, call him a liar and a bastard and a lot worse, but dared not. "I'm sorry," I said instead, breaking eye contact and transferring my attention to the worn surface of the table in front of me. There was a big divot near the edge, and I traced its outline with a finger.

Long, torturous seconds followed as Olavi worked himself into a fury. "No, you're not," he said finally, "because you told me last time it wouldn't happen again. And I told you what would happen if it did."

I sensed rather than saw the slap coming and raised both hands to protect myself. Yet I'd judged the distance between us well and the open-handed blow connected with empty air.

Coffee sloshed over the rim of Olavi's cup and onto the table. The mess and the botched attempt at corporal punishment only increased his anger. "Why you . . ." he said, leaning forward and raising his hand again.

"Enough!"

It was Mom. She stood between us, a plate of bacon and eggs in one hand, dishcloth in the other. "Can't we just have a peaceful meal for once?" With that, she made a show of wiping up the spilled liquid, then dropped the plate on the table with a thump and shoved it in front of my stepfather.

Olavi shot me a poisonous look before picking up his fork. I waited until he had stuffed some egg into his mouth before asking in a small voice, "Can I go now?"

He swallowed, took a gulp of black coffee, and paused long enough to keep me in suspense. "Go chop some wood first. Then you can feed the horses."

I fled.

Ninety minutes later, I was working my way through several shelves of junk in a long log building not far from the barn. The place was a repository for all manner of items, some useful, most not. I found what I was looking for amidst the detritus of several decades, a dirty wooden thing that looked like an oversized mousetrap.

That evening, after spending the afternoon familiarizing myself with the device's mechanism, I baited it with a lump of mouldy cheese, placed it behind my toy box, and settled into bed.

I waited, hopeful and too strung out to sleep. After what seemed like an epoch, there was a loud snap and several seconds of frantic thrashing, followed by silence. I waited a minute or two, long enough for the trap to do its dreadful work, then lit a candle and crept toward the attic corner. I stood there rigid for a bit, took a deep breath, and pulled my toy box from its cubby hole beneath the rafters.

The trap was empty.

Mom whispered from the foot of the stairs. "Did you catch it?"

"No," I said, miserable. "It got away."

"Well, go to bed and try again tomorrow."

Olavi didn't wake up, and the rat didn't return that night, allowing me at least a few hours of rest.

"Perhaps you scared it away, and it won't come back," Mom, always one to take the high road, said the following morning.

"Maybe," I replied. "I set the trap again just in case."

For a time, it seemed Mom might be right. Nothing returned to the attic that night or the next. Feeling optimistic, I sprung the trap and returned it.

Removing the Mike Turkki Home Defense System proved premature because the creature returned two nights later. I awoke from deep sleep to hear it rummaging in my toy box.

"Psssst," I said as quietly as possible.

The creature paused for a few seconds, then resumed its explorations. I hissed again, a little louder, and there was another short break in the proceedings, followed by a bump and the sound of sharp claws scuttling across the floor toward me. The rodent came hesitantly at first, one or two paces at a time, then quicker when it encountered no resistance.

Terrified, I made as if to get up. The scuttling stopped. "Get out of here," I whispered into the darkness, raising myself higher and waving both arms.

The thing scampered back toward the corner of the attic. I lay back and, after an eon, fell asleep.

With interdiction no longer a threat, the creature grew bold. It ventured further into the room each night, roaming across the pine floor and even scampering under my bed. When I offered only token opposition, it scaled the wall and ran along a narrow shelf above me, knocking my ship models helter-skelter and causing panic in the fleet.

Not content to disturb my sleep, it delighted in destroying the things I valued most. Navy GI Joe had his face disfigured and one hand gnawed off—a harbinger, I felt, of my fate—and great half-moons appeared in the uppers of my new hockey skates. The rat stole my tin sheriff's badge, then made off with a 1911 silver dime left unguarded on my dresser. And what it couldn't chew or swipe, it pissed on: a metal canteen, my precious Beatles LPs, diecast metal cars I'd owned since kindergarten.

I dared not oppose these nightly raids for fear of waking Olavi, who made it clear he would brook no further disturbances. I complained to Mom regularly, yet it did little good. While somewhat sympathetic, she maintained that the creature represented no threat.

"Oh, Mike," she said with growing impatience, "just leave it alone, and it will eventually go away. It's nothing to be afraid of."

But I *was* afraid of the rat. Some people fear insects, others snakes or water. For a select few, clowns and homeless people instill panic. None of these things bothered me, yet the smelly creature that entered my room each night and stayed until dawn was terror in four-legged form. There was something insidious about its actions, its single-minded determination to own my space, its fearlessness. It never squeaked, merely scuttled, and though I never saw it, I sometimes sensed it watching me in the darkness.

And despite Mom's assertions, the rat didn't leave, nor did it venture into Kelly's room or raid the pantry. It had chosen me. Night after night, it returned to my room in the attic to make me feel small and insignificant and alone.

Weeks of torment turned into months. I grew increasingly paranoid and sleep-deprived. It all came to a head one snowy night in early March.

Olavi had by this time taken a job at the Andrew Bay logging camp and was working the night shift. I was drifting toward sleep when something landed on the blankets covering my feet. The weight was so slight that I first thought it was the product of my overactive imagination, but then it started to move. At the same time, a fetid stench reminiscent of underarm sweat and sewage caused my nose to wrinkle.

I screamed and kicked, launching my tormenter into the air. It landed with a soft thump and scurried into the corner.

Mom grabbed the flashlight and rushed upstairs.

"It was on me," I said, nearly in tears. "It was crawling on my bed."

Mom was dubious. "Are you sure?"

"I can't take this anymore," I said with finality. "The rat can have my room."

With Olavi out of the house, Mom let me sleep downstairs in an armchair beside her bed. I dropped into it, drew a thin comforter over me, and settled in for the night's remainder.

It was warm downstairs, and the old lounger felt softer than my bed. Tired beyond words, I felt myself sliding toward unconsciousness. Then there was a familiar scratching from the corner of the room.

Horrified, I snatched the flashlight, trained its feeble beam toward the sound, and saw my nemesis for the first time.

The packrat's head protruded through a knothole in the ceiling less than six feet away. The creature had ears the size and colour of old quarters, a sharp, pink-tipped snout studded with coarse whiskers, and eyes that gleamed like black pearls in the lamplight. It peered down at me, unblinking, with a look that seemed more curious than malicious.

Mom started to laugh. "It misses you."

I didn't find the situation amusing. "Leave me alone," I yelled, leaping from the chair.

The creature's face disappeared, but I retrieved a broom from the kitchen and banged its handle on the ceiling anyway. Then I curled up in the chair and tried to sleep.

We had school the next day. I took my customary seat on the bus in front of Sean and Nicky but didn't say much.

"What's up, man?" the blond boy asked me after the bus picked up Diggory. "You look like shit this morning. Sick?"

"No, just really tired," I replied, trying to rub the exhaustion from my face with one hand. "Haven't been sleeping much."

"Probably too much of this," Nicky said, curling his hand into a fist and making an obscene pumping gesture.

The guys laughed. "Not funny," I said. "There's a rat in our house, and it's driving me fucking nuts. Last night it ran over my feet, and when I went downstairs, it followed me."

Diggs asked if I had tried catching the interloper.

"Yeah, but it got away," I replied.

"What did you use?"

I told him. He frowned and shook his head. "Those things are no damn good. You've got to use a leghold trap with peanut butter on the pan. Then, when the bush rat sticks his head in to eat the peanut butter . . ." He demonstrated the gruesome result by laying a forearm along each side of his neck, tilting his shaggy head to the left, and mimicking a death grimace.

I got the point. "You sure?"

"Yeah, it always works," he said. "Caught dozens of them that way. I'll bring you a trap tomorrow."

He did. It was a rusty old Victor No. 1 with a single spring and long tether chain. After showing me how to set it, he demonstrated the device's power by triggering it with a pencil. The pitted jaws snapped his Crownline HB cleanly in half.

"You don't have to wire it down, but I always do," he added before handing the trap to me. "Set it on a beam or a board where there's a lot of rat crap. You'll catch the bastard."

I took the trap home in my lunchbox. Mom wasn't keen to have the thing in the house but consented because she was tired of my complaints.

I set the trap just before going to bed. I followed Diggory's instructions to the letter, smearing a healthy glob of peanut butter on the pan and even wiring the chain to a rafter before leaving it behind my toy box.

Given my previous failures, I didn't expect immediate results. Yet I had been in bed just a few minutes when there was a loud snap and some frantic thrashing.

Jumping out of bed, flashlight in one hand, Louisville Slugger in the other, I ran to the corner and pulled out my toy box. Shone the torch into the dark recess beyond.

The trap had been sprung, and the steel jaws had slammed shut on the rat's front legs. Both were broken, yet the creature struggled to free itself despite this grievous injury.

The scene triggered something primitive and ugly in me. Anger and despair rose like black bile, contorting my face into a grim rictus. I raised the bat and brought it down on the small, writhing form.

Powered by unreasoning hatred, the weapon rose and fell, rose and fell, until at last, I felt a gentle pressure on one shoulder.

I turned my head, the bat poised for another strike.

Standing in the darkness behind me was my mother, a look of horror on her face.

"It's dead, Michael," she said. "You can stop now."

I glanced back at the trap. Seconds earlier, the old steel had held a live animal, but what remained was unrecognizable. Blood, gore, and matted fur were everywhere: on the floor, on the wall, on the bludgeon, and the hands that clutched it.

I lowered the bat and started to cry. Tears of sadness and relief rolled down my cheeks, but I didn't care.

Mom dropped to her knees and wrapped both arms around me.

"It's okay," she said, her breath warm on my face. "It's over."

I slept soundly that night for the first time in months.

Brody

For a brief period in the mid-1970s, Olavi found seasonal employment on a barge that cleared snags from the Nechako Reservoir. He was gone almost an entire summer, living on board and coming home only when the operation broke down or needed supplies.

On one of his furloughs, my stepfather mentioned a co-worker named Brody. He suggested the man be invited to visit when underwater logging shut down for the winter.

My mother was intrigued. So was I. Olavi, a hardcore introvert like the rest of us, had never voiced a desire to socialize with anyone. His preferred activity was holding down our overstuffed armchair and binge-reading science fiction novels like a chain smoker with unlimited tobacco. While he could be charming and engaged when it suited his purposes, he was generally aloof around strangers, saying little unless asked a direct question. He preferred his own company, and I got the impression he didn't much care for ours.

"I guess we could have this Brody over," said Mom with surprise. "But why?"

Olavi was evasive. "Well, he's . . . interesting."

Mom wanted to know more about this mysterious stranger, but my stepfather provided few details. "He's from around here," was all he would say. "He's twenty-five, maybe thirty. Single. Reads a lot. You'll probably like him."

Olavi worked out the arrangements during his next shift on the barge. Mom made some discrete inquiries.

People who live in small communities have an opinion about everything, including their neighbours. "Hmmm. How shall I phrase this?" said one woman. "Brody is . . . well, there's no way around it. He's odd. He marches to a different drum than the rest of us. But I don't think he's dangerous, just strange." Another recommended that we avoid the bachelor. "If you invite him over," she said, sniffing as if an unpleasant odour had been detected nearby, "better nail everything down. Can't say for sure he's a thief, but things tend to go missing when he's around."

Our landlord at Rainbow Lake delivered the final verdict. "He's one of the Johnsons. They're newcomers. Only been here twenty years or so," she said as if the family's failure to arrive with the first wave of settlers was a crime.

Mom filed the information away for future reference. I doubt she gave it much credence, though. Most people in Wistaria thought we were weird too. It was an accurate assessment, but it didn't make us criminals.

A week later, we had just started eating supper when someone pounded on the door.

"Hello, this place," said a loud male voice. Without waiting for a response, its owner opened the door and stepped into our lives.

The enigma that was Brody had arrived.

He was about five foot seven and as skinny as a utility pole, with a close-cropped ginger beard and moustache, hair the same colour, and a small but expressive mouth beneath a snub nose tossed haphazardly in the centre of his tanned face. The blue eyes that glittered in the light of our Coleman lantern viewed the world through thick glasses with heavy black plastic frames mended at several critical junctures with electrician's tape. His clothing consisted of steel-toed work boots, loose-fitting wool pants bunched well above the waist with a length of manila rope, and a long-sleeved cotton dress shirt with one cuff missing.

"Well," he said, pulling off his bright orange hard hat and hanging it on a nail by the door. "What are we eating tonight?"

A hush fell over the dinner table. The fork my mother was wielding paused halfway to its destination. Her mouth opened in surprise, but the piece of stew meat she had just speared never made it there. The grisly chunk fell off and landed in the gravy on her plate with a loud plop.

Olavi recovered first. "Hi, Brody," he said, sliding over. "Mike, give him your chair. Coffee?"

"No . . . well . . . Sure, why not," said our guest as he dropped into my seat. "I'll be up ten times tonight to pee, but what the hell." He ended the statement with a raucous laugh.

Mom got Brody a plate and cutlery while I went outside to find a block of pine to sit on. I wasn't gone long, but our guest had already finished his first helping of food by the time I returned.

"More?" asked my mother politely when he was done.

"Don't mind if I do," he said, wiping a sleeve across his mouth before reaching into the pot for seconds. "It's good."

Kelly, seated on my right, watched our guest with interest. It was like passing a car accident on the highway: you felt compelled to stare no matter how gruesome the scene. She leaned over to me and quietly asked, "Is that man starving?"

"I don't know," I whispered back. "But keep your hands and feet away from his mouth."

Brody finished Helping Number Two and looked around the table. I got the impression he was scoping out what remained on our plates. Kelly must have thought the same because she offered hers.

"You can have this," she said, extending the remains of her meal toward him like a sacrificial offering. "I'm full."

"I couldn't," said Brody without a shred of conviction.

Mom, sensing that famine was only a word away, agreed. "No, you eat that," she said to my sister. "It's good for you."

"But Mom," said Kelly, "I don't like it. It tastes like bum, and he's so hungry."

"Oh, really, I'm not," said Brody, reaching for the last slice of white bread. I beat him to it and smiled with grim satisfaction.

When there was nothing left to devour, our guest sighed, pushed his plate away, and leaned back in the chair. "Thank you," he said with genuine appreciation. "That was delicious, the best I've had in a long time. What's for dessert?"

I knew there was a package of fudge cookies in the cupboard. So did my mother, but she decided to keep it a secret. "I'm sorry, Brody," she said, her response apologetic. "I'm afraid there isn't any."

"No worries," he replied. As a backup, he reached into the pocket of his shirt and pulled out a piece of hard candy. It must have gone into the cavity wet because there was quite a bit of hair and fluff attached. He examined the morsel for several seconds before pulling off the unwanted fiber and popping what remained into his mouth.

"So," he asked, rolling the candy around his mouth. "Do you play cards?" Olavi went looking for a deck while Mom and I cleared the table.

Over the next half hour, Brody taught my parents the basics of gin rummy. They played nonstop after that, pausing only to refill their coffee cups and pump the pressure lamp that hung over our kitchen table.

I watched from the sidelines for a while, then asked if I could play. To my surprise, Olavi agreed. He had won three games and was looking for another victim.

Brody shuffled the cards, and we started anew. As the evening progressed, our guest told us his life story. He had, we learned, three brothers and two sisters. His family moved to the area in the late 1940s, but unlike most who came for the Alcan boom and left, they stayed and bought land near Wistaria. After completing Grade Ten at Grassy Plains, he left home to attend trade school in Vancouver, returning after eighteen months without achieving certification in any field. The instructors, he explained, didn't seem to like him much.

We played into the night. Kelly lost interest in the proceedings and wandered away to do girl things. Laina fell asleep in the high chair, her face planted in a half-eaten bowl of Pablum.

Brody talked. And talked. And talked some more.

Around midnight, Mom said it was time for me to get some rest. She looked with undisguised longing at her bed in the adjacent room, but the gesture was lost on our visitor.

"Aw, Mom, not yet," I said. "There's no school tomorrow, and I'm having fun."

"Stop whining and go to bed," said Olavi with finality.

I did not want to surrender my spot at the table. Olavi had been right: Brody was fascinating. His mind was a reservoir of quirky knowledge, and he had a twisted sense of humour. And there was no sign that he was cultivating our friendship for personal gain. The man lacked guile; unlike me, he didn't even cheat at cards.

I retired for the night, but Brody's loud voice kept me awake for hours. He had no volume control. Every comment, no matter how mundane, was delivered as if there was a crowd present and he needed to make himself heard above the hubbub.

Despite the ruckus, I drifted off. When I awoke, the first light of a new day was slicing through the tiny window in our cabin's eastern gable. My head pounded as though someone had removed my brain during the night and used a broomstick to jam coarse steel wool into the cavity left behind. I could hear Olavi talking downstairs, his voice soft and low. Whatever he said was greeted by a barking guffaw that was now all too familiar.

Brody was still in the building.

I got dressed and went downstairs. The adults were sitting just as I'd left them the previous night. The ashtray on the kitchen table was full of crushed cigarette butts. There were rings of dried coffee on the red-checked plastic tablecloth, and an empty box of snack crackers sat in front of our guest. The naphtha lantern hissed dully overhead.

Mom and Olavi glanced in my direction. They looked exhausted.

Brody, on the other hand, appeared as fresh as spring flowers after a gentle rain. "Morning, sleepyhead," he bellowed at me with a wide grin. "Have a good snooze?"

"Not really," I replied, rooting for my rubber boots in the pile of footwear behind his chair. "You guys were awfully loud."

The implied criticism flew right over his head. "Well, I guess I better get going," he added as I pushed through the door and headed for the outhouse. "Got people to do and things to see."

He was still there when I returned.

"I'm hungry. What can I eat?" I asked, shooting Brody a harsh look. I still hadn't forgiven him for scarfing most of the previous night's meal.

Mom, her eyes like two pee holes in a dirty snowbank, got up and stuffed some kindling into the wood stove. "I'll make breakfast," she said.

We watched as she pulled a cast iron pan from beneath the sink and set it on the stove to warm. A can of bacon appeared unannounced on the countertop; she opened it, pulled the glutinous, paper-wrapped mass out with a fork, and unrolled it on a cutting board. Then she pried off a half dozen slices and arranged them in tight rows on the bottom of the hot pan where they hissed and spat defiantly.

The tantalizing aroma of frying pork soon filled the room. All conversation ceased.

"Gee, that sure smells good," said Brody, looking expectantly toward my mother.

Mom's face hardened. I saw a sharp-edged rebuke forming on her lips, but she took one look at the youthful smile on our guest's face and lost all resolve. Her shoulders sagged in resignation.

"Would you like some?" she asked, already knowing the answer.

"Well, twist my rubber arm," said Brody with another deafening laugh. "Why not? There's nowhere else I really need to be."

Mom sighed and started cooking more bacon.

That was our introduction to Brody Johnson, the man who, like a character from Tolkien's *The Hobbit*, came for dinner and stayed until breakfast.

Sometime around one in the afternoon, when no other food appeared to be forthcoming, Brody again announced that it was time to leave. This time, though, the blessed event happened. He clamped the safety helmet back on his blocky head, climbed into the green pickup he arrived in, and drove away—but not before thanking my parents profusely.

He came back that evening. And the next. And the one after that.

My parents liked him. We all did. But after four nights with little sleep and less food, our family of misanthropes had experienced enough Johnson amity to last weeks. We needed a break but could not seem to communicate it. Subtlety was lost on him; he didn't get the hint, even when my sister burst into tears on day three after learning that while he was at last headed out the door, it was only to relieve himself.

Something had to be done, but despite Brody's constant effervescence, there was an unmistakable aura of desperation and loneliness about him that made us hesitant to say anything that might give offense. Poor and rejected by almost everyone in the community, he devoured our groceries and companionship like a glutton at a banquet.

Finally, with our nerves frayed and larder depleted, we had no choice.

"Brody," Mom said with rare frankness after another of his fourteen-hour stays, "you need to go home for a while—and by that, I mean for a week or two. We've got things to do, and we're almost out of food."

Our guest did not take umbrage at the statement, perhaps because he had heard it so often. He grinned, expressed appreciation for our hospitality, said goodbye, and left.

He returned ten days later and never again overstayed his welcome.

We learned more about him as the months went by. In some ways, Brody's life was like ours. He was poor and survived by doing odd jobs in the community, most for a wealthy rancher named Richard Lawson. He lived in a dilapidated blue travel trailer that he pulled from one jobsite to another, never spending more than a few months in one place before moving on. Like Olavi, he was a packrat and, despite his itinerancy, had already accumulated an impressive array of junk by the time we met. He carted these treasures around the country and stored them in temporary sheds at each new location. Moving day for him lasted a week.

Brody's home had twelve-volt lighting, which he extended to his complex of warehouses and outbuildings with miles of eight-gauge wire. When his energy demands outstripped the capacity of a solitary automobile battery, he bought two enormous industrial cells and installed them in the box of his pickup. Using ingenuity, some mail-order components, and plenty of solder, he connected both to the vehicle's electrical system so they could be charged whenever he drove around. Upon returning from a trip, he simply plugged his house into his truck, went inside, and flicked a switch.

Of course, this jumble of wires and circuitry only worked if Brody had enough money for gasoline. This proved his greatest obstacle because he got more satisfaction from puttering than working. Steady, full-time employment eluded him, generally by design, which resulted in one home-grown energy crisis after another. These self-inflicted power outages created no significant hardships if they occurred during the sunlight-rich months of May, June, July, and August, but those that hit in winter sent our friend back to the Dark Ages. We sometimes didn't see him for weeks because electricity generation had trumped travel, but he would show up again as soon as good fortune or a wealthy Samaritan provided a few dollars for fuel.

He also collected cats and sometimes had two dozen four-legged boarders, most of them female. His trailer in Streatham became a halfway house for indigent felines. Word that free room and board was available at the Johnson residence must have spread like grassfire through the feral cat community, because they made a beeline for his place after getting pregnant. Grossly bloated Mollies were everywhere; they lounged around his trailer, slept under his bed, made nests for themselves in closets and walls. None of them ever went hungry, even if it meant Brody lived on short rations. Once, when he had been unemployed for an extended period, he asked us to pick up a few things in town. His handwritten shopping list, folded over a ten-dollar banknote, had six items on it:

- White bread (two loaves);
- Butter (one pound);
- Coffee (one can);
- Kraft dinner (twenty boxes);
- Evaporated milk (a case);
- Dried cat food (six bags, 30 pounds each, please).

We bought him other stuff and never sought reimbursement.

His mode of transportation varied, but, in general, consisted of whichever of his vehicles happened to be running at the time. For several months in the early '70s, perhaps out of necessity, he got around on a Honda 50 with no muffler. Every Saturday evening for ten weeks, he climbed aboard the child-sized minibike, stuffed cotton in his ears, and rode to our house for dinner. Fearing a mechanical breakdown, he kept to the main thoroughfares as much as possible, dodging automobiles and indignant black bears with his knees jammed into his armpits. We never asked how long the ten-mile trip took him, but it must have been like riding a chainsaw at Daytona.

At one point, he had a metallic green Oldsmobile 4-4-2. The muscle car must have been beautiful in its day, but that day was long past by the time Brody acquired it. The two-door fastback was not designed for gravel roads, a fact that had been lost on all ten of its previous owners. In a final act of disrespect, a gang of irresponsible teenagers flogged it unmercifully and eschewed routine maintenance.

Brody must have seen something in the car because he paid two hundred dollars for the privilege of towing it home. Perhaps it was the 455-cubic-inch engine, which remained strong despite having propelled almost two tonnes of iron, glass, and plastic the equivalent of five times around the earth. Maybe it was the Hurst shifter protruding through the abused centre console or the pair of fuzzy dice dangling provocatively from the cracked rear-view mirror. It couldn't have been the car's body, which by 1975 was disappearing faster than a nail in a bottle of cola.

Our friend got the Oldsmobile back on the road, and his mechanical genius would have kept it there for several more years if not for the failure of one critical component. For reasons that remain a mystery, the car's steering wheel broke. The first casualty was the upper half of the polyurethane ring, which left its disappointed owner with a mechanism not unlike the yoke of an airplane. At length, that too snapped off—at a most inopportune time. Brody, making his way down Wistaria Hill, turned a bit too abruptly at the bottom and found himself gripping two prongs of synthetic polymer no longer attached to the automobile. He survived by hitting the brakes and grabbing the remaining four-inch plastic circle with both hands. The rest of his journey to our house was made possible with the aid of locking pliers, which he clamped to the nub of the steering column. This fix proved adequate for a while, but then the steering nut rounded off, leaving him with no control over the front wheels. The car was retired in a simple ceremony not long after, but parts of it lived on in other Johnson vehicles.

Brody found a permanent home in the late 1970s. Kendrick Jones, a childless widower who was getting on in years, agreed to share four acres with the younger man if he helped around the place. Brody, ready to put down roots by that time, accepted the offer.

Our friend's salvage activities had always been somewhat held in check by his lack of a fixed address because he knew from painful experience that anything he collected would have to be moved at some point in the not-too-distant future. For this reason, during his peripatetic period, he practiced selective accumulation, hauling home only those items for which he had a short-term (i.e., five-year) plan.

Kendrick's generous offer of permanent tenancy removed this obstacle and paved the way for hoarding on a grand scale. With eviction no longer imminent, Brody began bringing all manner of stuff back to his new home: old vehicles, boxes of mildewed books, chunks of waste steel and plywood, other odds and ends that might, at some point in his lifetime, prove useful. The northern half of the Jones property started to look like a breaker's yard.

As his inventory grew, so did his need for more warehouse space. Desperate for building materials but with no money to buy them, Brody scoured the countryside for anything he could nail together in the form of rudimentary shelter. After weeks of fruitless search, he finally hit the jackpot. An abandoned sawmill near Mumford Lake yielded a mountain of trim ends and rough-cut slabs, the worthless by-products of railway tie manufacturing in the 1950s. He sorted through the pile and hauled the least rotten pieces home on a trailer borrowed from his landlord.

The exercise took weeks and gave birth to an impromptu lumber yard on another acre of Kendrick's property. When the landowner, feeling squeezed, tactfully expressed concern over the expansionist policies of his new helper, Brody promised to clean everything up before the winter.

He met this self-imposed deadline by knocking together a half-dozen shelters and stuffing everything he could lift inside them. Several larger items, including a rotting cabin cruiser and the burnt-out hulk of a John Deere bulldozer, remained exposed to the elements, but he pulled them behind his sheds so they could not be seen from Kendrick's living room window. All were still visible from the main road, though, and provided locals with a constant source of amusement.

Brody's primary dwelling unit, built around the decaying remains of his travel trailer, was separate from these sheds and outbuildings for many years. This proved inconvenient, though, because it required that he maintain the network of paths and trails that linked them to the manufacturing facility in his semi-detached carport. Snow removal and drainage control took time and effort better spent on more meaningful activities like small engine repair.

Brody solved the problem by building covered walkways between his residence and outbuildings. After a while, these also became superfluous because home expansion resulted in the closest sheds being incorporated into the main building. The result was a sprawling clapboard mansion comparable in size to Graceland.

Phase III of this consolidation program included changes to his pit toilet, which became an indoor outhouse in the west wing.

While our family had much in common with Brody, his life differed from ours in crucial respects. He had never known parental love, only censure and neglect from the two people who could have changed the trajectory of his development at an early age. While his siblings tolerated him, his dysfunctional mother and father—themselves abject failures in almost everything that mattered—made it clear to anyone who asked that they considered him a grave disappointment. They never understood him because they never bothered to try. He was allowed home at Christmas but seldom got an invite at any other time of the year, and no one did anything to give him a decent start in life. He became self-sufficient because his survival depended on it.

Brody became part of our family by default, and we soon learned that most of what people said about him was false. Contrary to popular belief, he wasn't lazy. Despite being a reluctant employee, he was a good one who arrived at work on time and stayed until his assigned tasks were complete. And while it was true that Brody collected things, the lion's share of them were objects cast aside by others. He was a regular at local landfills where he made more withdrawals than deposits and was on a first-name basis with the attendants. There was no evidence that his meagre possessions had been obtained through dishonesty or grift. In all the years we knew him, he never stole anything from us other than the misconception that every Canadian starts life with an equal chance at success.

Most people took one look at Brody—with his myopic eyesight, hand-me-down clothing, and lack of social graces—and wrote him off as a worthless incompetent. They were mistaken. Yes, he was eccentric and socially handicapped, and sometimes his behaviour was boorish. There were times when his hygiene was also questionable. Yet, how could he be anything else given his upbringing and financial situation?

That he possessed these qualities and lacked others did not make him stupid. Quite the opposite was true. Brody, we discovered, was a gifted mechanic who could fix anything without the benefit of a repair manual. Equipped with an adjustable wrench and a selection of screwdrivers, he could make a broken motor run like new in less time than it took the rest of us to read a comic book. He was MacGyver without manners or mullet.

How clever was the man considered Wistaria's village idiot? Consider this: in the mid-1980s, during one of his many forays to the dump, Brody found a Tandy computer beneath a bag of rotten garbage. He took the electronic device home, plugged it in, and depressed the power button. Much to his surprise and disappointment (but no one else's), it wouldn't start. But that did not deter him. He disassembled the machine, found the problem circuits, and fixed them. Then he taught himself BASIC and wrote computer games that everyone could play.

"The only things that separated Brody from Bill Gates and Steve Jobs," my sister Laina says in retrospect, "were upbringing and opportunity."

Yet Brody was more than just smart. He was also patient, kind, and generous, and these qualities earned him a place at our table. The winter after I left Wistaria, he spent hours shovelling a frozen swamp near his home so that Laina could learn to skate. He didn't do it for money, prestige, or even gratitude, but for the privilege of seeing joy on the face of a reticent seven-year-old. My sister remembers gliding unsteadily through a labyrinth of snow-covered evergreens at twilight, the rusty blades of her second-hand skates rasping over the pitted ice, her frosted breath trailing behind in the still air like an opaque ribbon while Brody watched from shore with a contented smile on his face. She says the experience was magical, like being in a fairy tale, and she will never forget the man who made it possible.

We accepted Brody for who and what he was: an outlier. While his own family considered him an embarrassment, a square peg that would never fit the round hole reserved for him, he was just one oddball among many in our household. None of us fit in, and I believe he found the knowledge comforting.

He became the older brother I never had. He taught me routine automobile maintenance and other valuable skills, like how to hotwire a car and fuse two pieces of steel with a welder made from a twelve-volt battery. When my reluctance to use drugs and alcohol alienated me from others my age, Brody took me fishing and exploring and second-hand vehicle shopping. We once bought two cars for two hundred dollars at a moving sale in Cheslatta, then drove them forty miles back to Wistaria without the benefit of spare tires or insurance. Mine, a decrepit station wagon that made more smoke than a torpedo boat at Jutland, lasted only long enough to get me home, but Brody's provided him with transportation and spare parts for months.

In my youth, I considered Brody's desire to avoid full-time employment a serious character defect. Now I think perhaps he had things figured out long before the rest of us. By his mid-twenties, he already understood that life is meant to be lived, not worked, and that the keys to happiness can be found in accumulating experiences rather than possessions (unless, of course, you can get the latter for free).

In Norse mythology, the Norns are three female beings who rule the destiny of gods and men. They sit at the foot of Yggdrasil, the world's tree, and weave the threads of fate into each person's life. It's a romantic notion but perhaps as good an explanation as any for what happens to us. One thing is certain: time has a way of tugging at the fabric of our lives, separating strands from it that were once important, and weaving others in their place.

I lost touch with Brody. I got a job in a demanding field, married, had children, and found other things to occupy my time. I stopped playing rummy; eventually, I stopped playing at all. Wealthier in financial terms but poorer in spirit, I crashed and burned faster than a B-17 hit by Messerschmitts.

A few years later, my wife and I drove to a secluded beach along Ootsa Lake for a weekend of rest. We had just started a fire and unpacked our lunch when we heard the unmistakable buzz of a small motor.

A yellow all-terrain vehicle crawled over a rise in the meadow several hundred feet away. It skirted the weathered remains of Wistaria's first post office, a log cabin abandoned after Alcan's dam project, and started toward the lakeshore.

I held my breath. Our campsite had been chosen because it was remote and difficult to access. We sought solitude, not company.

It was not to be. The four-wheeler made an abrupt turn and headed toward us.

"Ah, shit," I said.

"Who's that?" asked my wife.

"I don't know, but I didn't drive fifty miles to socialize."

As the four-wheeler drew near, I recognized a familiar figure in a bright orange hard hat.

My frown turned into a smile. "It's Brody!"

Our old friend stopped about ten feet from the campfire. He shut off the ATV's motor and peered at me for a second through cracked safety goggles.

"Well, fancy meeting you here," he said with enthusiasm. "What's for lunch?"

I started cooking more hot dogs.

Around noon the following day, we repacked our trailer and headed for the government ferry at Southbank. Realizing we were unlikely to get there in time for the next sailing, I decided to stop at Brody's place and tell him we were leaving. It seemed the polite thing to do, and it would give him time to make other arrangements for lunch.

We pulled up just as he was coming out his front door with what appeared to be a cardboard box full of kittens. His outfit consisted of a grubby calico shirt that hung almost to his knees, black rubber boots, and a smile.

My wife turned to me, her eyes wide with alarm. "My God," she said, "he's not wearing any pants."

"Nope," I replied. "But don't worry. It's only Brody."

And with that, a long-absent piece of my life slipped back into place.

A Home of Our Own

When they came north, my parents traded decent jobs and good rental accommodations for unemployment and a four-person canvas tent. The escapade, financed by the Unemployment Insurance Commission, was great fun for a while. We spent an idyllic month camped in the Rockies beside a backcountry lake so clear you could see eastern brook trout swimming in lazy circles twenty feet below the surface.

Yet living by the seat of your pants is not as Elysian as travel writers make it out to be. The first casualty of adventure is predictability, followed soon after by comfort and security. Collecting dole and sleeping in a tent is fine for a couple of months in warm weather, but it soon gets old when the money stops coming, and each night brings hard frost.

A succession of low-paying jobs in backwater communities across the Cariboo followed. In every case, the living quarters provided were uniformly poor, and we soon learned that "free accommodation in exchange for a few chores," when printed in the classified section of a small-town newspaper, meant trading months of indentured servitude for shelter in a building once occupied by farm animals.

After three years of this nonsense, my parents were desperate for a home of their own. Yet buying a house required money, a rare commodity in our household. When you are making next to nothing and getting paid whenever Scrooge McRancher finds it convenient, just putting food on the table is a challenge. Borrowing cash from an established financial institution was out of the question for the same reason. It did not help that Olavi felt debts incurred in one location need not be repaid if he moved to another.

Salvation arrived in the form of a short-term contract. My mother, who fell in love with words long before she met my father, discovered that her ability to string them together like pearls on silver filament was a marketable skill. The Burns Lake Historical Society wanted to publish a book but lacked one critical component: a capable writer who would do the work for next to nothing. The group promised her two thousand dollars, payable upon completion of the book, and another buck for every copy sold. She accepted with the enthusiasm of a drowning sailor reaching for a life ring.

The job took a year. She worked for less than a dollar per hour, but it was a fortune compared to Olavi's meagre salary as a ranch hand.

They started looking for property. A few acres of land were available near Wistaria Hall, but the asking price was too great, and the place had more hills than Tibet. They even thought about using the money to finance a move to the Yukon, then abandoned the idea after learning that homesteading was no longer an option there.

It seemed we were doomed to live in Jude O'Brian's ramshackle cabin forever, knuckling our foreheads and doing whatever was asked of us whenever she came around. Then, something caught my mother's attention on the way back from collecting her windfall.

It was a house trailer, a red-and-white monstrosity parked in a farmer's weedy boneyard beside a dozen other mechanical relics from the first half of the twentieth century. The trailer's starboard side had two doors, each pierced by a single porthole, and its rounded prow featured a generous picture window. Leaning against the wheel well amidships was a hand painted "For Sale" sign.

"Look," said Mom, pointing out the window. "Stop!"

Though Olavi hit the brakes immediately, it was at least three hundred feet before we screeched to a halt. He waited for the dust cloud we had been dragging to clear, then hacked a U-turn in the middle of the road and went back for another look.

We drove through a narrow gate and parked near the trailer. My parents got out and started inspecting it. The owner emerged from his cabin overlooking a vast swamp, and they talked for a while. Then he opened one of the trailer doors, and they went inside.

They reappeared five minutes later and motioned for us. Kelly crawled out the driver's door, and I exited the passenger side with Laina.

"Come take a look," Mom said when we drew near.

We followed her in.

The trailer seemed impossibly narrow compared to our cabin at Rainbow Lake. The front part, with its built-in settee flanked by a pair of two-drawer cabinets, was intended to serve as a combination living room and dining area. Next was the kitchen, with its four-burner gas stove, sink, and icebox, followed by a short central corridor between two bunks and a hall closet.

Aft of the wheel wells was a bathroom so small you could wash your hands while sitting on the toilet and soaking your feet in the tub. It looked great for a circus contortionist or anyone who valued economy of movement.

A tiny master bedroom took up the stern. The rear door was also located there so you could exit without turning around, which I figured would be necessary after my parents installed their double bed.

Everything seemed to have been built two-thirds scale. Still, the unit must have been top-of-the-line in its day, which I judged fell somewhere between the end of the Great War and the birth of rock and roll. The cabinetry and blond panelling were constructed of laminated spruce, likely stuff left over when De Havilland stopped making Mosquito bombers, and the floor was a checkerboard of scuffed black and white linoleum tiles. There were plenty of small windows to prevent hysteria among visiting claustrophobics.

"And look at this," said Mom on the way out. She was pointing with eagerness to a small kitchen table that folded down against some bookshelves between the living room and kitchen counter. It looked large enough to accommodate three people, provided each was no more than four feet tall and had an eighteen-inch wingspan.

"What do you think?" she asked as we exited the aluminum beast.

The first thing that came to mind was a photograph published in *Iron Coffins,* Herbert A. Werner's classic book about submarine warfare. The second was a story by J. R. R. Tolkien about small people doing big things on a long quest. It didn't seem appropriate to rain on Mom's parade by mentioning either, so I shrugged and said, "It looks all right."

"That's good," she replied, shooing us toward the truck, "because I think we're buying it."

Kelly, Laina, and I watched as they closed the deal. Mom and Olavi shook hands with the farmer and walked back.

"Wow, all that for sixteen hundred dollars," Mom said as we drove off. "What a bargain."

I wasn't so sure. I had a room in the trapper's cabin and was not eager to trade it for a cramped bunk in U-571. There was also a good chance I would grow taller than a hobbit one day.

"What about us? Where will I put my ship models?"

"We'll build a joey shack on one side," my mother said after giving the question some thought. "There will be lots of room. And the best part is, no one will be able to take it away."

I figured that would be okay. Mom and Olavi still had a problem, though. They had to get our new home from Grassy Plains to the O'Brian Ranch, a thirty-mile trip over rough gravel roads. The farmer, too busy to deliver it, recommended we hire a man named Erlon who had a new truck and towed things for a dollar fifty per mile. My parents dismissed the idea as a waste of money and decided to enter the cartage business.

"We'll tow it home ourselves next week," Olavi said.

Moving day came. Olavi checked the gasoline and filled the oil in our antediluvian Ford F100. We piled into the cab and headed for Grassy Plains.

We got there okay, though my stepfather had to pull over and add another quart of 10W30 to the truck's dented crankcase. He backed up to the trailer, dropped its hitch over the rusty ball on the Ford's bumper, and pulled out.

The thing was heavy, like towing Mount Robson. Our truck, which had difficulty reaching cruising speed under normal conditions, groaned under the load. We reached thirty miles per hour just as Ootsa-Nadina Road hove into view.

My stepfather removed his foot from the gas pedal and downshifted, but our speed remained constant.

"Slow down, Olavi," said Mom as the turnoff neared. Although she was trying to sound casual, I detected a note of panic.

"I'm trying," my stepfather said, pumping the brakes and throwing the helm hard astarboard.

There was, by God's grace, no one waiting at the junction, and we were able to negotiate the turn by crossing into the opposite lane and running along the shoulder for fifty feet or so. The trailer heeled over like a dread-nought at high speed, then righted itself just when I thought it would tip into the ditch.

Olavi proceeded with caution after that, never letting the speedometer's bouncing needle creep above thirty. There were exceptions. If the road ahead was straight, he stomped down on the accelerator as if there were a cock-roach beneath it. The Ford's tired six-cylinder howled in protest and vomited blue smoke.

"What's that smell?" my mother asked five miles farther down the road. She had to yell to be heard over the cacophony of slapping valves and ham-mering pistons.

There was a strange odour in the cab, an acrid cross between burning carpet and smoldering garbage. It got more pungent by the second.

"I smell it too," said Kelly, making a face. "Something's burning."

"It's the brakes," Olavi said, keeping his eyes on the road, "or maybe the clutch."

"Should we pull over?" Mom asked, her tone solicitous. "Let them rest for a bit?"

"Better not," was his response. "If we do, we might never get going again."

The Ford had the final say. It was over eighty degrees Fahrenheit in the shade that day, and it grew even warmer as we motored along. A series of small hills sent the little stick inside the pickup's temperature gauge into the danger zone.

Desperate to cool the engine, Olavi tried an old trucker's ploy. He reached over, pushed the heater control to the far right, and turned the fan on high.

Superheated air blasted out of the dash, and we were instantly bathed in sweat.

"For God's sake, open the window," Mom said. "I can't breathe."

I complied. Olavi could not. The driver's side window crank disappeared sometime during the late Jurassic period. All he could do was crack his tiny quarter vent.

It helped a little but not much. We were lobsters in a pot of boiling water.

Two cars blew past us, throwing up a curtain of dust. It rolled in the open windows and puffed through rust holes in the floor. Laina cried. Mom started coughing.

The F100 said enough was enough. Its inline-six missed a few beats, then threatened to quit altogether. Olavi glanced at the instrument panel and took his foot off the gas.

We coasted to a stop. I leaned forward and looked around the cab.

My family had disappeared, replaced by a quartet of New Guinea mud men in western clothing, their features obscured by ashen masks of caked dirt.

I laughed, felt something crack, and realized it was my face. A trickle of muddy water started down the temple of the stranger who had replaced Kelly, prompting me to run a sleeve across my forehead. It came away filthy.

We were covered in dust.

Olavi opened his door and shambled out. So did I. We met at the front of the truck, and he opened the hood. A mantle of steam billowed out.

My stepfather reached into his pocket, pulled out a greasy rag, and used it to loosen the hot radiator cap. More steam and gurgling noises followed.

He let the plug cool before twisting it off and peering into the abyss. After considering his options, he said, "There's a plastic jug of antifreeze behind the seat. Go get it."

I found it and hurried back. "Okay," he said. "I'm going to start the truck. You add the antifreeze."

He got back in the cab, depressed the clutch, and twisted the ignition key. The engine protested for a couple of seconds before coughing to life.

I poured until the jug was empty, then stepped back and held it aloft.

"How full is the radiator?" Olavi asked.

I leaned under the hood for a look. "I don't know," I said while trying to maintain a safe distance between my stiff hair and the whirling fan blades. "I think I see some bubbling, but it's a long way down."

"Well, don't just stand there," he said. "Find some more water."

I looked around and decided the guy was nuts. It was the middle of summer. The ditches were empty, and the swamps had dried up. There would likely be a trickle of water in the sluggish creek near Jim Hurdle's place, but that was at least two miles away. It was either the milk in Laina's baby bottles or . . .

One hand went to the fly of my jeans.

Olavi saw me and decided the truck's coolant level was adequate. "Oh, just put the cap on and get in," he said.

We continued the journey, stopping at the Hurdle homestead. The owner, a tall, skinny man with a kindly face the colour of tanned moosehide, came out of the family's clapboard shack with a five-gallon bucket of water. His plump wife and three children followed.

"Warm today," he noted, handing over the pail.

"It is," said my stepfather. He hefted the bucket and sent a stream of cold water into the radiator. Some spilled on the engine's exhaust manifold where it boiled and hissed for a few seconds while making the transition from liquid to gas.

Jim cast a critical eye over our rig and its bloated load. "That's a lot of weight," he said. "What you got under the hood, a six-banger and a three-on-the-tree?"

"Yeah," said Olavi with a measure of embarrassment.

Jim, bony hands jammed in the back pockets of his wool pants, was quiet for a few seconds. "Think you'll make it up?"

He was, of course, referring to the incline known as Chicken Creek Hill, a half-mile of road that groped its way over the height of land between Francois and Ootsa lakes. With an average grade of more than eight percent, and a three-hundred-foot section twice as steep, it was a formidable obstacle for any motorist.

My stepfather replaced the radiator cap and transferred the rest of Jim's water to our empty antifreeze container. "I think so," he said hesitantly.

Jim looked skeptical and shook his head as if to free himself of great doubt. "I don't know. It's a big hill, and that's a heavy trailer."

Olavi handed the pail back. "We'll make it," he said with more conviction.

"Okay," said Jim slowly. "What then?"

Olavi gave him a vacant look. "What do you mean?"

"Well," said our host, "don't forget about the downhill on the other side."

On the far side of Chicken Creek Hill, after weaving around Verdun Mountain and Stump Lake, Ootsa-Nadina Road dropped precipitously toward the Nechako Reservoir. While there were a couple of short flat spots en route to what had been Bennett's Landing in pre-flood days, the final stretch past Ootsa school looked like it had been lifted from Vancouver's North Shore. It made an excellent toboggan run in winter if you were willing to dodge oncoming traffic.

Judging from the look on my stepfather's face, he had not thought that far ahead. He was, however, an eternal optimist. "I'll go slow. We'll be fine."

"Okay. Good luck," said Jim. His intonation suggested that he'd enjoyed knowing us and would attend our funerals.

Olavi added another quart of oil to the truck and got us on the road again. There was a long straight stretch and a slight dip a few miles south of Jim's place, and he tried to make the most of it. The truck almost reached fifty miles per hour on the downslope while threatening to fly apart and dump us without ceremony on the gravel road surface. A hubcap came loose with a clatter and winged its way into the ditch as if launched from a skeet thrower. I tracked its progress in the side mirror, noting with interest that it skipped twice before disappearing into the tall grass.

We reached the bottom of Chicken Creek Hill and started up. My stepfather had the accelerator matted and looked like he would gladly cut the floor out beneath it for a few more RPMs. We negotiated the dogleg turn. Ahead lay the steepest section.

The Ford's speed drained away like blood from a butchered hog. Olavi downshifted to second, then first. He looked down at the lever as if rare sorcery might conjure another gear, but the transmission faery was otherwise occupied that day.

Progress slowed to a walking pace. The five of us tried to generate more momentum by rocking back and forth, but it did no good. Halfway up the hill, the old truck stopped and strained in its traces like an exhausted draft horse.

More foul-smelling smoke rolled into the cab. Sensing that disaster was but a second or two away, Olavi depressed the clutch while at the same time jamming down on the brake pedal. Taking no chances, he also deployed the emergency brake. He had forgotten that it did not work.

For a moment, time and the truck stood still. Then we started rolling backward down the hill.

"Oh no," said my mother.

"Get out and throw something behind the wheels," my stepfather said.

I jumped out and started looking for anything that might serve as a wheel chock. There were a couple of large rocks in the ditch, and I tried those. The Ford rolled merrily over them.

A grinding noise from the rear hubs sent Olavi into a panic. "For Christ's sake, hurry," he implored. "I don't know how much longer I can hold it."

Necessitas est ingenii mater, loosely translated, is Latin for "necessity is the mother of invention." While the phrase is sometimes attributed to Plato, no one knows for sure who coined it.

The unknown author would have been proud of me that day regardless of his nationality. As the pickup and trailer slid down the hill, I remembered our earlier trip to the laundromat. The truck box held six black plastic garbage sacks full of washed clothing, all of it still wet because we had run out of quarters and the change machine was broken.

I reached over the side, grabbed two bloated Hefty bags, and threw them behind the rear wheel closest to me. One popped and sent a river of soapy water cascading down the hill, but the second bundle held, and the truck stopped.

Spontaneous cheering exploded from the cab.

I walked forward and looked in the window. Mom was ecstatic. Olavi appeared relieved but unwilling to let his foot off the brake. "Find something else too," he said, "and where does this Erlon guy live?"

I found a couple of big logs in the bush and dragged them behind the trailer wheels. When my parents were satisfied our new home would not roll down the hill, they unhooked the truck and went looking for a tow.

Kelly and I stayed behind. When our parents disappeared in the direction of Grassy Plains, we walked back to Chicken Creek for a drink. The water at the bottom was clear and cold and tasted like heaven.

Mom and Olavi returned an hour later with Erlon, who hitched our trailer to his two-tone GMC and easily towed it home.

We slept well that night. The next day, Olavi borrowed Mickey O'Brian's bulldozer and scraped a level patch on the hillside above our cabin. We backed the trailer onto it and used slabs and rough lumber to build a full-length addition along one side. The result was not pretty, but it gave us extra storage space and room for a wood stove.

Kelly and I shared the bunk beds. While I missed having a room of my own—the trailer's top bunk had so little headspace that sleeping there was like being the guest of honour at a closed casket funeral—the set-up had some advantages. If my eldest sister said something to me that gave offense, I waited until we retired for the night before exacting revenge. She often slept with one arm extended into the trailer's narrow hallway. With practice, I could lean over the bed railing and dribble spit into her open palm. Then it was just a matter of waiting for a mosquito to land on her face.

While I thought this hilarious, Kelly did not. She found a way to get even with me, though. Not long after I started these air raids, my best ship models sustained significant damage from unknown forces. Several had their radar masts bent at impossible angles, and the long barrels of *USS Arizona's* primary armament were snapped off at the root. When Kennedy's PT-109 disappeared after a massive nighttime slobber-bombing, I ceased hostilities and negotiated an uneasy truce.

While the new sleeping arrangements were less than ideal, my parents felt they were adequate. Finding a place to put Laina at the end of each day was more difficult. They solved the problem with minor renovations. To this day, I am convinced my youngest sister's short stature can be attributed to her sleeping for years in what had once been a hall closet. With space in the trailer at a premium, she dared not outgrow her share.

We lived in the trailer at Rainbow Lake until my parents had a big fight with the property owner and were asked to move. A charitable widow offered to rent us land along Wistaria Boat Landing Road for forty dollars a month, and we started packing.

Olavi pulled the house trailer there first. The move was made without incident, but he could not figure out how to get the eight-by-thirty addition down the road in one piece. Brody came up with a solution. He and my stepfather cut two large spruce trees, lifted the joey shed with hydraulic jacks, and slid the logs beneath it. After hammering a lift of rough-cut two-by-fours to the bow and stern of this makeshift sledge, they borrowed Richard Lawson's D-6 bulldozer and dragged our home to its new location. The five-mile exercise took an entire day. By the time it was complete, the skids were half their original size, and the building was almost level. Olavi, tired from all the effort, chose to leave them in place.

But no matter how hard he tried, my stepfather could not get the addition flush with the trailer. For months we lived in a house divided. We slept and cooked in the trailer but had to cross six feet of broken No Man's Land to get to the living room. We stopped trying to reunite the two halves and built a new structure between them just before winter arrived. The changes increased our square footage by nearly a third.

The only real casualty of this move was our old Ford F100. It died not long after and defied Olavi's repair efforts. We pulled it into the bush and got another vehicle.

The truck is still there. It would be a good project for someone, provided they can evict the packrats that now call it home.

Wooding

Humans have used fire for eons. The earliest unequivocal evidence dates to paleolithic times, but an international team recently unearthed charred animal bones, plants, and stone tools in a South African cave inhabited by our early ancestors more than a million years ago.

My family learned to use fire in 1970. Not that we were some obscure and soon-to-be-pruned branch of the hominid tree. Before that, like most city-dwellers, we did not need to master the skill. If we were cold, we turned the thermostat up; when we were hungry, we cooked something on the electric stove. And if we ever required a tool, we bought it from Simpsons-Sears.

If necessity is the mother of invention, deprivation is the father of redis-covery. When it is -30 Fahrenheit outside, and there are no switches to flick or knobs to turn, you soon tap into skills learned by your predecessors a millennium earlier. A year after leaving the city lights behind, we were so accustomed to using fire that even I had stopped staring and hooting at it.

At Ootsa Lake, we could start a blaze anywhere with the speed and effi-ciency of legendary arsonist John Leonard Orr. It was the principles associ-ated with fuel collection that eluded us.

To keep a fire burning, as most advanced primates know, you need to feed it. In Northern BC, accumulating a ready supply of combustible mate-rial, while time-consuming and labour-intensive, is not difficult. It involves getting a sharp tool (a saw, we discovered, is better than a dinner fork), finding a vehicle (preferably one with wheels and an operable engine), and going to a place occupied by tall, flammable objects called trees. Once there, you select a handsome candidate from the thousands in attendance, cut it down using your sharp tool, reduce it to pieces that will fit your stove, and haul the fruits

MIKE TURKKI

of your labour home. Alternatively, you can take your wood home in longer lengths, and then chop it into blocks as needed. Regardless of the method, it is not quantum physics.

Most Northerners collect firewood in autumn when temperatures are cooler, and other essential chores like food gathering are complete. By the time snow flies, they are barricaded behind several cords of dry pine and prepared for winter's onslaught.

Not my stepfather. For some inexplicable reason, Olavi did not start cutting firewood until there was snow on the ground.

We implored him to follow the example of our more evolved neighbours and start the process early. Mom tried to light a fire under him, both literally and figuratively. Her actions caused him to jump out of bed and dowse his feet with lukewarm coffee but did not result in any long-term behaviour modification. Every year, he waited until we were down to our last six sticks and facing extinction before venturing out of the cave. Making a sustained effort to get wood was also out of the question. He preferred to sally forth for an hour or two every seven days.

Olavi's intransigence made hunting for fuel necessary regardless of the weather. Every weekend, no matter how cold it was or how much snow had fallen, we jammed into the pickup and looked for something to burn. It was a cold, wet, and exhausting exercise that Kelly and I hated.

One year not long after Halloween, a freak storm dumped two feet of snow on the Southside within thirty-six hours. Trees collapsed from the weight, knocking down electrical lines and leaving Wistaria in the dark. As if that weren't enough, Old Man Winter then unleashed a cold front that sent the mercury in our thermometer plunging toward the reservoir bulb.

The power outage did not affect our family because we weren't BC Hydro customers. Wood stove blazing, we hunkered down and waited for the government plow trucks to arrive.

By the time they did, we were almost out of firewood.

Olavi showed no concern when I told him the woodpile had shrunk to an all-time low. Another day and a night went by.

"That's the last of it," I said early the following morning, dropping an armload of wood into the crate beside our stove. "We have two blocks left."

- 146 -

My stepfather, parked in his armchair with a science fiction novel, took no notice. My mother did, though.

"Why didn't you say something earlier?" she asked me with annoyance.

"I did," I said, brushing sawdust off my arm. "I told the Finnish Flash yesterday that we only had a bit left."

"Olavi," she said, turning toward my stepfather.

"Huh?" he asked without looking up.

"We're almost out of wood. Mike says he told you yesterday."

"Yeah. So?"

"So why didn't you do something about it?"

"Because he's a lazy jerk," I muttered, thrusting my cold hands toward the heater.

I thought I said it low enough to avoid detection, but Olavi's head snapped around. "What was that?"

Eager to avoid a confrontation, I improvised. "Uh . . . because it's crazy work?"

Kelly, staging a Barbie doll fashion show on the couch, snickered.

Olavi glared, but I had planted enough doubt in his mind to preclude physical retaliation. "Don't get smart with me," he said.

Mom got the conversation back on track. "Olavi, we need firewood. What if the truck doesn't start? Do you have gas for the chainsaw?"

My stepfather put down his book. Sighing as if the world's weight rested upon his rounded shoulders, he levered himself out of the chair. "All right, all right. I'll start the truck. You two," he said, pointing in our direction, "get your stuff on."

Kelly started to cry. "No, Dad, not wooding. I don't want to go. It's cold outside."

"Oh, stop it," he said, heading for the door. "I want you ready in five minutes."

Mom tried to rally the troops. "Come on," she said. "We'll all go. Afterward, we'll have a fire and a picnic like last time. It will be fun."

In recent years, Mom and Olavi had tried to turn wood-gathering into a social event by taking along a Thermos of hot chocolate and a basket of pre-cooked food. When the unpleasant chore was complete, they built a bonfire with leftover tree limbs, and we sat around in wet clothes eating Prem and other delicacies.

Kelly cried even harder. "No, it won't. It will be awful, and I don't like mystery meat."

"We'll have fun," Mom repeated. "And if you don't like Prem, why did you eat so much of it last time?"

"Because I was starving," Kelly replied. "We were out there so long I thought we'd have to eat our boots."

I got ready to leave while Kelly threatened job action. In my opinion, it was better to be cold for a few hours than slowly freeze to death after the home fires burned out. Besides, I liked Prem. It was almost as good as Spork and far superior to the stuff that contained macaroni, chunks of pimento, and slivers of unidentified greenery. Two years earlier, after reading the latter's product label, I had asked my parents what "meat by-products" were. They had not provided a definitive answer.

I was zipping up my coat when Olavi returned. "Might as well hold on," he said as he removed his boots. "Truck won't start. The battery's dead."

"Oh, no," said Mom. "What now?"

Olavi joined me beside the wood stove. "We've got a spare battery in here," he said. "I'll start the process after I warm up."

Our latest vehicle was a 1967 Ford pickup with about a quarter-million miles on its odometer. The decrepit two-wheel-drive had started life turquoise with chrome accents, but years of exposure to salt and grime had given it the mottled appearance of a song sparrow's egg. Its original owner, a local man with strong religious convictions and few friends, had placed it on the market after vandals spray-painted two words equating to an anatomically impossible sex act along one side. My parents bought it at an attractive price but never got around to removing the graffiti, which made us the talk of the town whenever we ventured out.

Old Rusty-But-%#&!-Reliable was hard to start in cold weather. We were told it had a functioning block heater when we purchased it, but our lack of electricity meant this claim could never be put to the test. Olavi devised a workaround, though. When temperatures dropped below freezing, he lit a kindling fire in a length of seven-inch stovepipe and slid it under the truck's oil pan.

It was a delicate operation. Feeding the blaze too much fuel was inviting disaster; giving it too little ensured the engine never thawed. After scorching several feet of wiring harness, he learned how much heat was required to get the engine up to operating temperature in a reasonable length of time.

He passed this arcane knowledge on to me. After the fire had been lit, my job was to keep it going without destroying the family automobile.

Sometime around noon, after I had burned our last block of firewood in the stovepipe, Olavi got the truck running and announced it was time to leave.

Kelly could have taught Gandhi a thing or two about passive resistance. Mom coaxed her into winter clothing, but my eldest sister lay by the back door and refused to move. She flattened herself into seventy pounds of dead weight whenever anyone got close and chanted, "Heck no, I won't go." The house was growing cold when my parents dragged her outside.

"Help me, I'm being kidnapped!" she cried on her way to the truck. "This isn't fair. I'm just a little kid."

No one came to her aid. After considerable pushing and shoving, we sardined ourselves into the single-cab pickup and headed out. The truck's tires, frozen and a bit flat from the extreme cold, banged madly on the icy road surface. It was like riding in a Neolithic cart with hand-carved wheels.

Olavi stopped several miles from home near a stand of decadent evergreens he had spotted the previous spring. He climbed out and left the truck running. "You stay here. I'll cut the trees down first," he said before closing the door.

We watched him lift our chainsaw, a yellow McCulloch that weighed as much as a farrier's anvil, out of the truck box. After filling the monstrosity with a concoction of leaded gasoline and used engine oil, he hoisted it on one shoulder and waded toward the treeline.

Olavi spent some time selecting his first victim. Then he put the chainsaw down and began yanking vigorously on its starting cord.

Kelly, who a month earlier had begun attending church with the neighbours, started praying. "Please, sweet baby Jesus," she intoned beside me, eyes clenched and fingers intertwined. "Don't let the saw start. I don't care if we all freeze to death this winter. I hate wooding, and I want to go home."

Her orison went unanswered. The McCulloch coughed twice, belched blue smoke, and roared to life. Eager to go home, Olavi got it chewing on the frozen pine.

"Okay," my mother said when the tree fell a few moments later. "You can probably get out now."

I complied. "Come on, sis. It's time to start."

My sister was having none of it. "No way, Jose," she said, shaking her head. "I'm not getting out. It's colder than a witch's boobie out there."

"You have to help, Kelly," Mom said. "My emphysema is bad today, and I have to look after Laina."

Kelly sensed an opportunity. "I'll look after her. I love my little sister."

"No, you won't," said Mom. "The last time you babysat Laina, you told her yellow snow was lemonade from heaven. Now get out and help, or I'll take away your dolls."

"I don't care," Kelly said, leaning back in the seat. "You can burn my bed if you want to. I'm not moving."

Mom sighed. "Okay, suit yourself. We'll see what your father has to say about it."

That got my sister moving. When it came to discipline, Olavi preferred action over words. Further non-compliance would likely earn her the belt.

"All right," she said with obvious distaste, "but Mike can haul. I'll stack."

Kelly got out and climbed into the truck box. I clambered over the snowbank left by the plow trucks and followed Olavi's tracks toward the treeline. Progress was slow; the white stuff was waist-deep, and my wood-getting gear consisted of a toque, thick parka, a sweater, two layers of jeans, wool mitts, and heavy snow boots. It was like trudging through gumbo while wearing Jacques Cousteau's deepwater diving suit.

My clothing was drenched with sweat by the time I reached Olavi. The chainsaw screamed like a woman possessed, spewing tangy sawdust and exhaust thick with the stench of unburnt fuel. I picked up the first block, a mammoth forty-pounder sliced from the tree's butt, and headed back the way I'd come.

"Here you go," I told Kelly, depositing the chunk of wood on the tailgate. "These are heavy."

My sister slid it into place at the far end of the truck box. "Haul faster," she said. "I want to go home."

I repeated the procedure twenty times. Olavi finished cutting up the first tree and moved to another.

I was on my way to the truck with a chunk of wood under each arm when the chainsaw's wailing dropped to an uneven growl. There was a prolonged groan of distressed wood behind me, followed by what sounded like a rifle shot.

Acting on instinct, I turned toward the sound.

A dead pine was falling slowly toward me. It was massive, the same diameter as a garbage can at the base, and at least eighty feet tall with a crown of twisted limbs and red needles. It had probably stood in that location for a hundred and fifty years before succumbing to the bite of Olavi's chainsaw.

My stepfather was pushing it in my direction, the idling McCulloch in one hand and a grim smile on his bearded face.

My legs felt as though they were encased in cement. At the last second, with the conifer's gnarled trunk filling my field of vision, I dropped both blocks and threw myself to the left.

There was a massive whump. The earth shook, and a blinding curtain of snow rolled over me.

I lay still for several seconds, heart pounding, ice water running down my neck. I tried to move my legs and discovered with relief that they still worked. Then I dug myself out and stood up.

The tree was buried in the snow an arm's length from the trail. Olavi was already cutting it up.

I glanced toward the truck. Kelly was as stiff as a totem pole, shock on her face.

"He tried to hit you with that tree," she said when I got near enough to hear her.

I shrugged. "It was probably an accident. I just didn't hear him yell 'timber.'"

"No," she said with conviction, "it wasn't. He never said a thing. You know he hates us."

We needed only two trees to fill the truck that day. The blocks from the second one were so large that Kelly had to help me lift them onto the tailgate.

As promised, we had a fire afterward and roasted sausages on willow sticks. I liked them. Even Kelly had some, though she complained later that they gave her the runs. When all the food was gone, we went home, stuffed the stove, and peeled off our wet clothing.

No one mentioned my near mishap, but on future expeditions, I never ventured into the bush until Olavi left it.

Twenty years later, my wife and I bought a mobile home on two acres of swamp west of Burns Lake. The trailer's oil furnace had failed by the time we arrived on November 1, leaving us with nothing but a rusty wood stove and eight pieces of waterlogged birch.

For three straight weekends, I drove alone into the hills behind Decker Lake and cut firewood with an old Homelite chainsaw we bought at a garage sale. I packed the logs out in six-foot lengths and took them home in our tired Landcruiser, never quite sure if the vehicle's brakes would survive the long descent from Boo Mountain.

The Homelite packed it in after my seventh load. Still a few cords of wood short, I bought a new chainsaw and continued the exercise for another month.

The snow was three feet deep by the time I finished.

We survived the winter, but the experience brought back unpleasant memories. In subsequent years, we started getting wood as soon as the snow melted. While I enjoyed the work, my children did not.

"No, Dad," they cried every time I picked up the chainsaw, "not wooding."

"Oh, stop complaining and get in the truck," I would reply. "It's not that bad, and it beats getting wood in winter. If you work hard, we'll have a picnic afterward."

Some things, like the knowledge of how to make fire, are meant to be shared.

Twenty-five Cents a Box

It was Friday. My mother, seated at the kitchen table in a rectangle of late evening sunlight, was pounding away on our old Underwood typewriter. Kelly was playing with her dolls; judging from the monologue, Steve and Steffie Sunshine were embroiled in a bitter custody battle over Baby Sweets, and the grandparents could do nothing about it. I was reading a borrowed copy of Stephen King's *Night Shift* and trying not to think about what might be lurking in our walls.

"We have to leave for town early tomorrow," Olavi said loud enough to penetrate the din from the other room. Ensconced in his scarred armchair under the bay window, he was smoking a cigarette and reading the newspaper. Laina squirmed in his lap.

Mom stopped typing. "Why?"

"There's an auction sale in Decker Lake," he said. "It starts at ten."

Kelly's version of *Divorce Court* recessed. I held my breath and prayed for clemency.

Olavi loved auctions. He became obsessed with them after reading a story about a lucky bidder who found a diamond ring in a box of worthless junk. Determined to duplicate the feat, he scoured the classifieds each week for impending sales. If there was one within driving distance and he had enough money for gasoline, we went. It didn't matter what items were on the block or whether they were useful. We attended vehicle auctions, estate auctions, consignment auctions, silent auctions, and blind auctions where you bid on stuff before you saw it. Once there, he made an offer on almost everything. The result? We carted home truckloads of stuff no one else wanted: boxes of mismatched ice skates, water pumps that only worked for a month, kerosene refrigerators that kept things sort of cold.

He once purchased a pallet of old newspaper printing plates and used them to re-roof the outhouse. After that, there was no need to take reading material with you to the loo; all you had to do was "look up, way up" like a guest on *The Friendly Giant*. We left another auction treasure in there, a cracked Wallace hand mirror, for visitors who had difficulty reading backward, and I kept the material fresh by replacing the "shingles" regularly.

Olavi's auction habit complemented his principal hobby, hoarding. We had enough second-hand dinnerware to outfit the enlisted men's mess of *HMCS Haida* and more ten-speed bicycles than the Tour de France. Our backyard looked like a subsidiary of the Burns Lake landfill. Mom made him erect a "No Dumping" sign at the end of the driveway after someone left three bags of garbage there.

Don't get me wrong: not all his purchases were bad. He bought my second car, a 1976 Dodge Monaco that had once been a police cruiser, at a government surplus auction for $250. Equipped with a 440-cubic-inch engine and a four-barrel Holley carburetor, the purple beast served me well for three years.

Most auctions were a bust, though, and Kelly and I resented having to attend them. We knew from experience that our stepfather would not depart until the last lot sold or he ran out of money, even if it meant inspecting prospective purchases by lamplight.

We held our breath as Mom considered his proposition.

"And there are two garage sales in Danskin," he added as if this were a rare celestial event akin to the planets aligning.

Mom's eyes glazed over as she did a mental calculation involving words per minute and pages untyped. "Okay," she said after a moment. "I can be ready by seven. Almost done here." She slapped the Underwood's carriage return before continuing her assault on the keyboard.

Kelly and I groaned in unison. We were doomed.

"Do we have to go?" my sister said. "They last so long."

"Don't whine," said Olavi. "There'll be some good stuff there."

"What, like school supplies?" I asked, setting aside my book. The previous year, aggressive bidding had netted Olavi the contents of a failed entrepreneur's home office. We still hadn't forgiven him for sending us back to class with chewed pencil stubs and water-damaged notebooks.

Our stepfather glared. "Keep it up, wise guy," he said. "That'll cost you a week's allowance. Want to try for two?"

"I was only telling the truth."

Mom heard the exchange and tried to intervene. "Oh, come on, Olavi. Don't dock him for that."

"Maxwell Smart over there always has something to say," my stepfather noted. "He's got to learn not to talk back."

I shut up. Registering my displeasure wasn't worth another twenty-five cents, not if I wanted that model ship in Mort's Variety Store. My truculence had already delayed the purchase by six weeks. The way things were going, the Turkkish fleet wouldn't get a new vessel until I was old enough to join the real navy.

The Bearded Wonder had everyone up at six the next morning. Kelly feigned illness, but it did no good. He had us on the road by seven.

The garage sales were a bust, perhaps because we didn't give the vendors adequate time to unpack their merchandise. By the age of fourteen, I was convinced that if Merriam-Webster ever added the phrase "early bird" to its dictionary, the definition would include a line drawing of a fat Scandinavian with abundant facial hair and a dirty plaid jacket.

Mom gave her stories to the newspaper editor, and we arrived at the auction sale a half-hour before its start. The venue, an open field across from the Decker Lake Hall, was already packed with bargain hunters.

Olavi found a parking spot and went looking for the registration desk. Mom spotted an artist friend and headed in that direction with Laina.

"You coming?" I asked Kelly, getting out.

My sister was still peeved at having her Saturday pre-empted. "Nope, I'm staying here. Auctions are stupid." She crossed her arms and settled back in the truck seat.

"Not as stupid as sitting in the car all day," I said and closed the door.

She glared.

I crossed the road and entered the crowd. The event had a carnival atmosphere. Elderly farmers crawled over rusty agricultural equipment while their women gossiped nearby. Mennonite men in white shirts and charcoal dress pants clustered around a table of woodworking tools, their wives and children trailing behind like disassembled Russian nesting dolls. Pimple-faced teenagers bought hotdogs and soda pop from a concession stand on the periphery, the boys then gravitating toward a row of used automobiles while their female counterparts formed whispering cliques just out of earshot. Younger kids, some clutching bits of pilfered flagging tape, chased each other through the crowd. Music blared from the auctioneer's sound system. Babies cried, and dogs barked.

The merchandise was as varied as the clientele. There were the usual household items and dusty boxes of hardcover books. One table held sports equipment, including an impressive collection of military surplus firearms, another an assortment of power tools with taped handles and frayed electrical cords. There were kitchen appliances and burned-out wood stoves, old tobacco tins filled with nuts and bolts, ancient chainsaws and double-bitted axes that had not tasted wood in decades. A woman in a lime-coloured pantsuit hovered possessively around two cabinets filled with costume jewellery while her husband examined furniture that looked as though it came over on the *Mayflower*. There was even a livestock section; two knackered horses and three milk cows shared a temporary corral at the rear, while the adjacent cell held a black-and-white hog the size of a Volkswagen.

I was swinging a desiccated baseball bat and watching six little hoodlums throw dirt clods at the farm animals when a voice boomed over the crowd.

"Well, ladies and gentlemen, we're going to get started here. For those of you who don't know how this works, you need a number to bid. The beautiful Miss Hayley and her equally lovely colleagues at the registration table can help you with that," said the auctioneer, a short man with red sideburns. Despite having a pronounced Austrian accent, he sported a white Stetson and hand-tooled cowboy boots. "Lot Number One is two crates of women's undergarments. Hold that up, Fitch. Have you ever seen anything like it, folks? The stuff in there looks like it came from Vancouver Tent and Awning. Seriously, though, there's got to be a use for it. What did you say? Shop rags? There you go.

"Do I have a bid? How about a dollar? No? Throw those rubber boots and that set of crutches in with it, boys. Someone give me twenty-five cents for this mess. I got a quarter in front. Can I get fifty cents? No? Going once, going twice . . . sold to bidder eighty-seven, eight seven. Good to see you again, Mr. Turkki."

I put a hand to my forehead. It had started.

I heard Olavi's number called four more times over the next two hours. Around noon, when the auctioneer halted trading for thirty minutes, Mom came looking for me.

"Your father wants to see you," she said.

"Where is he?"

"Near the front."

I found him surrounded by his purchases. He appeared to have bought, in addition to the lady's underwear, most of her kitchen utensils and *True Romance* magazines. There was also a cracked fireplace screen, three rolls of stained carpet, and a coffee table that had been born with four legs but now had three.

"Take this stuff to the van," Olavi said.

"Can I have money for a pop?" I asked. "I'm thirsty."

"Talk to your mother," he said, "after you haul the stuff."

I picked up a box and weaved my way through the crowd.

Kelly was still in the van. "What did he buy?" she asked as I opened the rear doors and slid my burden inside.

"The usual crap," I replied.

She reached over the back seat and began poking through the junk.

"Ew, gross," she said, holding up a canning jar that contained an amorphous blob suspended in yellow liquid.

"What is it?" I asked, half hoping it was something interesting, maybe a calf's head or a human fetus.

"I'm not sure," Kelly said, inspecting the container. "It might be fish, but it could also be vegetables because it looks green. Yuck." She tossed it back in the box.

"Jeez, be careful," I said. "Break it and you'll start a plague."

I made two more trips to the van. On the last, I thought Kelly had ended her sit-down strike and left. Then, as I jammed the carpets inside, a small hand clad in a dirty brown knee sock rose like an apparition over the back seat. Clenched between the thumb and fingers was a set of bright pink dentures with one front tooth missing. Something was also bunched below the wrist to give her makeshift puppet a large, distended belly.

"Hi, Mike," said a disembodied voice with a Finnish accent. "Look what Kelly found beside the jar of mystery meat. Who do I remind you of?"

I tried not to laugh. "Stop fooling around. I need your help hauling a table."

"Wait a minute. I'll ask." The sock puppet disappeared below the seat. After a hushed discussion with my sister, it popped back up. "Nope," the Sock Father said, shaking its woolen head. "Kelly don't want to. Too bad, so sad."

"Come on. I'll buy you a pop," I said, though I had no idea where the money was coming from.

There was a moment's hesitation. Then the puppet belched mightily, sending the teeth flying.

"Okay," said Kelly, sitting up. "But I want Orange Crush."

My sister put her socks and shoes on and followed me across the road. We hauled the table to the truck and tossed it in with the other artifacts. In the process, its three good legs became two.

"Shit," I said. "We broke it. The Scandinavian Scourge will be pissed."

"Tell him somebody tripped us," said Kelly. "Now, where's my drink?"

We tracked Mom down. She was changing Laina's diaper on a picnic table near the concession while a couple of thumb-sucking preschoolers watched with interest.

"Dad said to ask you for money for pop and hot dogs," I told her.

"Yeah, Mike promised me an Orange Crush if I helped him haul a table," Kelly added. "A mean kid knocked us down and broke two of the table legs off."

"One of the legs," I corrected. "The other was already missing."

"Right, one of the legs," Kelly said. "Can we go back to town soon? We've been here forever, and I have to pee."

Mom sighed. She dug around in her purse and produced a crumpled two-dollar bill. "Bring me back a coffee and the change," she said. "I'll go find your father."

After lunch, I filled Mom's order, and we followed the auctioneer's voice to the front lines. He was standing in the back of a pickup with a bullhorn. His singsong chant was hypnotic.

"Hey, bidder, bidder, I got a five-dollar bid, now seven. Seven, seven, seven, how about ten? Who'll give me ten, now twelve?"

My parents had ringside seats. Olavi was trying to buy three lawn sprinklers and a tangle of garden hoses despite the fact we had no running water, and our front yard was a ten-acre hayfield.

He quit when the bidding hit fifteen dollars. The auctioneer implored him to continue, but my stepfather shook his head. "Too rich for my blood," he muttered, stuffing the white bid card back in his shirt pocket.

He consoled himself by lighting a cigarette. I heard my mother breathe a sigh of relief.

"Here you go, Mom," I said, handing her the coffee. She smiled and took a sip.

The auctioneer consulted his clipboard before continuing. "Okay, Fitch, what do we have next?"

On cue, one of his helpers held a cardboard box up for inspection. The contents shifted, and we heard the brittle sound of colliding porcelain.

The auctioneer reached in, withdrew a painted miniature of a cow, and held it up for all to see. "There's a herd of these, some snow globes, three or four cats, and a really nice plastic bust of either Lou Costello or Winston Churchill," he said, making eye contact with Olavi. "What will you bid for this box of fine ornaments?"

Give the man credit: he knew his market. As anyone who visited our home could attest, my stepfather had a thing for small, shiny objects. We had more knickknacks than Woolworth's Five and Dime, and they covered every flat surface in our living room. He had constructed a special revolving base for his prized possession, a Bakelite sculpture of the Seven Dwarves forming a human pyramid while wearing Christmas attire. Mom had pointed out that Dopey, poised atop the heap, was missing an arm, but it didn't matter. The piece still occupied prime real estate atop the mantle of our faux fireplace.

I knew in an instant that the box was going home with us.

Olavi's face lit up. "Fifty cents!" he said, snatching his bid card and throwing caution to the wind. Much to my surprise, someone else wanted the tchotchkes. A plump woman in a calico dress offered a dollar, and the war was on.

Olavi's hand rose and fell as often as a semaphore operator's at the Battle of Trafalgar. In the process, he knocked the cigarette out of his mouth. It fell into the pocket previously occupied by his bid card where it came to rest, we surmise, against a wad of discarded toilet tissue.

"Mom, Daddy's smoking," Kelly said thirty seconds later.

"I know, dear," said our mother, who was doing her best to ignore the train wreck in progress. "He smokes all the time."

"No, Mom," my sister said, pointing to our stepfather. "He's on fire."

He was indeed. Mom turned in time to see a small tongue of flame dart out of her husband's pocket and lick upward toward his beard.

"Fire!" she yelled.

Olavi felt the heat. He looked down, gasped, and started beating his chest with the bid card while doing a reasonable facsimile of James Brown's *Mashed Potato*. The auctioneer, thinking this display was an extreme manifestation of auction fever, continued the proceedings.

Sparks flew. The price of the box of gewgaws climbed as Olavi transitioned neatly to *The Jerk*.

"I've got four dollars . . . four-fifty . . . five dollars on the right, five-fifty down in front," the man with the megaphone intoned.

Mom finally realized what was happening. "For God's sake, Olavi, stop!" she implored and threw her coffee on him.

The fire went out, and the woman in calico stopped bidding.

"Going once . . . going twice . . . sold to Mr. Turkki for six dollars and fifty cents!" the auctioneer said with glee, slamming down his hammer. "What's your number again?"

"Eighty-seven," Olavi said as he wiped his face.

A lesser man would have surrendered the field after such misadventure. Not my stepfather. Shirt dripping and beard singed, he continued bidding throughout the afternoon, amassing a staggering amount of rubbish even by his standards. To the morning's take, he added a horse collar, three buckets of oxidized nails, two and a half bags of fossilized Portland cement, and the entire twenty-two-volume *Collected Works of Carl Jung*. The Travelall's leaf springs were bending backward by 3 p.m., and I was exhausted from hauling stuff across the road.

I was admiring his latest purchase, a velvet painting of a busty African nude, when a pair of men shuffled forward with a large mahogany cabinet. Taking great care, they deposited it in front of the auctioneer and stepped back. The guy named Fitch darted forward and opened the unit's two rectangular doors, revealing a smoked glass panel about a foot and a half square.

It was a television.

I put Nefertiti aside. This had potential.

The previous year, Eurocan Pulp & Paper had erected a telecommunications tower on Mount Wells. As a gesture of goodwill, the company was rebroadcasting CFTK-TV, Telemedia's Terrace station, giving Ootsa Lake residents access to programs like *Happy Days* and *Gunsmoke* for the first time.

Most of our neighbours had televisions. We did not, and I considered it a significant hardship. When my friends discussed the adventures of Arthur Fonzarelli and Matt Dillon, all I could do was change the subject.

I wanted the television. Badly.

I poked Olavi. "Can we bid on it?"

My stepfather looked surprised. To the best of his knowledge, it was the first time I had expressed interest in something on the auction block.

"I don't know," he said. "All I have left is a $1.05."

"Can't we give some of this other shi . . . stuff back?"

He shook his head. "Doesn't work that way."

I remembered the change left from lunch. "I've got some money."

"How much?"

I pulled a handful of quarters, dimes, and nickels from my pocket and quickly did the math. "A dollar twenty."

Olavi's eyes glinted with avarice, and he reached for the coins. A vision of him using them to buy another box of doodads jumped into my mind. "Uh-uh," I said, stuffing the money back in my jeans before he could snatch it. "Only if we get the TV."

He looked from me to the television. I could tell he wanted it too. "Okay," he said, "but don't get your hopes up. Two twenty-five is probably not enough."

The auctioneer got things rolling. "All right, next on the block is an RCA Victor TV, a nice, clean little black-and-white unit with a 19-inch screen. It's not new, but it was in 1959, and I am told it works. Who will give me twenty-five cents for this treasure?"

Enthusiastic bidding pushed the price to six bits, then a dollar. My stepfather got in at a dollar fifty but was immediately outbid by a grey-haired guy in plaid pants. Then a hippie with two dollars put up his hand.

The situation appeared desperate. What we needed was divine intervention. *Please, God,* I prayed, *let us get the TV. I really want it. I won't talk back to Single Fang Big Belly for at least a week, and I'll try not to fight with Kelly.*

Olavi went all in.

The hippie was about to offer more when fate intervened.

The gang of miscreants I had seen earlier at the corrals chose that precise moment to release the farm animals. Two wild-eyed horses and an aggravated milk cow tore through the crowd, followed by a small boy riding an enormous pig.

People scattered. The auctioneer, true to form, never missed a beat. "I have two dollars and twenty-five cents in front," he said from his perch atop the truck. "Going once . . . going twice . . . Sold!"

I jumped up and down, hugged the stranger standing next to me, and gave my stepfather the money. Then I said a heartfelt "thank you" to the Big Guy who answered requests for outdated technology.

We managed to cram the television into the back seat of the Travelall, but only after removing its legs. Two of them went AWOL on the way home, probably when Olavi unloaded everything to change a flat tire just south of the ferry landing, but he cannibalized the end table for replacements. The following night, after hooking up a set of rabbit ears, we sat on the couch and ate popcorn while watching *The Beachcombers.*

I thought I had died and gone to heaven.

The set worked for years. Sadly, the generator that powered it—another auction purchase—did not, but I had left home by that time. Olavi removed the cabinet's electronics and repurposed it as a display case.

Dopey and the other six dwarves got a permanent home behind glass.

Going to Town

The first homesteaders to pre-empt land around Ootsa Lake came in from Bella Coola on a narrow trail worn deep in the forest floor by generations of Indigenous traders. It was such a long and difficult trek that most returned to the coast only once each year.

Burns Lake replaced Bella Coola as the source of all things necessary for modern living in 1914, and by the time we arrived almost six decades later, a journey that had once taken weeks could be completed in less than a day. But when fifty miles of gravel road and a twenty-five-minute ferry ride stand between you and your sources of resupply, you learn to make the most of each visit.

We went to town every week, which was far more frequent than most of our neighbours, many of whom felt that two visits to civilization per annum was an outrageous waste of time and money.

"You're going again?" asked Granny Keighley upon learning that we were headed to the metropolis of Burns Lake for the second time in a fortnight. "It's so busy and dirty there. You shouldn't need to go that often. Ach, such extravagance."

The old girl was right: you *could* get enough stuff in one trip to last months. But our circumstances were different. We had to go to town at least once every seven days because my mother was a journalist in the technological Dark Ages before fax machines and email. She had to file her copy with the local newspaper each week, and her delivery options were limited. Surface mail was too slow, and there wasn't a courier company on God's green earth willing to set one eight-ply tire south of the ferry landing. Sometimes, if we lacked money for gasoline, Mom would jam her typewritten stories into a manila envelope and send them with another outbound traveller or borrow Mona Cullen's telephone and read each story to a luckless typesetter fifty miles away, but these were less reliable methods of getting her product to market. She preferred to hand-deliver it.

Saturday was town day. While it was always an adventure, one trip made Livingstone's wanderings through Central Africa seem like a short hike in fine weather.

The day started like any other. Olavi had us up at 6 a.m. so we could load eight bags of dirty laundry into the truck and leave home in time to catch the third ferry sailing from Southbank. Our weekly forays to Burns Lake always included a lengthy visit to the town's solitary laundromat, a Shangri-La with a vending machine and twelve coin-operated washers.

"Laundry is in," I told Olavi after heaving the last sack aboard.

"Good," he said. "Garbage loaded too?"

No visit to Burns Lake was complete without a stop at the landfill. "Yeah, it's in there," I said.

"Okay. Get in."

Jamming two adults and three children into a single-cab pickup takes finesse. By 1975, we had it down to a science.

Olavi and my mother boarded from the port side. Mom got in first and sat spread-eagle in the middle with one foot planted on either side of the bulging transmission tunnel. She then took Laina from my stepfather and placed the four-year-old between her knees. Centrifugal force, leg pressure, and my mother's loving arms kept my youngest sister in place when the vehicle was in motion, though she sometimes squirted free during panic stops and rolled around the floorboards like a jellybean.

Next came Kelly. She entered from the passenger side and settled beside Mom with her back pressed hard against the seat and her skinny legs pointed like sticks toward the bow. Finding a spot for her upper extremities proved challenging under this arrangement, but she solved the problem by adopting a position of earnest prayer whenever we hit the road. I have since learned that she petitioned the Almighty for a larger vehicle.

I got whatever seat remained visible on the starboard side after the others had staked their claims. Most of the time, so little ass room was left that I had to sit forward for the entire journey with my hands and feet braced against the dash.

Olavi was always the last person to enter the vehicle. This was strategic as well as ceremonial; someone had to close the passenger door after we had shoehorned ourselves into the cab. Battening the hatches was most difficult in winter because the old truck's heater was substandard, and everyone had to wear at least three layers of clothing to prevent frostbite. The extra gear so exacerbated the overcrowding that my stepfather often had to slam the door three or four times before it latched. My right arm bore the brunt of these weekly assaults and, by spring, it looked like it had been beaten with a kendo stick. Every year on parent–teacher day, at least one well-meaning educator quietly asked Mom if "everything was all right" at home—and looked skeptical when she explained that the bruising on my body resulted from frequent collisions with a door.

Exiting the Turkki Express was tricky, too. Some thoughtless imbecile once turned the door handle before his travelling companions were ready and dumped everyone in a heap on the sidewalk like poorly dressed circus clowns.

Seatbelts were not required but would have been helpful. If our Ford F100 had rolled off the assembly line in 1961 with a passenger restraint system, we could have used it to ensure no one got more than his allotted space. Fistfights often broke out en route as Kelly and I battled leg cramps, back spasms, and each other for a few more inches of *lebensraum*. No one worried about what might happen in the event of an auto accident, though. We were jammed in the cab so tight that nothing short of a nuclear blast would have dislodged us.

It was seven o'clock by the time we got everyone in the truck and headed down the road.

The first ten miles of our journey on that beautiful August morning were pleasant. The sun was shining, and the day was full of promise. We made good time. There was no one else on the road, and we only had to brake for one herd of itinerant cattle. It appeared we would make the eight o'clock ferry sailing.

Then everything went to Hell in a handbasket.

We were halfway up Ootsa Hill when calamity struck. As the truck pointed its rounded nose up the final incline, Olavi tried to select a gear more appropriate for the terrain. Grabbing the column shift, he slammed the transmission from third to second.

The lever broke off in his hand.

He stared at it dumbly for several seconds. Then, as the pickup slowed, he panicked.

In the heat of the moment, Olavi's command of the English language evaporated like summer dew. He looked at my mother and tried to speak. His mouth opened and closed several times, but no sound came out. When at length he managed a sentence, it was gibberish.

"Hanki ruuvimeisseli," he said.

Mom turned and gave him a curious expression. "Hank, who?"

Olavi dropped the metal shift lever to the floor and held his empty hand out palm up.

"Ruuvimeisseli," he said again with increased urgency. "Hanki ruuvimeisseli nopeasti."

Mom cocked her head in a question, which only added to my stepfather's frustration.

"I think he's speaking Finnish," I said.

Olavi nodded his head and glanced at the truck's speedometer. The white needle inside the circular gauge was moving in the wrong direction.

My mother was baffled. "For God's sake, man, speak English."

He tried, but his tongue remained locked into the language of his homeland. "Ruuvimeisseli," he pleaded. "Ruuvimeisseli, kiitos." To emphasize the point, he made a fist with his free hand and rotated it repeatedly from left to right.

The trip became a game of charades played at thirty miles per hour, then twenty, and finally ten. Olavi, his apprehension growing, tried to communicate with hand gestures while the rest of us attempted to guess what he needed.

"You want us to roll down the window?" asked Mom.

Olavi shook his head and rolled his wrist some more.

"Turn the truck off?" I asked, reaching for the ignition switch.

More emphatic headshaking. He swatted my hand away with annoyance, then made a blade with his own and pushed it forward as if to engage an unseen object. Once more, the appendage rotated slowly from left to right.

"You need a spatula?" asked Kelly.

All heads swivelled in her direction. "Don't look at me like that," she said. "It looks like he's flipping pancakes."

Our forward progress had slowed to a crawl by this time, and the pickup's ancient six-cylinder motor was gasping. In a last-ditch attempt to communicate, Olavi let go of the steering wheel. He made a circle with the thumb and first finger of his left hand, then jammed the index finger of his right into it repeatedly.

Mom looked away in disgust. "There's no need to be crude, Olavi. It's not our fault we can't understand you."

Something clicked in my sex-obsessed teenage brain. "Screwing!" I exclaimed. "He needs a screwdriver!"

Olavi nodded with enthusiasm. "Ruuvimeisseli," he said. "Screwdriver. Find me one before the engine quits."

I looked on the dash. Nothing there. Tried the glovebox and only came up with a notice from something called the Insurance Corporation of British Columbia. According to the document, our automobile liability coverage had expired a year earlier.

"Stop reading that and look under the seat," said Olavi. My inability to locate the tool was pushing him toward apoplexy.

Discarding the soiled document, I slammed the glovebox, stuck my head between my legs, and peered into the gloom beneath me. Way in the back, next to a rusty tire iron and a couple of discarded candy wrappers, was something that looked like a yellow Phillips screwdriver.

I groped for it, got my fingers around its plastic handle, and pulled it out. "Roomy-smelling," I said in triumph, holding the implement aloft like the Holy Grail.

Olavi snatched the tool from my hand, rammed it into the cavity once occupied by the Ford's shift lever, and yanked down hard. The truck, a heartbeat from stalling, groaned at the mistreatment and bucked several times before resuming speed.

We all breathed a sigh of relief.

The rest of the trip to Southbank was uneventful. As we rolled down the hill toward the ferry landing, the truck's engine backfiring like an overtaxed draft horse, we saw a long line of cars ahead of us. They stretched from Knelsen's Store to a point halfway up the hill.

The *M.V. Jacob Henkel* was a 152-tonne ferry named after one of the first white men to set foot in the country. Constructed in 1949, it shuttled passengers and freight across Francois Lake every half hour at the speed of a recalcitrant mule. The vessel had a maximum capacity of sixteen vehicles, and there were more than twenty ahead of us.

"Crap," said Mom as we pulled behind the last car in line, a purple station wagon covered in dust. "We're late, and now we'll have to wait."

Olavi took her comments as criticism. "Well, if Mike had found the screwdriver quicker, we'd have got here in time. Stupid kid started reading the insurance papers."

I was offended. If not for my heroics, we would have drifted down Ootsa Hill and into the lake. Everyone on board would be sleeping with the fishes instead of waiting for a boat.

My belligerence bubbled out like slag from a melting pot. "It's not my fault you can't speak English," I said, staring straight ahead so as not to make eye contact. "How was I supposed to know what you wanted? It's not me who is stupid."

Olavi heard me and growled. He reached over the others and gave my skull a hard rap with his calloused knuckles.

The blow sent me reeling. When I looked in his direction, there was a glint of amusement in his green eyes. "How's that feel, Mr. Smarty Pants?" he asked. "Want another?"

I lost it. All my anger and resentment boiled to the surface, and I launched a roundhouse punch at his fat, bearded face.

Mom chose that moment to lean forward and say something.

My fist struck her between the eyes. She dropped like a stone or would have if there had been room.

Kelly was horrified. Olavi looked surprised. Laina, sensing something terrible had happened, started to cry.

I bolted from the car and walked toward the ferry, gingerly touching the knot produced by Olavi's blow. Lord, how I hated the man.

There was a one-sailing wait, and the delay gave everyone a chance to cool off.

"How is your noggin?" my mother asked when I got back in the truck. The ferry was approaching Northbank, and a pair of deckhands dressed in white shirts and dark blue dress pants were getting the vessel ready to dock. They moved from vehicle to vehicle, pulling scuffed wheel chocks from beneath tires and waving to passengers they recognized.

"Better," I replied. "How is yours?"

The lump between her eyes matched the one on my head. "It's okay," she said. "Does it look bad?"

"No," I lied. "You can hardly see it."

We covered the final sixteen miles to town in silence and went straight to the newspaper office. The structure had previously served as a police station and was allegedly haunted. After hearing these rumours, I implored Mom to wear a crucifix when delivering the news each week, but she declined. Such blatant disregard for her safety might, I feared, put us all at risk, so I made the sign of the cross whenever we got within a block of the place.

Kelly and I exited the truck as soon as it pulled even with the old building. Mom slid out behind us with all the news that was fit to print clutched in one slender hand.

"Go with God," I said as she walked away, then added three hail Marys and a Hallelujah. You can never be too careful when it comes to ghosts.

Olavi rolled his eyes before glancing at his watch. "Getting late," he said out the side window as Mom crossed in front of the truck with my little sister. "We're going to the laundromat."

My mother nodded and kept going.

Gurten's Family Laundry was only two hundred feet away, so Kelly and I ran there while our stepfather circled the block.

As soon as Olavi found a parking space, I started yanking bags out of the truck box and dragging them toward the laundromat. Kelly acted as an advance party and went inside to case the joint.

The establishment had only been open an hour but was already a madhouse. Washing machines rattled and shook, and, in the bank of dryers along one wall, apparel in a kaleidoscope of colours danced inside each revolving drum. Canned music competed for auditory ownership of the space with the whirring of electric motors and the idle chatter of a half-dozen patrons.

A fat woman in a muumuu was pulling wet clothes out of a machine on the right. She was there most Saturdays and did not like kids. Then again, maybe it was me she didn't like. If so, the feeling was mutual.

As soon as she was clear, Kelly claimed the washer and started looking for another.

I tore open a laundry bag and stuffed dirty clothes into the metal drum. They smelled of sawdust, week-old perspiration, and stale petroleum products.

"Don't rip the bags open. We'll reuse them," said Olavi as he dropped a load of laundry at my feet.

"Okay," I replied and silently cursed him again.

Kelly called to me from farther down the line. "There's an empty one over here."

An elderly man with a small box of detergent clutched in one bony paw shuffled toward the vacant machine. Kelly blocked his path by placing her back against the washer's glass porthole.

"No way, grandpa," she said. "This one's ours."

"But I was using it," the old guy said. "I just went to put my wet stuff in the dryer and get more soap. Those are my things on top."

Kelly stole a look over her shoulder, confirmed his statement, and sighed. Though only eleven, she was well versed in laundromat etiquette. She knew that if you stepped away from a machine for less than two minutes while leaving personal items atop it, your license of temporary occupation remained valid.

"Okay," she said. "But we get it when you're done, right?"

The old guy nodded. Having finalized the verbal contract, my sister went looking for easier pickings.

Olavi returned with another bag of dirty clothing and a container of soap. He looked around before putting both down.

"Which machines are ours?" he asked, pulling a handful of quarters from his pocket.

"Just this one so far," I said. "Kelly's looking for more."

My stepfather grimaced. "All right. Get out of the way so I can put the money and soap in."

I stepped aside. To my right, another machine stopped shuddering and went silent. The whale in the Godawful print dress came over and transferred its wet contents to a steel trolley. Almost every article of clothing that came out of the spinner was adorned with at least one floral species. A few had several, and there was something the size of a wall tent covered with stylized teddy bears. It was wrapped around a lacey off-white bra that looked as though it had been plundered from a medieval siege machine.

"Are you finished with the washer, my dear?" Olavi asked in a honeyed tone. *God,* I thought, *he's flirting.*

Mrs. Esmeralda Dick, a direct descendant of Moby and, until recently, a resident of the South Atlantic, returned his smile and batted her fake eyelashes. "Yes, you're welcome to it," she said before swimming away with the cart.

"Thar she blows, matey," I whispered in my best Captain Ahab voice as soon as she was out of earshot.

"What?" asked Olavi.

"Nothing," I replied.

The empty machine was a top loader. I untied the knot on one of our bags and dumped its contents into the washer's gaping maw. Much to my horror, a flood of greasy paper towels, tin cans, and mouldy food waste spilled out.

"Shit," I said, peering down at the garbage. "You brought in the wrong bag."

Olavi looked over. "So I did. But don't just stand there staring at it. Get it out and put some clothes in."

I complied. After fishing out most of the refuse—some of the more disgusting bits, including a dollop of potato salad that was well on its way to becoming liquid, earned the right to stay due to their offensiveness—I opened another bag and filled the washer. Most of the clothing that went into the machine after the garbage had been retrieved belonged to my stepfather, which gave me satisfaction. Sometimes revenge is a dish best enjoyed in secret.

By the time Mom showed up, we had corralled three washers and crammed a quarter of our laundry into them. The machines were pounding away like power hammers in a blacksmith shop, but with all the others in use and none even close to the rinse cycle, Olavi announced it was time to leave. He said we were tight on time and still had four stops to make.

One of us had to stay behind and guard the machines. "I don't care who it is," Mom said to my sister and me. "You decide."

I turned to Kelly and opened negotiations. "If you stay, I'll find you some books at the library."

"Mom will get me some," Kelly said. "She knows what I like. You've got to give me something."

Babysitting the laundry, in my opinion, was not time well spent. I had my list of priorities for the day, and one of them was paying a visit to Mort's Variety Store. A plastic model kit there had caught my eye two months earlier. Short on funds at the time, I had hidden it behind a Paint by Number set. Since then, I had sold myself enough war bonds to make the purchase.

I fingered the coins in my pocket. Maybe my sister could be bribed.

"If you stay behind, I'll give you a nickel," I said.

Kelly screwed up her face and gave the matter some thought. I saw her eyes stray to the pop machine in the corner.

"I want a dime," she said at length, "and a Mountain Dew."

The soda would cost me ten cents. When combined with the stipend she was seeking, it amounted to almost a week's allowance. There was, however, a compelling argument in favour of paying her. No new ships had been commissioned into the Turkkish Navy for months, and something had to be done if I wanted to stay ahead of Sean Alcott in the arms race.

"Seven cents and a pop," I countered.

Her face brightened, and she held out one hand. "Deal. Hand it over."

When I walked out the door with my parents a few minutes later, Kelly was drinking soda and sitting a short harpoon's throw from the Great White Whale.

We dropped Mom and Laina at the library before heading to the dump. When we got to our destination, Olavi made me open every black sack that remained in the truck to ensure they contained refuse and not someone's wardrobe. Then he went into salvage mode and filled the truck box with items reclaimed from the refuse heap.

A filthy couch and some bits of plywood went in, followed by scrap steel and a broken chainsaw. I thought we were done, but Olavi spotted a lift of nail-infested two-by-fours and decided they also needed to come home with us.

We were about to pull out when I heard a hissing sound. Olavi traced it to our Ford's port side rear tire, which now sported a half-dozen roofing nails and was rapidly going flat.

He swore and consulted his Timex for the second time in forty minutes. "Start unloading," he said to me. "The jack and spare are under all that stuff in the back."

The sun had reached its zenith when we left the dump. We proceeded to the library without passing "Go" or collecting two hundred dollars. Olavi stayed in the truck and kept the motor running in preparation for takeoff.

"Get your mother and sister," he said, "and no looking for books. We don't have time."

"Aw, come off it," I said. "I've got nothing to read. Just a few minutes?"

"No," he said. "We need to be home by six. Now hurry up."

Mom was inside talking to the librarian. I took advantage of the opportunity and made a beeline for the world history section. But I didn't tarry there. Mindful of my instructions, I scooped up enough dissertations on the Second World War to get me through another week and headed for the checkout desk. Shakespeare's *Hamlet* caught my eye on the way out. After reading the dust jacket, I thought it might offer some practical advice on dealing with difficult people, but a closer inspection revealed it was not a DIY manual.

"Mom," I said, interrupting her conversation. "The Lapland Louse says it's time to go."

She looked startled. "Sorry," she said to her friend. "I don't know why Olavi is in such a rush today, but I better go. See you next week."

I tossed my accounts of global death and destruction into Mom's book bag, and we left. Olavi drove like a maniac to the laundromat where we transferred our wet clothing to the dryers and reloaded the washing machines. Kelly demanded another dime to stay behind and watch the stuff, but I pleaded poverty. Mom paid her.

Olavi fired up the Ford, and we tore away from the curb in a cloud of blue smoke. He took the dogleg turn in Burns Lake's crooked Main Street hunched over the wheel like a Formula 1 driver. As we entered the downtown core—a two-block stretch of stores dominated by the town's pride and joy, a drab three-storey hotel built during the Alcan era—I prayed for a slow-moving pedestrian, tire blowout, or mechanical failure, anything that would result in an unscheduled stop. It didn't happen. Mort's Variety was just a blur in the side window as we flashed past.

At the grocery store, my stepfather was out of the truck almost before it stopped rolling. He raced across the blackened expanse of asphalt toward a tangled line of shopping carts near the entrance. The rest of us tried to catch up, strung out like a gaggle of ugly ducklings in his wake.

"Good Lord, Olavi, slow down," my mother said. She was jogging behind him, my youngest sister in tow. The poor kid had to take long, leaping strides to keep pace with the adults, and the awkward movements made her look like Neil Armstrong running across the grey surface of the moon.

My stepfather looked over his shoulder and slowed his pace to a quickstep.

"What on earth is your hurry?" Mom asked as she drew even with him. The man didn't usually move this fast unless he was evading employment.

He muttered something, grabbed a shopping cart, and hoisted Laina into it. Then he entered the store and took off as if he were a contestant on *Supermarket Sweep*. Mom trailed behind with the shopping list, reading it aloud like an ode to mercantilism.

When it came time to pay, my mother found herself four dollars and fifteen cents short. She looked skyward as if expecting currency to rain down like manna. When it did not, she poked my stepfather, who responded by digging in one pocket. The exercise netted him two dollars in quarters and a mittful of lint. He handed both to the teller, who winced, tossed the coins in her hand a few times to winnow out the pocket fluff, and deposited them in the cash drawer.

"Still two dollars and fifteen cents short," she announced, popping her chewing gum aggressively. "You want to put some of this stuff back?"

The store's bag boy looked aggrieved, and there was a murmur of discontent from the growing lineup of shoppers behind us.

I saved my parents further embarrassment.

"I've got some money," I said. Though it pained me, I followed Olavi's example and deposited a handful of change on the rubber conveyor. The teller took what she needed and shoved the rest back.

My good deed left me with eighty-six cents. There would be no addition to the Turkkish Fleet this week.

Mom, relieved, put a hand on my shoulder. "Thanks," she said. "I'll pay you back when I get my cheque."

"With thirty percent interest?" I asked.

"Don't push your luck, Don Corleone," she replied.

Olavi shepherded us to the pickup and found room for the groceries amidst his dump finds. We followed the access road along the railway tracks back to the laundromat.

"No time to dry any more clothes," my stepfather announced over his shoulder as he pushed through the establishment's front door. "We'll take everything home wet."

Kelly lugged dry stuff to the curb while Mom and I ran from washer to washer like hens after grain. Olavi took the wet laundry to the pickup as fast as we could bag it. When he ran out of stuff to toss into the hold, he urged everyone to move faster.

"Hurry," he said, glancing at the clock on the laundromat wall. "We've got to catch the four o'clock ferry."

"What is the rush?" Mom asked again.

He picked up another bag and went out without answering.

At length, the task was complete. My stepfather hacked a U-turn on the street and headed in a direction opposite the one we expected.

"Where are we going?" asked Mom.

"Gas station," said Olavi.

Mom looked puzzled. "I don't have any money left."

"That's okay," he replied. "I do." Reaching into his shirt pocket, he pulled out a crumpled ten-dollar bill.

My mother was incensed. So was I.

"Why in God's name didn't you produce that in the grocery store?" she asked him. "We had to use Mike's money, and now he doesn't have any."

My stepfather, the ten-spot clutched in one grubby hand, shrugged. "I had to keep it for fuel. What's the big deal? Mike still has ninety cents."

"Eighty-six," I corrected, "and I wanted a ship model."

"You didn't have time for that today anyway," he said.

"I had the time. You didn't," I said under my breath.

We pulled into the Esso station and watched the gas jockey fill our tank. Olavi handed over the money and drummed his fingers on the steering wheel while the kid went inside to record the transaction. Then we were off again as though shot from a cannon.

Tchesinkut Lake was visible through the driver's side window when I realized there was enough room in the cab to draw a breath. Something was amiss.

"Where's Laina?" I asked.

Mom leaned forward. Her eyes looked like two full moons as she searched for the missing kid.

"My God," she said. "We left her in the laundromat."

Olavi let out a groan of frustration and started looking for a place to turn around.

We were ten minutes south of town when Laina's absence was noted. It only took us six to get back. Mr. Ford's wonderful creation hadn't moved that fast in at least a decade. Every moving part in the vehicle howled its disapproval.

My youngest sister had her face pressed against the laundromat's plate glass window when we arrived. She had been crying, and there was a muddy streak down each pink cheek.

I went inside to get her.

"Gaggy!" Laina said, using my nickname. She climbed off the bench and attached herself to my right leg like a limpet. I patted her head and shuffled toward the exit.

"You came back for your sister."

The woman in the muumuu was standing near an open doorway at the rear of the building. Both arms were crossed over her immense bosom, and there was a look of censure on her round face. It suddenly dawned on me that she ran the place.

"Yeah," I said, still trying to reach the doorway. Walking is difficult when you have a toddler strapped to one leg.

The woman took an aggressive step in my direction. "We're not running a babysitting service here," she said. "I would have called Social Services, but it's Saturday. Maybe I'll do that on Monday. What's your surname, boy?"

Olavi started honking the truck's horn, which added urgency to my efforts. I stumped along like a sailor with a peg leg. Upon reaching the door, I turned and gave the leviathan her due.

"Oh, shut your blowhole, Moby." To make sure she got the message, I filled my cheeks with air and let it out in a blast.

She gasped and tried to respond, but I was already gone.

It was well after four by the time we arrived at Northbank. The ferry was already out of sight, and at least two dozen cars were waiting for the next sailing.

Olavi consulted his wristwatch and made a snap decision.

"We'll go around the head of the lake," he said and crushed the accelerator.

The rest of us groaned, and I had a sudden desire to throw myself from the vehicle.

There are two ways to reach Ootsa Lake by car. The first and fastest is to take Highway 35 to Francois Lake, ride the government ferry to Southbank, and motor along Keefe's Landing Road at something approximating the speed limit for three-quarters of an hour. The alternative is a much longer journey that involves driving west along Colleymount Road to the head of Francois Lake, and then taking a hard left on Ootsa-Nadina Road.

Taking the second route is known locally as "driving the head," and it was an ordeal in the 1970s. The road had more twists and turns than ticks on a moose, and it rolled through hill country reminiscent of the Scottish Highlands. The final insult, which also had the potential to inflict grave injury, came in the form of wildlife corridors. Platoons of suicidal animals lurked around every bend in the road and liked to hasten their demise by playing chicken with approaching automobiles. Kelly swore that a porcupine we encountered on one trip showed abject disappointment when we chose to enter the ditch rather than hit him.

My sisters and mother had an additional worry. They all suffered from motion sickness, and Colleymount Road was famous for creating it. By the time we reached Clemretta, an unincorporated hamlet named after two calves, they were always on the verge of hurling.

It didn't help that Olavi had, by this time, developed a unique driving style that the rest of us dubbed "stop and go." According to page 21 of the British Columbia Drivers Handbook, the responsible motorist maintains vehicular speed by subtly applying variable pressure to the accelerator. My stepfather disagreed. He was a vociferous advocate of "stomp and squash," which involved mashing the pedal to the floorboards and holding it there for several seconds before removing his foot from it entirely. This technique resulted in sudden, rapid acceleration followed by slow deacceleration. When our rate of progress dropped below the speed limit, he repeated the exercise.

Passengers subjected to "stop and go" for an extended period exhibited symptoms consistent with whiplash. Because I sat forward on the seat and was better able to predict the go-fast cycle, I was immune to it. Mom, Kelly, and Laina were not, and their discomfort was a source of great amusement to me. When you're a teenage boy whose day hasn't gone as planned, there is nothing more enjoyable than seeing members of your family in mild distress. Adding to it only sweetens the experience.

We had only put a few miles behind us when Kelly started to look green around the gills. Then Mom dug into her purse for some Gravol, and I knew the game was afoot.

I started with a few mild belches. They soon escalated to lengthy burps followed by prolonged dry heaves.

"Don't make that sound," Kelly said as she struggled to retain ownership of the soft drinks she had consumed. "You're making me sick."

I retched again, this one by far the most disgusting, and was rewarded with an answering heave to my left.

Mom gagged and swallowed. "Stop it, Mike. I'm going to barf."

"I can't help it," I said, trying not to laugh. "I don't feel good."

She turned to my stepfather. "Olavi, if he does that again, hit him."

Knowing that the man would be happy to accommodate her, I quit making foul noises. It was just one more disappointment in a day filled with them. People were always wrecking my fun.

The Ford negotiated a few more turns and hills. Then, as we entered a long decline, there was a clang from the rear of our vehicle.

The noise was not loud, and nothing happened right away, so Olavi ignored it. Of considerable interest, though, was the single tire that passed him in the outside lane.

Chaos broke loose a heartbeat later. There was a massive crash, and we listed violently to port. The Ford's rudder started behaving erratically, and its stern slewed back and forth across the road, throwing up a thick screen of dust and flying gravel.

We came to a grinding halt, but the renegade wheel did not. It veered left after rolling perhaps fifty yards farther down the hill, jumped the ditch, bounced once, and escaped into a grassy meadow.

The dust cloud enveloped us. We sat there coughing and choking until it cleared, then got out.

Olavi and I went aft to survey the damage. The rear axle was cocked at an impossible angle, and one brake drum was half-buried in the dirt. Behind it was a deep gouge that snaked along the road for at least a hundred feet.

My stepfather stated the obvious. "Tire came off."

That's when it dawned on me. Back at the landfill, in his eagerness to hit the road, he had failed to tighten the lug nuts. They had worked themselves free over forty miles, releasing the tire and sending us into a skid.

I knew better than to suggest he was the architect of our misfortune. Instead, I restricted my comment to two words and delivered them with as much impertinence as possible.

"You think?"

He glared at me before consulting his wristwatch. "Better start unloading," he said. "Spare and jack are in the back."

We piled everything at the side of the road. By the time we were done, it looked like a pop-up garage sale was in progress. My mother and sisters threw a clean blanket over the dump couch and watched from the sidelines, taking hits from a large bottle of lukewarm soda from time to time.

Olavi didn't remember the spare was flat until our excavations reached the lowest strata. Then he swore and led us on a search for the missing wheel.

We went to the spot where Mr. Goodyear had disappeared. He had left tracks in the dry grass, but they went on forever because the meadow beyond sloped gently toward the lake. We followed his spoor down the hill, through a stand of cottonwood trees, and onto the sandy beach where it went cold at the water's edge.

"Can you see it?" asked Mom, shading her eyes against the setting sun.

"Yeah, I think so," I said, pointing to a spot offshore. "It's out there about fifteen feet, just before the drop-off."

"Good," said Olavi. "Go get it."

I peeled off my shoes and socks, rolled up my trousers, and recovered the tire. Olavi carried it back up the hill to the road where we discovered our baggage had drawn a crowd.

A murder of crows and an unkindness of ravens had descended on our temporary encampment. They had ripped open most of the bags and strewn the contents over a wide area. It looked like a bomb had gone off in a Chinese laundry, causing collateral damage to a farmer's market. And the birds were still at it; everything edible was being devoured with utmost speed and efficiency by the first wave of invaders while a second waited nearby. Late arrivals not actively engaged in destruction perched in the trees like extras in an Alfred Hitchcock film and showed their enthusiasm for the proceedings by raining copious amounts of white shit down on everything below. It was terrifying.

Mom saw what was happening and ran toward the truck. The birds scattered, but not far enough for her liking. She shook her fist and hurled insults at them. Coarse language came next, followed by a volley of rocks. Then she just sat down in the dirt and wept.

There wasn't much said after that. Olavi jacked up the truck and reattached the tire. The original lug nuts had disappeared in the crash, so he swiped one from each of the other three wheels and added an extra from the glove box. We gathered what remained of our groceries, decamped, and continued down the road at reduced speed.

The sun disappeared behind Nadina Mountain, turning the western sky a deep vermilion. It was very late when we got home. Fearing another airborne assault, Olavi made us drag everything inside before heading to bed.

Just before I fell asleep, I heard Mom ask the question that had been on everyone's mind.

"Olavi, why were you in such a rush to get home?"

My stepfather, realizing that deception was no longer necessary, did not dissemble. "Tommy Hunter had a special on TV tonight. I wanted to see it."

"You're telling me you put us through all that for a television show?" Mom said. "Haven't you heard of reruns?"

Judging from the silence that followed, my stepfather did not feel a response was necessary.

We surveyed the wreckage the following morning. Birds had eaten all the bread and three-quarters of the eggs. Our only piece of red meat was pecked almost beyond recognition. What had left the store as round steak now looked like hamburger.

The biggest disappointment, though, was the laundry. Three of the eight bags we brought home contained women's apparel, none of it my mother's. She didn't object to the floral pattern but said the undergarments were too large.

Mrs. Dick must have had a whale of a time with our clothing.

THE END
(Sort of)

The BIC

The pen was a good one, a ballpoint with a clear barrel and ink as black as anthracite, and it had a mind of its own. The brass tip glided across the fools-cap in front of me, leaving in its wake an eight-word sentence in penmanship that was not mine.

I let the pen have its way again, and it wrote the same thing. I studied the handwriting, provided some constructive criticism, and repeated the exercise. When the vowels in each word were nicely rounded and the consonants bold and looping, I found a clean sheet of paper and wrote the message a final time. The pen moved confidently and without hesitation. When it was done, I looked at the result and could find no fault in it.

Satisfied, I signed my mother's name at the bottom of the page with a flourish.

I was seated at my desk in the Grade Nine classroom and admiring the pen's handiwork when Diggs returned from the washroom.

"What do you think?" I asked, handing him the masterpiece.

My friend read the note aloud. "'Please allow Mike to go to the store. Sincerely, Pat Turkki.' I thought you said you didn't have a permission note?"

"I didn't until a minute ago," I said. "Now I do."

"Did your parents show up while I was in the can?" Diggs asked, passing the foolscap back to me and looking around suspiciously. If there was an adult nearby, he wanted to know about it.

"Nope," I said. "I wrote it myself."

Diggs snatched the paper from me and stared at it. "Holy shit. I've seen your mom's writing, and this looks just like it."

"Pretty good, huh?" I said, pleased with myself. "Now give it back because it's not quite done."

"Looks good to me," Diggs said as he surrendered the page a second time.

"The writing is fine, but the whole thing looks way too neat. Don't forget, it's supposed to have been in my pocket since six o'clock this morning."

With that, I crumpled the freshly minted note into a loose ball. Diggs was about to protest this willful destruction when I unfolded the page, lay it flat atop my desk, and smoothed the wrinkles with a forearm. The document looked better for it but not perfect, so I took a bite of the mealy apple that had come to school with me that day, chewed the granular flesh three or four times, and dribbled the slurry onto the page. I left the mess in situ for a few seconds, just long enough to dampen the paper, then wiped it off. The ink of my mother's name was smeared, and there were still random chunks of fruit pulp clinging to the paper, but now the document looked as though it was at least five hours old.

"Okay, now it's ready." Folding the note and sticking it into my shirt pocket, I added, "Let's go find a teacher to give this to. I'm hungry."

The Grassy Plains Store was located kitty-corner from the school at the junction of Keefe's Landing Road and a dirt track that led west into the rolling hills. The two-storey log building, its walls blackened with age and grime, had sat there since the 1930s when a local man concluded it was more profitable to sell things to his neighbours than work the area's marginal farmland. A family of wayward Germans bought the place in the early 1970s, and it didn't take them long to figure out their target market was across the road at Grassy school. The store still carried staples like rice and flour, but the primary ingredient in most of the merchandise was sugar. Shelves near the cash register groaned under the weight of empty calories.

Diggs and I loved the store, but we couldn't go there whenever we felt like it. You needed parental authorization to leave the school grounds, which had become problematic for me by 1976. Faced with mounting dental bills and a cratering bank account, Mom tried to curb my sugar intake by withholding store permission notes. It didn't work. I promised to get clean and tried eating fruit instead of candy, but the sugar had its claws in deep, and the withdrawal symptoms were awful. After a day of sweating and crying and begging my friends for a nibble of something sweet, I decided I wasn't ready to go cold Turkki.

I needed a hit of sugar, which is why we were on our way to the office with a document that appeared to have been written by my mother.

We found the on-duty teacher, a recent recruit named Sheary who was unfamiliar with our reputation for skulduggery, and handed him the permission notes. He accepted Diggory's without question, but mine got a little extra scrutiny.

Butterflies tickled the inside of my stomach as I waited for him to pronounce judgment on the pen's handiwork.

"Hmmm . . ." Sheary said as he perused the note. He was holding it by the corners to avoid getting his fingers soiled. "Everything appears to be in order, but this looks old. When did your mother write it?"

I tried not to smile. "Late last night. Sorry it's such a mess."

"It *is* a little worse for wear," the teacher said. "What's this stuff on it?"

"Something blew up in my lunch bag," I answered. "I think it's apple, but I'm not sure. It was kind of slimy."

My words had the desired effect. Sheary's mouth curled up in disgust, and he said, "Okay, you two can go. Be back before the bell rings."

"We will," I assured him.

"Man, you were as cool as a cucumber," Diggs noted when we were safely out of earshot.

"No reason not to be," I said. "The note was perfect."

Diggs and I pushed through the school's big double doors and started down the well-beaten path that ran straight as a taut cable across the playing field toward the store. A crowd of sugar junkies was hanging around the weathered snake fence that enclosed the school grounds, and some of them accosted us as we drew near. We elbowed our way through the rabble, climbed the fence, and crossed the road.

Ralph was coming out of the store as we were going in. He had a bag of potato chips in one hand and a giant bottle of cola in the other. An Eat-More bar protruded from the breast pocket of his snap-button shirt. The food must have cost him at least eighty-five or ninety cents—a small fortune at the time. Where did the guy get his money? It would have taken me a month to save that much.

"What are you doing here?" he asked me. "I thought you weren't allowed to go to the store anymore."

Diggs answered on my behalf. "He's not, but he wrote himself a permission note."

Ralph was impressed. "You wrote your own note? That takes balls." To illustrate the point, he walked in a tight circle with the sixty-four-ounce soft drink bottle dangling between his skinny legs.

The pantomime elicited a barking laugh from Diggs. I just shrugged. "I needed something."

Ralph gave me a knowing look. "Can't kick the Stix, huh?"

My battle with sugar addiction was well known, and Pixy Stix, those paper straws filled with fine sugar and chemicals with long, unpronounceable names, were my candy of choice. Most kids cut the tops off these little tubes of goodness and consumed their contents over five or ten minutes. Not me. I dumped all the powder into my mouth and waited long enough for the dust storm to dissipate before chewing and swallowing. The sugar rush that followed was phenomenal, like pulling the pin on an adrenalin grenade, and I couldn't get enough of it.

Pixy Stix were cheap and readily available, which was fortuitous because I was going through about two dozen a week by Ninth Grade. Still, Ralph's suggestion that I had a problem irked me.

"They're just candy," I told him. "I could stop eating them any time I want. And what about you and Coke?"

He gave his jug of soda a companionable hug. "Yeah," he said, "I like my pop. But I don't get the shakes if I don't have it."

He had me there, so I changed the subject. "Hey, don't tell anyone about the note, eh?"

Ralph gave me a pained look. "Of course not," he said as he walked away. "Oh, by the way, the Krauts got something new in there. They're called Pop Rocks, and, according to Adolf, it's candy that explodes in your mouth." Having conveyed this nugget of information, he gave me a stiff-armed salute and headed back to class.

I couldn't get inside the store fast enough.

Ralph didn't tell anyone about my forgery. Days later, though, he sought me out. "Hey, Turkki Lurkey," he said. "Can you copy anyone's handwriting or just your mom's?"

I ignored the jibe. "Don't know. Probably, if I had the right pen. Why?"

"Well," he said. "There's a kid down by the fence who was supposed to pick up some stuff for his parents today. The dork has the list they gave him, but he lost his note from home. He's freaking out, trying to get someone to go for him."

"What's the big deal? There's always someone going to the store."

Ralph shook his head. "No one will do it. The first item on the list is Tampax and the second is Preparation H."

Now the student body's recalcitrance made sense. No self-respecting kid would be caught dead buying that stuff. Still, I couldn't see any reason to get involved.

"That's a bummer, but why should I care?"

"Because," Ralph said with an avaricious leer, "he's willing to pay."

That got my attention. I came from a long line of poor people. My parents and their forebears had possessed so little money for so long that my sister Kelly and I were convinced poverty was a congenital disability, like heart valve problems and Down syndrome.

"All right," I said. "Give me a couple minutes, and then send him to the john."

As soon as Ralph left, I grabbed a selection of pens and paper, then made my way to the rendezvous point. I barely had time to lock myself in one of the toilet stalls before the bathroom door opened and someone entered the room. There was silence for a moment, followed by the sound of rubber-soled tennis shoes squeaking across the cold linoleum floor.

"Hello?" a prepubescent voice asked hesitantly. "Anybody here?"

"Yeah, kid, someone's here," I said, trying my best to sound like a gangster. "Whaddaya want?"

He was quiet for a moment. Then the words tumbled out of him. "I got a problem. I need to go to the store, but I lost my note. The redheaded guy said he had a friend who could help. Can you write me a note?"

"Maybe, maybe not. You still have the grocery list?"

"Yes," he said.

"Good. Give it to me."

The kid followed the sound of my voice to the bathroom stall. He stopped a few feet away, close enough that I could see his dusty Chuck Taylor running shoes and the rolled-up cuffs of his blue jeans. He pushed a tattered sheet of paper under the door.

It was your run-of-the-mill grocery list, six items written in blue ink on the upper half of a sheet of lined paper torn from someone's notebook. The penmanship was decent, and—despite being hurried—there was an elegance to it. Judging from the way the handwriting meandered across several lines and listed to port, I suspected the author was a left-handed, thirty-something female under extreme stress. I decided to test the theory.

"Your mom, was she upset when she wrote this? Moody and irritable? Spending a lot of time in the bathroom?"

There was a sharp intake of breath on the other side of the door. "How'd you know?"

A smile of satisfaction crept unseen across my face. "It's a gift, kid."

"So, can you do it? Copy her handwriting?"

I looked at the list again and gave the matter some thought. "Yeah, but it's going to cost you twenty-five cents."

The kid didn't hesitate. "Okay, but I need it before the end of lunch hour."

"No problem," I said. "What's your name?"

"Bobby Thompson."

"And your mom's name?"

"Mrs. Thompson?"

I grimaced and rolled my eyes. "No, kid, her first name. How she signs stuff."

"Molly. Her name is Molly, but she usually just writes, 'Mrs. M. Thompson.'"

"Okay, now get out of here so I can work. Come back in . . ." There was a pause as I consulted my cheap wristwatch. "Ten minutes."

The kid bolted from the washroom, and as soon as he was gone, I set about forging him a permission note. It appeared Molly Thompson had used a commercially available medium ballpoint to craft her grocery list, and I happened to have a similar one with me. After a few false starts and a good but not great effort, the pen produced something I judged would pass inspection—provided the kid didn't hand over his grocery list at the same time. It wasn't perfect, but an artist needs time to work.

Bobby came back just as I tore off the document's left margin to give it authenticity.

"Is it ready?" he asked.

"Yeah, but first things first," I said, extending my right hand under the door palm up.

Bobby got the hint and handed over two dimes and a nickel. I pocketed the change, then stacked the two pieces of paper and pushed them through the gap at my feet. I saw his hand come down and collect the documents, after which there was a long silence as he examined them.

There was awe in his voice when he at last spoke. "Wow. Who are you?"

Now it was my turn to hesitate. How to answer? Part of me wanted to take credit for a job well done, yet intuition told me that might not be the wisest course of action. I was looking down at the pen in my hand and silently debating the matter when it came to me.

"They call me," I said, pausing for dramatic effect, "the BIC."

That permission note was the BIC's first commercial success. Everyone was happy: Bobby made it to the store, his long-suffering mother got temporary relief from what ailed her, and I earned enough money to keep me in Pixy Stix for a week. Even the German shopkeeper across the road benefited, albeit in a small way, and as far as I could tell, no one was hurt. It was the perfect, victimless crime. In Ralph's learned opinion, I was just Stixing It to the Man.

I thought the note would be a one-off. I was wrong. Grassy Plains was a small school, and word got around that there was a guy in junior high who could supply false documents for a fee. Soon I was spending my lunch hours in the bathroom dealing with clients. At first, I used Ralph as a go-between and gave him fifty percent of the take. But when he went AWOL, and teachers began asking questions about the long lineup for Toilet Stall #2, I moved my office outdoors and became my middleman. The arrangement worked well and cut operating expenses in half, leaving more money for candy. Working conditions were better, too, with plenty of natural light and no noxious odours.

Every day, between twelve and twelve-fifteen, I hung out at the rusty steam tractor that graced the school's rock-strewn front lawn. Potential customers were easy to spot because they were the kids striding toward me while casting furtive glances over their shoulders.

The conversations that followed were predictable.

"Are you the one they call the BIC?"

"No," I would reply, "but I can hook you up for a nickel."

The prospective client would make his request, hand over the consulting fee, and leave. As soon as he disappeared, I went inside and stayed there long enough to fill the order before strolling back to the steam tractor. Then it was just a matter of collecting the money.

Business boomed. I wrote permission notes, notes explaining short absences from school, notes asking that the bearer be excused from music class forever because he was tone-deaf. Heathens paid me to get them out of reciting the Lord's Prayer each morning, and religious kids paid me to get them into sex education class. A few wicked souls wanted both, and I obliged them. Everyone, it seemed, needed a note from home and was willing to pay for it.

Demand for my services spiked whenever report cards were issued because parents had to sign off on their child's progress or lack thereof. As I soon discovered, students would hand over a week's allowance in exchange for one signature acknowledging their academic failures. I charged a premium for report cards that already featured a bona fide parental autograph because they were the hardest to fake. None of my customers objected. They said it was better to pay the BIC than get a whupping at home, and forty cents bought them time to get their academic act together. Most of them did, but there were exceptions. I signed one dullard's report card so many times during his years at Grassy that when he brought a real note from home, it was rejected as a forgery. I got him out of the jam by signing his father's name on a long and tedious letter that claimed the change in his mother's handwriting resulted from a broken wrist suffered in an industrial accident. The teachers felt so bad when they read it that they signed a get-well card for the woman—and unwittingly gave me specimens of their signatures.

By May, I estimated the BIC was responsible for half the communications between home and school. The volume of counterfeit mail going in both directions was astounding. Favours were granted on the strength of a forged signature, sensitive and often fictitious issues were resolved with the stroke of a pen. Does little Johnny need to impress his parents? No problem. For fifty cents, the BIC could supply a letter of commendation signed by Johnny's teacher or (for only a dime more) Principal Dunford.

Typing class had never been so much fun.

The money rolled in. Some of it was used to buy pens and stationery, but most ended up at the Grassy Plains Store. My candy habit grew to epic proportions. The class diabetic, after watching me wash a dozen Pixy Stix down with a chaser of Mountain Dew, suggested I cut back on the sweets before I had to start giving myself needles. I didn't care because I was higher than a kite on sugar most days.

It seemed the good times would never end. Then Ralph came to me with a dilemma.

"You gotta help me, Mike," he said. He was fidgety and nervous, like a packrat on a corrugated iron roof at midday, and there was a desperation in his eyes I hadn't seen before.

"What's up, man?" I asked.

Ralph told me his story, and when he was done, I understood where he got his money and why he had been Missing in Action since early spring.

My redheaded classmate, eager to make some additional coin, had taken a part-time job with a childless Mennonite who lived a mile down the road in Tatalrose. The work was good and the pay decent, a dollar an hour with a home-cooked meal thrown in at midday, but there was a problem. The guy always needed help around the farm between the hours of nine and two when Ralph was supposed to be in school.

Unwilling to turn down the offer and unable to negotiate an alternative work schedule, Ralph did the unthinkable: he started cutting class.

Three days a week, Ralph pounded posts and fixed fences for a bible-thumper while the rest of us tried to master the three Rs. He might have gotten away with it had he not used the school bus for his daily commute. Mondays, Wednesdays, and Fridays, he rode with us as far as Grassy Plains, then got off and walked to his place of employment. Sometimes he came to class for an hour before disappearing until late afternoon, but he was gone most of the time.

His absences came to the attention of the authorities. No one, when questioned, could account for his whereabouts, and Ralph wasn't there often enough to shed any light on the matter. Bob the Bus Driver was as mystified as the rest of us.

"All I know is that he's on the bus every morning and evening," Bob told Miss Albrecht, the school's self-appointed truancy officer. "What he does after that is anybody's guess."

The jig was up. Albrecht communicated her findings to Principal Dunford, and Ralph was summoned to the office during one of his rare appearances in class. To his credit, he didn't crack under questioning. Instead, he blamed his chronic absenteeism on an undisclosed illness.

Despite being a walking fossil, Old Man Dunford had a mind that was not yet petrified. He called Ralph's bluff and demanded documentary evidence.

"So, I need a doctor's note," Ralph said to me when his tale was complete. "How much is it going to cost?"

The question was a good one, and it gave me pause. This was uncharted territory. The BIC had never been called upon to fabricate a document of this nature or import. While I didn't doubt a convincing signature could be produced—physicians, after all, have terrible handwriting—the form and language were unfamiliar.

"I don't know," I said. "Can I just type you something?"

"No," Ralph said. "Dunflop says it has to be on doctor paper. What do you think? Can you do it?"

In retrospect, I should have refused. It wasn't like medical stationery could be purchased at the corner store. Yet I liked a challenge, particularly one that might prove lucrative, so I accepted the commission.

"All right," I said. "Give me two bucks now, and I'll get back to you."

Ralph didn't give me time to change my mind. "Okay," he said, pushing a crumpled banknote into my hand. "Just don't take too long. I need it by Monday, or I'm dead meat."

Armed with Ralph's money, I started plotting the crime of the century. After binging on Pixy Stix and staying up all night, I came up with a plan that offered a reasonable chance of success.

During an earlier visit to the Burns Lake Medical Clinic, after spending what felt like a lifetime in the facility's holding area surrounded by sick people, I had been ushered into a small examination office. Another interminable delay followed, during which I amused myself by exploring the room and its contents. I discovered I was sharing the tiny space with an antique rolltop desk, several fine pens, a cool recliner with adjustable footrests, and some instruments that were popular during the Inquisition. And stationery, lots of it, in various sizes and colours, all bearing the clinic's name, address, and telephone number. Some of the legal-sized stuff, marked "Laboratory Referral," included a convenient list of the area's practicing physicians and a long series of checkboxes beside what I assumed were test procedures. It was quite illuminating to a curious fifteen-year-old with nothing better to do.

At the time, I had no use for anything but the pens, three of which found their way into my pocket. Later, though, I realized the place was a forger's gold mine, and I had left the real bounty behind. Everything the BIC needed to get anyone out of trouble was inside those four institutional green walls. Five minutes alone in there while wearing loose jeans with deep pockets, and I would never again want for candy.

"Mom, I need to go to the doctor," I announced Thursday morning before school.

"Why?" she asked. "What's wrong?"

"I'd rather not say," I answered with mock chagrin. "It's kind of personal. Can you get me an appointment for Saturday?"

The concern on her face was touching, and I hoped it would translate into prompt action. "Is it serious? Should I try to get you in earlier?"

"No, that's okay. Just as long as it's before Monday."

"I'll walk to Mona's today and call the clinic," she said.

"Thanks, Mom. And don't worry, I'll be fine."

She looked relieved. I felt the same way.

My mother kept her word, and by ten o'clock Saturday morning, I was following an overworked nurse through the medical clinic's narrow hallways. The woman took me deep into the belly of the beast before stopping outside a room not much larger than a broom closet.

"In you go," she said without fanfare. "Dr. Hastings will be with you shortly."

Then she closed the door.

I looked around. The place was a claustrophobe's nightmare, a windowless compartment lit by one unadorned light bulb. Two folding chairs faced each other across a metal table, and the walls were bare but for a small medicine cabinet and two anatomy charts. It reminded me of a Gestapo interrogation chamber, and I half expected Heinrich Müller to walk in with two brownshirts. There was no rolltop desk, no nifty recliner with stirrups, and—worst of all—no stationery.

I was rifling through the medicine cabinet when I heard heavy footfalls in the corridor outside my cell.

The door opened, and a tall, middle-aged man with a well-tended Van Dyck beard entered. Dropping a thin manila folder on the table, he settled into one of the folding chairs and encouraged me to do the same with a casual wave of his hand.

"And what can I do for you today, young man?" he asked as I sat down.

His question caught me off guard. Operation Doctor's Note was based on the premise that every room in the clinic would be stocked with letterhead. I had intended to infiltrate the facility, seize the necessary documents, and then exfiltrate before the authorities arrived. I was never provided with a cover story because I assumed one would not be needed. There was no Plan B, and I was about to tell the doctor that my parents had taken a wrong turn at Francois Lake when he opened the folder in front of him.

Nestled inside, atop a bundle of handwritten reports, was a virgin block of prescription paper.

Success was within reach. All I had to do was improvise.

"Well, I've been having some . . . problems . . ." My words trailed away as I tried to think of a malady worthy of a prescription but not lab work.

Dr. Hastings mistook my hesitancy for embarrassment. He waited for me to continue. When I did not, he leaned forward and raised his bushy eyebrows in expectation.

I looked around that barren room in search of inspiration. At first, I found none. Then my gaze landed on the anatomical charts. The female schematic was interesting; I would have liked to study it for a while, but there was no time, so I turned my attention to the other one, which proved to be a diagram of the male reproductive system. The germ of an idea began to form just as my bladder reminded me I had downed two sodas before entering the clinic.

"I have to go," I blurted out.

Relieved to hear something come out of my mouth, the doctor leaned back in his chair and looked thoughtful.

"Are you saying you have to urinate a lot?" he asked.

"Yeah," I said.

"Hmmm," he said. "Do you ever have trouble going? Does a burning sensation accompany it?"

The ball was now in play, and there was no going back. "Sometimes," I said cautiously, "maybe a little?"

"Are you sexually active?" he asked.

Male hubris prevented me from answering truthfully. "Oh, definitely," I replied.

"And how often are you having sex?"

"Oh, regularly. Three or four times . . ." There was another pause as I tried to decide what might constitute a lot of sex to someone of Dr. Hastings's advanced age. I couldn't imagine any amount being excessive, but it was hard to tell what a thirty-year-old might consider aberrant behaviour. In the end, I decided the term was relative and simply added, "a week."

The statement left my confessor stunned. Then the first hint of doubt appeared on his face, and it convinced me to lay my cards on the table.

"The reason I'm here," I said before he could ask any more questions, "is that I've missed a lot of school because of this problem, and the principal says I need to bring him a doctor's note."

What sounded like skepticism crept into Dr. Hasting's voice. "I see," he said. "Very well. I can give you that, and perhaps some penicillin as well. But before I do, we should check something. Stand up and drop your pants, please."

"Excuse me?"

Dr. Hastings produced a pair of rubber gloves from somewhere and pulled them on as he spoke. "You're a bit young for problems of this type, so a prostate exam is in order. That can only be accomplished if you are naked from the waist down."

"No way, man." I pushed my chair back and tried to leave, but the good doctor barred the way.

"Come now. There's no need to be shy," he said. "It will all be over in a minute." With that, he stood and moved toward me.

What to do? Ralph's money was long gone, spent on junk food within hours of being received, so reimbursing him was out of the question. Yet this wasn't just about money; my professional reputation was at stake. People counted on the BIC to get them out of difficult situations, and failing to deliver the goods could have serious consequences for everyone. Public confidence in the con artist would be shattered. Kids with poor academic performance might feel they had no recourse but to work harder, and boys like Bobby Thompson would be doomed to disappoint their parents. The whole system, built as it was on greed and grift, could break down. At the very least, it would be bad for business, and bad business meant no Pixy Stix.

It was a sobering thought.

There was, it seemed, only one road out of this mess, so I took it.

My recollections of what happened next are hazy. I recall loosening my belt and feeling my trousers slip to half-mast. Then my mind went on vacation for a while. When it returned, Dr. Hastings was handing me two slips of paper.

"Here you go," he said. "Top one is your doctor's note, bottom one is a prescription. If the problem persists, come see me again."

Papers in hand, I murmured something and fled.

Hours later, in the privacy of my room, I examined the documents. The prescription found its way into the outhouse, and I turned the BIC loose on the doctor's note. The result, while nothing to write home about, was acceptable.

"You got my doctor's letter?" Ralph asked as soon as he boarded the school bus on Monday morning.

"Yeah, but the price has gone up. You owe me another three bucks."

The truant was not impressed. "What the fuck? That's almost a day's pay for me."

"Don't complain. You have no idea what I had to do to get it for you. It was like being abducted by aliens."

"Well, it better be worth it," he said, handing me the money.

I let the BIC's work speak for itself.

"This is good," Ralph said after inspecting the forgery. "Real authentic. Can you get me another one next month?"

"Not a chance," I said.

The BIC never forged another doctor's note, and I avoided Dr. Hastings like the plague.

Employee of the Month

Getting a job is a rite of passage. It's a first halting step toward adulthood and gives us a measure of financial independence from our parents.

Finding work was easy on the Southside in the 1970s. There were dozens of small sawmills churning out rough lumber and railway ties, and farmers made hay every summer. Even an idle wretch like me could make money.

Like most teens, my first paying job came at the behest of my parents. It was a less than ideal appointment because they had far more work than money. I chopped firewood, hauled water, and did a hundred other things in exchange for twenty-five cents per week. The rate of remuneration fluctuated depending on the state of our family finances. If my parents got paid, so did I. If not, they issued promissory notes of dubious value. Olavi kept track of his indebtedness to me on a small blackboard that hung near the door. The ledger was periodically erased, sometimes after payment of arrears, sometimes for reasons that he alone knew and seldom shared. When the slate got wiped, he started with a clean one, and so did I. It was frustrating.

My worst chore was dumping our communal chamber pot, a five-gallon Esso can fitted with a toilet seat. During our three years at Rainbow Lake, I earned a small but steady income as the family's liquid waste disposal expert, though I would have gladly subcontracted the work to Kelly if she had been able to do it. Pay was by the pot-load, and the rate—five cents per bucket—was not adjusted for inflation. My parents also tended to call Mike's Poo-B-Gone less frequently when strapped for cash, making the job harder and more disgusting. And sadly, it was something other than Worker's Compensation that covered me if I had an accident on the job.

Striking for higher pay and better working conditions was out of the question. When your employer controls the means of production as well as your sources of food, clothing, and shelter, you have no bargaining power. Perhaps these early experiences explain my penchant for Marxism. Nothing sows the seeds of rabid discontent quite like poverty and oppression.

The chamber pot job was terminated without notice after my parents moved us into a used travel trailer. Despite being secretly pleased by the development, I complained about the lost revenue and threatened to sue for breach of contract. We reached an out-of-court settlement.

Our new home featured indoor plumbing. Before any of us could use it, we needed a septic system.

After consulting *Mother Earth News* and other eminent publications that catered to the "back to the land" movement, my stepfather decided that our family of five needed a sewage lagoon at least twenty-five feet long, ten feet wide, and six feet deep. He chose a location for the proposed facility two lengths of sewer pipe from the trailer's rounded stern and direct awarded the excavation work to me as compensation for the loss of the effluent disposal deal. Remuneration was set at 10 cents per hour, $1.90 below the provincial minimum wage but still a fortune for a money-hungry teenager.

I accepted the offer. Not that I had a lot of say in the matter. I had no other prospects at the time, and it was either do the work or continue making what was now a long walk to the outhouse each morning with nothing in my pockets but toilet paper. Besides, I figured the project would make me wealthy beyond my wildest dreams. By expending minimal effort when my overseer was in attendance, and next to none when he was absent, I figured I could make the job last the entire summer. There were at least twenty dollars in it for me, even by conservative estimates, and perhaps as much as thirty if I worked to rule.

Alas, to paraphrase Robbie Burns, "the best-laid plans of mice and men often go awry." The Hoarder from Helsinki was a step ahead of me. I had no sooner accepted the contract than he amended it. Remuneration was capped at five dollars, and the agreed-upon work was to take no more than two weeks. At the end of a fortnight, I had to deliver a ready-built septic lagoon or face stiff penalties for non-compliance. Every day it took to finish the project beyond fourteen, my stepfather chirped as he handed me a shovel and pickaxe, would cost Mike's Poo-B-Gone a quarter dollar.

I attacked the ground behind our trailer. Initial progress was good because the first six inches were soft, black loam, and easy to dig. After four hours of concerted effort, there was a shallow depression inside the stakes Olavi had pounded into the ground to denote the lagoon's parameters.

Day Two started with high hopes. They soon disappeared. At a depth of eight inches, I hit a plethora of tree roots, all of which had to be severed with a double-bladed axe before any serious digging could be done. When I dropped the shovel in disgust at 6 p.m., the hole was only a handspan deeper.

The going did not get any easier the following day. Compacted glacial till lay beneath the tree roots. Progress slowed to a snail's pace, and the pickaxe threatened to become a pick hatchet after I stuck its point in the ground and exerted too much force trying to free it. Olavi offered to fix the implement if I forked over two dollars for a replacement handle, but I waited until he wandered off and then reinforced the defective one with about sixty feet of stolen duct tape.

The weather turned hot and dry. I drank copious amounts of water and soldiered on. When my enthusiasm for the endeavour began to wane, I tried to generate a bit more by thinking about everything Olavi's five dollars could buy me. When that, too, proved inadequate, I speculated on the chance of finding gold beneath the hardpan. Perhaps a fortune lay mere inches beneath my scuffed tennis shoes, and all I had to do was dig a little deeper. One thing was certain: if I found any, it would not be shared with my employer.

By the end of the week, what I hoped would be a goldmine had become the pit of despair. The palms of my hands were a mass of broken blisters, and the tools Olavi had given me were failing. What had started the project as a long-handled shovel had become the equivalent of a garden spade, and the only reasonable substitute was an aluminum snow scoop. I confiscated it, borrowed a hammer and chisel from the toolshed, and kept burrowing.

The excavation reached a depth of four feet on Day Nine. Given my rate of progress, I figured that if I put in sixteen-hour days until the deadline, I might get down another twelve inches. While not thrilled by this pronounce-ment, Olavi admitted a hole that deep might be adequate for a lifetime of excrement.

I met something more unyielding than hardpan at eleven o'clock the following morning. Thinking my pickaxe had struck a large boulder, I tried digging around it. There was no "around it." I scraped away the loose dirt to reveal an unbroken slab of brown rhyolite.

I had hit bedrock.

Olavi refused to believe me. "That's not bedrock," he said, peering into the pit.

"Yes, it is. Watch this." I swung the pickaxe overhead and brought its blunt end down hard on the rock. Sparks flew, and there was a loud metallic clang.

"That's not bedrock," my stepfather repeated with less certainty. "It can't be."

I sighed. "Well, if it's not, it's a monster freaking boulder."

Olavi reached into the pocket of his jack shirt and produced a steel measuring tape. He lowered the yellow strip until it contacted the pit floor, then consulted the markings on its side.

"Fifty-three inches," he said, shaking his head and letting the tape snap back into its silver container. "Not deep enough."

"Well, what do you expect me to do about it? Unless you have dynamite, this is as deep as I can go."

My stepfather returned the tape measure to its resting place and extracted a dog-earned notebook. He made a few scribbles with a pencil stub, looked thoughtful, and then announced, "You can quit, but I'll have to dock you for failing to reach depth. Fifty-three inches is eighty-eight percent of five feet, so that will cost you fifty-eight cents."

Though the math was Chinese to me, the implications were not. I was furious. "Come off it. You said you'd give me five dollars for digging this shit pit. Don't be so cheap. It's not my fault I can't dig deeper."

Olavi stood up. "Don't complain," he said over his shoulder as he walked away. "Technically, the original deal was for a hole six feet deep. If I went by that, you'd only get three dollars and sixty-eight cents."

I took the matter to an arbiter, my mother, who ruled in favour of Mike's Poo-B-Gone. I thought Olavi might appeal it, but he recorded the transaction on his blackboard. I hoped it would still be there on payday.

With the lagoon complete, he had me dig another hole under the joey shack. It was like participating in the Great Escape from Stalag Luft III. There was no room to swing the pickaxe, and all the dirt had to be hauled out of the crawlspace in a galvanized bucket. The garden trowel came in handy, though, as did the vintage miner's lamp Olavi found in a box of auction junk—a least for a while. I wanted to use candles for illumination after our meagre supply of calcium carbide ran out, but Mom said the risk of a catastrophic fire was too high. Go figure.

When I crawled out from under the house for the last time, my stepfather cut a hole in the floor of the joey shack and lowered a prefabricated wooden box lined with plastic into it. I wondered why he had not cut the hole first so that I didn't have to lay on my stomach and chip away at the hardpan for a week in near darkness, but at that point could not be bothered to ask. All I wanted was the dollar he promised me.

I was curious about the hole's function and hoped it was not designed as an overflow tank for the sewage lagoon.

"What's the thing for?" I asked.

"It's a cistern," Olavi announced with pride after capping the underground infrastructure with a plywood hatch. "It will hold about forty-five gallons of water, and it won't freeze in winter because it's under the house."

It seemed a good idea in theory because we were hauling drinking water from the lake in plastic garbage cans that took up most of our boot room during the winter months. In practice, though, it was a poor investment. Olavi could not get the water into our trailer's plumbing system. We did not have electricity, and my mother felt that a mechanical pump placed in the middle of the hallway would be inconvenient. The rectangular box sat empty beneath the house for years, though I often wondered if the body of a certain Finnish immigrant might fit inside it.

My parents had a never-ending list of projects for me. Sadly, they did not have a never-ending supply of money. After a few years of this nonsense, I looked elsewhere for employment. Ranch owner Jude O'Brian was happy to help, or at least seemed to be. She hired Olavi to put her hay up one year, and he, in turn, hired me. I was responsible for stooking bales and hauling them to the barn. At the end of the season, when all of Jude's hay was in, Olavi submitted our combined invoice. The old girl took one look at it and refused to pay. Olavi settled for half of what was owed to him. Once again, I was left holding the empty bag, though forgoing my cut ensured our family ate for another month.

I had better luck working for Richard Dyck, the father of one of my classmates at Grassy school. The Man with Two First Names and No Last One—or, as my mother called him, "the African antelope"—hired me part-time one summer to help him lay a new water line. My digging prowess had preceded me.

Dik-Dik was a short, squat farmer with a humungous bald head that looked as though it had been designed as a flesh-toned projectile for *HMS Victory's* thirty-six-pound cannon. Two decades later, while watching ABC's *Wide World of Sports*, I thought he had graduated from farming to prizefighting because he bore an uncanny resemblance to boxer Eric Esch, the man better known in pugilistic circles as Butterbean.

Nearly illiterate and taciturn in the extreme, Dik-Dik preferred to communicate with me using hand gestures and subtle-yet-incisive grunts. He got annoyed when I failed to interpret his instructions.

Dik-Dik and I were standing at the bottom of a deep, muddy trench in late June. He had a length of plastic pipe in one hand and was motioning with the other at something on the ground. In addition to his feet, there were four objects in attendance: a shovel, a large boulder, a sixty-foot piece of flex hose, and me.

"You want the piece of hose?" I asked.

Dik-Dik shook his round head, which on the day in question was topped by a green hunter's cap that would have made Elmer Fudd proud. He repeated his initial gesture with greater emphasis.

"Hand you the shovel?"

Judging from the explosion of guttural noises that escaped his mouth, I had guessed wrong yet again.

"Move the rock out of the way?" I was so sure of his intent this time that I bent down, wrapped both arms around the giant lump of conglomerate, flexed my legs like a weightlifter, and raised it waist high.

More exasperated hooting. I dropped the rock and stared at him with incomprehension.

A deeply religious man, Dik-Dik sighed and looked skyward as if asking God to give him patience and not idiot farmhands.

"No, boy," he said at length. "Move out of the way."

I did.

Working with Dik-Dik was stressful for another reason. A decade earlier, he had been diagnosed with a severe cardio-pulmonary condition. Doctors had fitted him with a mechanical pacemaker, one of the first of its kind in BC, and you could hear its miniature valve ticking whenever he was near. When the work we were doing grew tedious, I fantasized that I was Captain Hook, and my thickset boss was the crocodile that swallowed a clock. It was entertaining, though a bit unnerving at times. I feared the ticking might cease at some point during my employment, perhaps due to a failure of the battery that powered the medical device or maybe a bout of apoplexy, and I would be forced to save him by way of mouth-to-mouth resuscitation. The man's fondness for homemade garlic sausage potent enough to deter vampires made the prospect too horrifying to contemplate. I vowed to try jump-starting him with booster cables and a twelve-volt battery before placing my lips anywhere near his.

Dik-Dik didn't pay well. I spent the better part of a summer working for him, earning just enough to buy new hockey skates and better equipment, but at least he settled his accounts. It was better than a kick in the butt with Jude O'Brian's frozen mukluk.

Despite the obtuseness I displayed while in his employ, Dik-Dik gave me a decent reference. It earned me another job in Streatham, a wide spot in the Ootsa-Nadina Road a few miles east of Wistaria.

Buford Atkinson ran about three hundred head of Hereford cattle on his sprawling ranch in the foothills above Ootsa Lake. By local standards, he came to the area late—right after the Second World War—but his work ethic and goodwill had earned him the respect of locals with longer tenure. The fact that he'd married the daughter of a well-known pioneer had helped cement his status as a citizen of note.

Buford was no more than fifty when he hired me, but a lifetime of hard work in adverse weather conditions had given him the dignified patina of someone far older. The man looked like he had been formed from the gnarled trunks and branches of coarsely trimmed willow trees. His appendages were uniformly long and bony—all knots and gristle and hard, stringy muscle—and he had a prominent Adam's apple that slid up and down his thin, leathery neck like a bead on an abacus rail whenever he swallowed or talked. He never left the house without a dusty cowboy hat parked on his head, and the intelligent blue eyes below its brim were countersunk in an angular face that had more lines than a topographical map of Tweedsmuir Park. He abhorred haste, did everything with an economy of movement, and walked with his body thrust deliberately forward as if heading into a strong wind.

A born-again Christian, Buford believed God was firmly in control of his life, and it gave him a humility and quiet confidence that others found reassuring. Nothing seemed to faze him because he had faith that his future would unfold as it should despite the clumsy attempts of people like me to change it, and he had infinite patience with creatures four-legged and two.

With no children of their own, the Atkinsons were forced to hire day labourers during haying season. This put them at a disadvantage because, like most hardscrabble farmers, they could not afford to pay more than minimum wage, and the only people willing to work long hours in the hot sun for such a pittance were under the age of majority. The number of available workers was further diminished at that time of the year because most kids with experience were seconded by their parents for the harvest and thus unavailable. When combined with a robust lumber market, these factors often reduced the labour pool to a single drip: me.

Buford approached my parents at the Wistaria Hall on Dominion Day and asked if I would be interested in helping him around the farm. They, in turn, asked me, and I agreed.

Mom made the necessary arrangements, and Olavi dropped me at the Atkinson home on an early morning in late July. The summer had been unseasonably wet, but the clouds had parted for the first time in weeks, and my employer was eager to make hay while the sun shone.

"Ever drive a tractor?" he asked as we headed toward a voluminous equipment shed. His movements, while not hurried, were more brisk than usual.

"Yeah," I said. "Not a lot, but some. My dad taught me."

"Good," he said, looking up at the sky. "That will save some time. The pay, by the way, is two dollars an hour. That okay with you?"

As if I had a choice. "Sure."

Buford explained the intricacies of his International Harvester Farmall to me. The dusty red beast, a relic from the 1940s, had the customary number of large rear tires in the usual locations, but its two front ones were smaller and set twelve inches apart on either side of a single steering spindle. The configuration was one I had not seen before.

"Front wheels are a bit different, eh?" I noted.

"Yes," said Buford. He placed one knobby, elongated hand on the tractor's hood and gave it a loving caress. "This old girl is what you call a narrow front tractor. She turns sharper than a regular one, so when you drive her, you have to be aware of it."

"Okay," I said.

Buford walked me through the machine's starting and stopping procedures, then familiarized me with its gearbox pattern. "Keep her in second or third when you're towing a trailer full of hay, and don't apply too much throttle. Any faster, and the bales will fall off. No need to rush. The weatherman says we've got a couple of good days ahead of us."

"Okay," I repeated.

"I've still got some baling to do, so we'll get you hauling the stuff that's already on the ground." He looked back the way we had come as another vehicle drove into the yard. "That'll be your helper."

I followed Buford into the bright sunlight. The car's rear passenger door opened, and a tall, slender figure got out.

It was a girl.

Buford walked up to her. "Good morning. Have you two met?"

We hadn't, but I had seen her at the Dominion Day celebration a few weeks earlier. She was of Indigenous descent, my height or taller, maybe a year or two older, and as slender as a spring foal. Her hair was the colour of jet and fell in a thick mantle to a spot well below her strong shoulders; her eyes were almond-shaped and perfectly spaced on either side of a short, delicate nose. But the girl's most striking feature was her mouth, which was wide and full and made my heart flutter.

I mumbled something and looked away. Buford took it as a sign that introductions were necessary.

"This is Roberta. She's staying with the Chapmans for a while and has offered to give us a hand. Roberta, this is Mike. He's one of the Turkkis."

"Hi," she said with a trace of amusement.

"Hi," I replied and shuffled my feet. Why did the old geezer have to use my last name?

"Well, we best get started," said Buford. He pointed to a flatbed trailer across the yard. "You two hook that up and follow me out."

We did as we were told. Roberta climbed beside me and sat on a rear fender without speaking. I was aware of her closeness and tried hard not to think about it.

Buford stopped his tractor and walked back when we got to the first meadow. I throttled down so I could hear him.

"You start here and work your way around this field," he said, yelling to make himself heard above the thumping of two old gas engines. "If you have any problems, I'll be in the next one."

"Where do you want the bales?" I asked.

"In the barn near the house," he replied. "When that's full, put the rest in the pole shed up the hill."

I nodded. As soon as he was gone, we left the beaten track and started loading.

The field was a large one, and it produced a lot of hay. Unlike Jude O'Brian, Buford had a stooking machine that he dragged behind his baler. It stacked the bales in pyramids without human assistance, which afforded the hay some protection from the elements and made it easier to load.

I showed Roberta how to pile the hay so it would be stable. She was a quick learner, and her strength surprised me. We soon fell into a rhythm. I would drive as close to the bales as possible before jumping off and tossing them onto the trailer. My partner stacked them, and I climbed up and helped her when the load grew too high. When the process was complete, we moved to the next stook.

Drive. Park. Load. Stack. Repeat.

It took us forty-five minutes to get the first hundred bales on the trailer. By that time, we were both sweating and thirstier than camels at a dry oasis. The chaff and hay dust stuck to us, making our skin itchy.

"How are you doing up there?" I asked as Roberta jammed the last bale in place ten feet above me.

"Fine," she answered. She had somehow found time to braid her hair, and the thick ebony plait hung down the middle of her bronze back.

"Okay, let's get this in the barn," I said. "Hold on."

I decided to show off by leaping aboard the tractor like a superhero. I had to stretch my legs wide to make the footboard, and when I did, I heard the unmistakable sound of tearing fabric.

I looked back at Roberta and took my position behind the steering wheel. My butt felt unusually warm, which caused me to look down. What I saw filled me with horror.

The ass of my pants was ripped from stem to stern. A wardrobe failure of this magnitude would not have caused me great concern most of the time, but knowing the day would be hot and dusty, I had elected to forgo underwear that morning.

It had been a poor decision. Mr. Bobbsey and the twins had escaped captivity and were sunning themselves on the broad tractor seat.

I was mortified. It was not yet noon, there were no replacement trousers within five miles, and my parents did not have a telephone. Oh, and if anyone had forgotten, my workmate was the prettiest female to set foot on the Southside in a decade.

My head slumped to the steering wheel. Why me? Why now?

"Are you all right?" I heard Roberta ask from her perch atop the bales. The concern in her voice was touching or would have been under normal circumstances. "You want me to come down and ride with you?"

I panicked. "Yes. I mean, no, I'm fine. Everything's cool, great. Just stay where you are."

I slammed the tractor into gear and pushed the throttle forward. This was going to be a long day.

As soon as we got to the barn, I leaped from the tractor and found a place of concealment from which to survey the damage to my pants. The news was not good. The seam that joined both trouser legs at the crotch had suffered a catastrophic failure, leaving me clad in what appeared to be a pair of riding chaps made from blue jean material. The only thing holding the tattered halves together was the brass button at my waist. If it gave way, there would be nothing standing between me and a charge of indecent exposure.

The situation was dire. My mind raced. How to mend the tear? Safety pins, I thought, might be a temporary fix, but even if Mrs. Atkinson had the dozen or so needed to close the gap, they would put me on pins and needles for the rest of the day. And what about my well-being under such an arrangement? Should one of the pointed tips spring out of its metal sheath, the potential for a sudden, life-altering injury would be great. Male tackle was not designed to serve as a pincushion and would object strenuously. The trauma could make having sex, both now and in the future, impossible and not just improbable.

I couldn't figure out how to remedy the problem. Eager to avoid Roberta, I climbed through one of the barn windows in search of a piece of burlap, tarp, or leather—anything that might cover me below the waterline. Sackcloth and ashes would have been appropriate and not unwelcome, but the only grain bags nearby were made of paper. Knocking the bottom out of a wooden barrel and slinging it over my torso seemed viable until I realized I had no suspenders and driving a tractor in it would be impossible.

Desperation set in. I decided my best bet was to remove the long-sleeved plaid shirt I was wearing and wrap it around my waist. Five minutes later, after careful adjustment, I had supplemented my ass-bereft jeans with what appeared to be the cross between a kilt and a loincloth. The results were mixed: my skinny, hairless chest was now on full display, but at least my genitals were not.

I crawled back out the window and rejoined Roberta. She had climbed down from the trailer and leaned against the stacked bales, arms crossed over her small breasts.

"There you are, Mike," she said. "Where did you go?"

"Nowhere. Just looking around," I replied.

She consulted her wristwatch. "For seven and a half minutes?"

I improvised. "Yeah, just checking the barn. Buford told me to make sure there were no cows inside before we started unloading."

My answer seemed to mollify her but did not end the interrogation. "Oh. Why didn't you go in this door?" She nodded toward the one behind the hay trailer. "And why are you wearing your shirt like that?"

I skipped her first question and responded with one of my own. "Oh, this?" I asked, looking down at the tartan miniskirt around my hips as if for the first time. "It was so hot and itchy that I took it off."

"Yeah, I hear you," Roberta replied, absently scratching one brown shoulder. Without warning, she stepped toward me and held out a hand. "Here, let me take your shirt. We'll leave it with my jacket in the barn."

"No!" I said with more force than was necessary. "It's fine where it is. Now can we get this hay off the trailer? It won't unload itself."

My brusque reply gave offense. "Okay, Cranky Pants," she said. "No need to get your knickers in a knot."

I don't have any knickers, I thought as I unlatched the barn door, *and I'd kill for any kind of pants.*

We unloaded the hay in silence and went back for more. I tried to ease the tension between us by telling her goofy stories about my family. She made no mention of hers; it sounded like they were a part of her life she would rather forget. After a while, though, she laughed and loosened up enough to talk about other things, mostly music and school. She attended Grade Eleven in Burns Lake and was looking forward to graduation.

I liked Roberta and thought she would make a great girlfriend if we could overcome the age deficit. But a man with ripped breeches is in no position to make advances.

By the time Buford returned, we were friends again and had hauled three hundred bales off the field.

"Mother says dinner's ready." He looked around the barn and whistled with appreciation. "You two have been busy."

I dropped the bale I was carrying and walked toward him. My outfit gave him pause, but he was of good breeding and said nothing.

Mrs. Atkinson was renowned for her cooking and did not disappoint. Lunch was fried chicken, fresh corn on the cob, and whipped potatoes smothered in thick, brown gravy. There was warm apple cobbler for dessert, sweet and crunchy and spiced with cinnamon, and a generous scoop of real vanilla ice cream if we wanted it. All of it was better than anything that had landed on my family's dinner table in recorded history. I ate everything within reach and washed it down with gallons of sweet tea flavoured with lemon wedges and honey.

We had been back at work less than thirty minutes when I realized that gorging myself on Mrs. Atkinson's rich cuisine might not have been a good idea. What started as a few belches and some generalized farting soon developed into full-blown intestinal distress. Then my guts started rumbling like Vesuvius on the eve of an eruption, and I knew the end was near.

I hoped to make it to the barn because there was an outhouse nearby that likely had adequate capacity to contain what ailed me, and, if it did not, there was enough manure around it that a few tonnes more would go unnoticed. My insides had other ideas. We were ten minutes from the target when they said the gig was up and called for immediate evacuation of the premises.

Warning klaxons went off in my head. I slipped the tractor out of gear and didn't bother waiting for it to come to a complete stop before disembarking. Roberta asked me something, but sticking around to deliver a slow, measured response was out of the question. I entered the nearest poplar grove at a dead run and kept going until it was no longer feasible. The loincloth disappeared in a flash, and an instant later, there was an explosion the likes of which had not been heard since the Commies touched off Tsar Bomba in '61.

When it was over, and I came to, it felt as though my world had changed. The landscape certainly had. The blast had flattened everything within a six-foot radius of Ground Zero, and I doubted much would grow there in the foreseeable future. The carbon released by the event might help, but even by conservative estimates, green-up was at least a generation away. I had to travel far afield to collect enough living flora for clean-up.

When a semblance of personal hygiene had been restored, I grabbed the shirt and reattached it. By that time, Roberta was calling from the edge of the road.

"Are you okay?" she asked for the second time that day.

My response was the same. "Yeah, stay where you are." I should have added a surgeon general's warning, something about the dangers associated with toxic waste, but I was too embarrassed by what had happened to comment further.

"All right," she said.

Deflated, I waddled back to the tractor and resumed the journey. We had travelled about the length of a hockey rink when the palms of my hands started tingling. The sensation rapidly spread to my nether regions and became an unpleasant prickliness. By the time the tractor wheels made another twenty revolutions, I was in Hell, and the devil himself was toasting my privates with a blowtorch.

I stood up, pulled back the loincloth, and peered between my thighs. Every inch of skin from my belly button to my knees was covered with angry red welts.

There could be but one explanation: I had wiped myself with stinging nettles.

I remained standing and pushed the throttle lever as far forward as it would go. The tractor bellowed and took off like a wounded buffalo. There was a scream, and I looked behind me. The sudden acceleration had put Roberta on her back. She transitioned to her stomach and was clawing her way toward the front of the trailer when we hit a series of large mudholes. The violent movement dislodged her a second time, and she bounced around like a Mexican jumping bean until finding a handhold near the stern. I heard her begging me to slow down but did not care.

We rolled into the barnyard, and I leaped from the tractor. There was a cattle trough a short distance away. I made a beeline for it and lowered my flaming butt into the cool water. It felt so good.

I stayed in the trough until my skin stopped itching. Roberta watched me for a few minutes. I could tell from her body language that she was furious, but she got over it and started unloading the trailer.

"Sorry about that," I said when I got back. "Must have sat on stinging nettles."

She nodded and kept working.

We went back to the field for another load. Because I still had the loincloth and precious little else covering my bottom, I tried to stay on the ground where there was less chance of Roberta getting an impromptu peepshow. She got tired later in the afternoon, though, and I had no choice but to take over the stacking job. It is, I discovered, impossible to pile hay while keeping both legs clenched. At least my workmate had the decency to look away when she handed bales to me.

By four o'clock in the afternoon, the barn was full and the field almost empty. We took what proved to be our last load of the day to the Atkinsons' alternative storage facility.

Buford kept his surplus hay in a massive pole shed located atop a knobby hill overlooking the homestead. The road to it was steep, and the land on all sides sloped precipitously away. To this day, I don't know why he built it there. His corrals, barn, and other outbuildings were all down below on the flat, which meant he had to haul every stalk of feed twice. Maybe he just liked the view. Even I had to admit it was impressive; Mount Wells and the Quanchus Range seemed close enough to touch.

I wasn't sure where to park the tractor and its long load until I saw a bale conveyor sticking out of a doorway on the structure's south end. I pulled the trailer up as close as possible but left the tractor running with the transmission in neutral and the parking brake applied.

Roberta plugged the conveyor's electrical cord into an outlet on the wall, and I started sending her bales. We had unloaded about half the hay when I heard a clang and the trailer beneath me began to move.

The parking brake had let go. Pushed by the trailer's weight, the tractor gathered speed. I ran beside it for a short distance, but the Atkinson Express had left the station, and there was no way to jump aboard without killing myself. All I could do was watch as it rolled merrily away.

There was a boulder at the bottom of the hill. It was about a foot high and protruded through the thin soil like the stub of a broken tooth. If the International had been anything but a narrow front tractor, it might have rolled over the rock unimpeded. There was also plenty of room on either side of the obstruction for the tractor and trailer to pass, and a long, flat stretch beyond that would have allowed them to slow of their own accord. But fate had other ideas.

Buford's beloved Farmall struck the boulder squarely, snapping the tractor's steering pivot like a dry twig. With this crucial support member no longer present, the front wheels migrated toward the back ones. The rounded bow slammed into the ground and plowed a deep, wide trench through the gravelly soil for several yards before stopping. The Farmall's back wheels churned ineffectually for several heartbeats until friction took over and stalled the engine.

"Holy shit," said Roberta. She had left the pole shed and was standing beside me.

"Yeah," I said. "I better go find Buford."

The old farmer must have had a sixth sense for disaster because he found me. He drove to the bottom of the hill, shut his John Deere off, and stared wordlessly at the carnage before him.

I walked down.

"Sorry, Mr. Atkinson. The brake came off, and it rolled away before I could do anything."

Buford said nothing. After a few seconds, he climbed down from his tractor and walked over to what remained of the one we had been using. Its front wheels were jammed under the back ones, and the hot engine was ticking as it cooled. Yellow antifreeze bubbled through a hole in the radiator and seeped into the dry earth beneath.

Too afraid to follow him, I jammed both hands in the front pockets of my jean chaps and tried to look contrite. It was not difficult.

After a suitable period of mourning, Buford turned to me. To my surprise, he didn't cuss or throw a fit.

"Well, darn it," he said, removing the dusty Stetson from his head and running a soiled handkerchief over his sweaty brow. He refolded the cloth with care and returned it to his shirt pocket before continuing. "This tractor's not going anywhere today. You better unhook the trailer and use mine. Next time, shut the motor off, and don't leave her pointed downhill."

His words made no sense. "You still want me to work for you?" I asked.

"Of course," he said. "It's just a tractor. I've got another one, and there's still a lot of hay in the field. Besides, it looks like you could use some new trousers." Then, having said everything he needed to, St. Buford clapped the hat back on his rectangular head and walked toward the house.

I relaxed and let my breath out in a rush. I still had a job.

Roberta joined me at the bottom of the hill. "You get fired?"

"No," I said, shaking my head in disbelief. "He just said take the other tractor and keep hauling."

Roberta started to laugh, and I couldn't help but do the same. We kept it up until our stomachs hurt.

"Well, Mike," she said when we were done, "you might still have a job, but you're not going to be Employee of the Month."

"You think?" I asked, which kicked off another fit of giggling.

Roberta stayed until haying season was over, then moved back to town. I never saw her again, but I remained in Buford Atkinson's employ for the entire summer. There were no more accidents, and he paid me the agreed-upon rate without deducting anything for the damage to his machinery.

When I went back to school in the fall, the chain drive wallet in the back pocket of my new bell-bottoms had more than two hundred dollars in it.

The Streatham farmer must have been a slow learner because he tried to hire me again the following year. By that time, though, I had other irons in the fire.

The Dance

Adolescence is difficult. Experiences are magnified: successes are twice as sweet, failures doubly heartbreaking. Events that earlier or later in life do not rate consideration become crises when you're between the ages of twelve and twenty, as any teenager who has looked in a mirror and seen something less than perfect can attest.

Man, can't wait for the sock hop today. Looo-king good! Wish I had a moustache like that guy on Chico and the Man. *If I had a moustache, the girls would go crazy. Oh well, it'll come. I can already see a few hairs starting. There's a long, dark one right next to the . . . Wait, what is that thing right below my left nostril? Oh crap, is that a . . .? Oh my God, it's a big, ugly zit! Sure, it's in the early stages of gestation, but it will probably look like a third eye by lunch hour. I'll be Quasimodo. No girl will go out with me. I'll never get laid. My life is over. Might as well shoot myself and rid the world of my hideousness. I shouldn't have eaten those four chocolate bars. Where's the flesh-toned Clearasil? Oh, sweet baby Jesus, please make this a dream . . .*

Life is high drama at that age, and intense emotions, some of which we are experiencing for the first time, are the norm. We love greater, hate deeper, trust easier, and feel loss more profoundly—or we think we do. Perhaps that is why our childhood friends are remembered with such fondness. The bonds of camaraderie we formed as children are amplified by our innocence and, when viewed years later through the lens of experience, seem more meaningful and uncomplicated than the ones forged during adulthood.

The same applies to our earliest relationships with members of the opposite sex. Who can forget the angst and excitement that accompanied Valentine's

Day? I remember sitting at our chipped kitchen table with a dozen greeting cards and agonizing over how best to use them.

Should I send this one to Karen and that one to Leona, or the other way around? Is the saying "Some Bunny Loves You!" too strong for Cathy? I like her a lot, but I'm afraid to tell her in case she doesn't like me back. She's so cute, though. *Sigh* Maybe just give her this one that reads, "You're the Purr-fect Valentine." It has a kitten on it, and she likes cats. At least, I think she likes cats. Or was that Nancy? Think, Mike, think. It was only a week ago, but there was that incident with Sylvia in the bushes behind the generator shed since then. Can't get that out of my brain. But as for Nancy, I asked her to go out with me last month, and she told me to buzz off. Still, she might not have meant it, although she looked serious when she kicked me in the shins. Hmmm . . . Maybe she'll change her mind if I send a nice card. How about this one with the dumb-looking bee and the words "My heart's buzzing for you." It's not too pushy but communicates how I feel. Okay, it's decided. I'm opening it up and writing "Dear Nancy" inside. Oh crap, this card's already got Valerie's name on it. When did I write that? What was I thinking? This is so hard . . .

Flirtation was delicious and sometimes more satisfying than dating. I once told my friends that it was better to think the girl of your dreams likes you than to find out she does and is nothing like you imagined. Learning she's a dud *and* thinks you're a lower life form is even worse. No one needs that kind of rejection.

Maddy smiled at me today during the Lord's Prayer. Does she like me? I've been thinking about her friend Kim so much that I forgot all about her. She is pretty in a plain kind of way. Not as pretty as Kim, though. Kim is hot, smoking hot, so hot that just looking at her makes me sweat. Still, I've been chasing Kim for weeks, and all she does is spit at me. Not words, actual goobers. At first, it was a bit of a turn-on—she can spit farther than any girl in school and almost as far as Diggs—but Sean says that's probably not a good thing. So why not try for someone else? How about Cynthia? Does she like me? Jeez, I need to know before busting a move on her. Can't just walk up and start talking; that would be totally bogus. What should I do? This is so hard . . .

Most of us remember our first significant romance, not because it was the most fulfilling or sexually gratifying, but because the experience was novel and exciting.

Julianna (or Jules, as she was commonly known) was the younger sister of a guy ahead of me in school. She was not the most attractive girl, but her short, blonde hair, delicate features, and expressive mouth gave her an ethereal quality I found irresistible. When we first met at Ootsa school, she was withdrawn and prone to brooding, as if weighed down by an unknown trauma that could not be shared with anyone. By her second year at Grassy, though, she had cast off her burden of despair and blossomed into an effervescent, funny girl with a thousand-watt smile and dazzling blue eyes.

We dated for a while during her dark period, but it was a letdown. For several weeks we shared a bus seat on the way home from school. There was no physical contact between us and little conversation. Most of the time, she stared out the window at the passing scenery while I tried to figure out how to reach her.

Man, what's with this chick? She doesn't speak and won't even look at me. It's like someone talked her into going out with me, and now she just wishes I'd disappear so she can go back to being bummed out and alone. What have I done? This is bogus and a complete rip-off and so hard . . .

Just before the end of school, one of her friends found me and said the relationship (if you could call it one) was over. While the news wasn't unexpected or traumatic because we had never connected in a meaningful way, it still hurt enough to trigger a chemical response in my scrawny adolescent body. My adrenaline and cortisol levels must have gone through the roof because I suddenly had enough energy to power a small city.

What followed is proof that even the darkest clouds sometimes have silver linings. The breakup occurred, fortuitously, on sports day about five minutes before the one-mile race. Though long-distance running was not my forte, I entered to extinguish the anger and resentment burning inside me.

Diggs, who participated in every track and field event and won most of them, was surprised when I turned up at the starting line.

"I thought you weren't going in this one," he said.

"Jules just broke up with me," I replied. "I'm so pissed I just have to run somewhere."

"Bummer," he said as a short teacher approached with a starter's pistol. "Well, see you at the finish line."

I left the starting blocks like a bullet and made no effort to pace myself. It didn't matter. Fueled by an overabundance of teenage hormones, my feet flew around the track. I was so far ahead by the halfway point that other contestants stopped to watch me run.

The result was a school record, though perhaps there should be an asterisk beside it and a footnote that reads: "Set after taking a blow to the ego. Subsequently tested positive for rejection."

"Man, you were trucking out there," Diggs said with his customary barking laugh as we waited for our awards. "I tried to keep up, but you were going like a dog with his tail on fire. Can't believe you lapped me. You should get mad more often. Or maybe I should."

The blue ribbon I received for my efforts provided little consolation.

Two years later, my friends and I crashed an adult dance at the Wistaria Hall. The Blakely boys were playing '60s rock and roll loud enough to make your ears bleed, and people were jammed into the old place tighter than herring in a can. Everyone was drinking and sweating and shouting encouragement to the band, and so many were dancing that the scuffed pine floor laid down a half-century earlier was bouncing underfoot. A glowing wood stove at the rear of the building near the bar was adding its heat to that of a hundred bodies, and smoke from as many hand-rolled cigarettes hung in a thick cloud at head height. It mingled with the smell of ripe underarms and spilled beer and amber Canadian Club whisky in white plastic glasses half-filled with cola, making breathing a chore.

Just before midnight, seeking respite from the heat and noise, I ducked outside for some air. A gaggle of teenage girls was having an animated discussion on the front steps. They saw me, and all conversation ceased. Then, as if by some prearranged signal, all but one of them melted away like August snow.

It was Jules. She was wearing flared blue jeans and a thin white sweater over a scoop-neck T-shirt. There were tiny gold studs in each of her delicate earlobes, and they glittered when she turned toward me. Despite the absence of makeup, she looked wonderful.

I walked past her and stood a short distance away. The late autumn night was refreshingly cool.

"Hey, Jules," I said with exaggerated politeness.

"Hi," she replied.

I stretched and pretended to look at something in the heavens. "Nice night, eh?"

"Yes," she said. "The sky is amazing."

"For sure. I think I just saw a shooting star, or maybe one of those new satellites." Behind me, the band finished one song to a chorus of cheers and started another.

"What do you think of the music?" I asked the girl on the step.

"It's okay, I guess. It's not Abba or Bachman-Turner Overdrive, but it's decent. How about you?"

"Same here. Wish they played newer stuff. I can only take so much Elvis. The guy might have been the king of rock and roll in the '50s, but he's old and fat and looks like a beluga now."

She laughed. "I know. My parents listen to him like he's Jesus. It's so harsh."

The conversation fizzled. I watched Jules, head down, make little wind-rows in the dust with her white tennis shoes. Sensing my gaze, she stopped shuffling her feet and looked up. Her eyes were dark sapphires, the colour of Ootsa Lake on a sunny day. She smiled and tilted her head to one side as if in question.

My insides flip-flopped. *She's so cute. What should I do? Should I take a chance and hit on her? What if she freaks out?*

Nothing ventured, nothing gained. I walked over and sat down beside her, careful to keep at least a foot of empty step between us. Afraid to look at her in case she was recoiling in horror, I focused on the back end of a car in the parking lot. A sticker on its bumper read, "Do It In A Chevy." I was about to comment on it but changed my mind.

"So . . . what are you doing out here by yourself?" I asked.

"Oh, it's so hot and smoky inside that I just had to get out." There was a pause equal to several heartbeats before she continued, and I felt the step beneath me move as she swivelled in my direction. "Besides," she added, her voice soft and inviting, "I'm not alone, am I?"

Her words were magnetic and pulled my gaze away from the Chevrolet and its bawdy message. She was regarding me with disconcerting frankness, but there was no censure in her eyes, only humour and a trace of uncertainty.

"I guess not," I said, trying to hold her gaze. "Is it okay if I stay here for a bit?"

"Sure," she said. "I'd like that."

We talked about music and other stuff important to our generation for what seemed like minutes yet proved to be more than a half-hour. After a while, one of my friends came looking for me.

"Are you coming in?" asked Nicky, running a hand through his thick mop of dark hair. "The band is going to play *Wipe Out*." He saw Jules for the first time and took a step back. "Oops. Sorry, man. My bad. Didn't realize you were grooving out here."

I looked at Nicky and wished he would go back inside.

Jules didn't seem to mind. "It's no sweat, Nicky," she said, getting to her feet. "I should probably find Lizzi and the others."

"Catch you later?" I asked, trying to match her nonchalance.

"Okay."

Jules and I kept to our respective circle of friends for the remainder of the evening. I couldn't stop thinking about her, though. She was bright, engaging, and nothing like the girl I had dated two years earlier.

In the days that followed, I replayed the experience, trying to remember how she looked and everything she said. Each iteration brought more excitement but little in the way of clarity. I hunted for signs that she was playing me or that her perceived interest was just wishful thinking on my part.

Maybe I'm reading too much into this. After all, we only talked. But she seemed to like me. Hard to believe given that none of the other girls do. Most of them think I'm a chump. Could it be true? The liking me part, not the chump part. Maybe I should ask her out. What if she says "no?" That would really blow, and I'd look like a knob. Still . . .

Fortune favours the bold. The following Monday, wearing my best jeans, hippest shirt, and coolest flat cap, I looked for her in the big hallway that ran down the middle of Grassy school. She was standing on tiptoes and pulling some textbooks from the top shelf of her locker when I walked up. The pose accentuated her long legs and slim waist. I gulped.

"Hey, Jules," I said, trying not to stare.

She spun around, and the sudden movement sent a lock of golden hair cascading over one gorgeous eye. She brushed it away before answering.

"Oh, hi. What's happening, Mike?"

"Nothing. Just on my way to class. Got Mrs. Raymond and Math. It's bogus. You?" I did my best to sound casual, but my heart was thumping like Keith Moon's bass drum.

"I have Socials with Rickman. It's okay. He's cool."

An awkward moment followed while I tried to recall what needed to be said. I had rehearsed it the night before but seeing the object of my affection had caused temporary memory loss.

A few seconds went by. Jules shifted the books to her other arm. "Well, I guess I better get to class," she said with disappointment.

Say something, you stunned idiot. She's about to walk away. You might not get another chance.

I tried to swallow, failed, yet somehow forged ahead. "Me too, but . . . I just wanted to say that I liked talking to you at the dance."

Jules perked up. Suddenly, getting to class on time seemed inconsequential. "Me, too. It was nice. We have a lot in common."

Okay, here goes nothing.

"Yeah, totally." My tongue felt like desiccated shoe leather, but the palms of both hands were wet. I could also feel my armpits getting damp. Did I smell? Why was moisture never where you needed it?

I blundered on. "Yeah, well, after the other night, which was fun, by the way, I was thinking that . . . It might be good—great, really—if we . . . you know, got to know each other better and . . . I was wondering . . . would you, like, go out with me? But only if you think . . . feel, actually, that . . ."

Her face lit up like a neon sign at sunset. "Yes, I would."

I thought I might faint. "Cool. Far out. So . . ."

The school bell rang, saving me further embarrassment.

"I've got to go," she said, touching my forearm with her free hand. The contact, though fleeting, sent a jolt of pleasure through me that was almost electric. "See you on the bus?"

"For sure," I replied. "I'll save a seat."

Jules ran down the hall. I watched her go.

Wow, she's ace, and now she's my girlfriend. I've got a girlfriend! How cool is that?

I spun around and almost collided with Diggs. "Smooth move, Ex-lax," he said, laughing and handing me my notebook. "Sounds like it worked, though. Now, are we going to math class? Or are you going to stand here all day like Meathead on *All in the Family*?"

I couldn't help but smile. He was happy for me and trying not to show it. "Yeah, guess we better. Can you believe she said 'yes?'"

"No," Diggs said as we headed for Raymond's classroom. "She must not know what a dink you are. But she'll find out." To emphasize the point, he bodychecked me hard into the lockers. "Ha! Esposito lays out Lafleur at the blue line. By the way, you better get that thing of yours lubed up. You might finally score."

I tried slamming him back, but the guy was as solid as Windsor Castle. "Sit on it, Potsy," I said instead.

"Right back atchya," he replied, giving me another playful shove. "I guess I'm sitting by myself tonight?"

"Yep," I said with unrestrained joy.

Jules and I shared a bus seat home that night. We got along famously. We were holding hands a few days later and saying goodbye with a lingering kiss by the end of the week. Our public displays of affection became so frequent and lengthy that Bob the Bus Driver told us to dial them down a notch. "The younger kids on the bus," he said, "don't need that kind of education."

We complied and laughed about it because we were young.

Our relationship deepened with time. Though limited to passionate necking, the physical side of it was intense. But for me, it developed out of something far deeper: emotional attachment. For the first time in my short life, I was involved with a member of the opposite sex for reasons that had little to do with sexual gratification. I liked Jules as a person and enjoyed being around her. She was smart, funny, and sensitive. She liked books and enjoyed being creative with words and fabric.

Jules became my closest friend and confidant, and I believe she felt the same about me. I told her things I couldn't even tell Diggs. She learned early in our relationship that I planned to make a life for myself beyond Ootsa Lake. I didn't have to justify my desire to be more than a farmer, logger, or hockey player to her. She accepted and encouraged my dreams because they were mine.

We became inseparable. We hung out every school day and as often as possible on the weekends when I walked four miles over meandering game paths to her home beside a shallow lake. We would read together, play board games, and talk until our throats were sore. And kiss, of course—sometimes for so long that our lips looked and felt as though they had been stung by bees.

But mostly we danced. Her parents had a battered Magnavox phonograph that looked like a suitcase. The sound quality wasn't great, but that didn't matter. We would lug it upstairs to her room and play Fleetwood Mac, Elton John, and the Bee Gees. Sometimes I'd bring over my old Beatles albums, and we'd groove to the sounds of yesterday. When exhaustion set in, we put on Joe Cocker and slow danced with our bodies plastered together like wallpaper on shiplap. To this day, I can't hear *You Are So Beautiful* without thinking of Jules and those afternoons in her room.

Focusing my attention on Jules made the two of us happy, but it didn't please my friends. I saw much less of them, and they didn't like it.

Just before spring break, Jules went on a two-week vacation with her family. While she was away, I sought the company of old friends.

Sean looked askance when I dropped into the seat beside him. "What are you doing here?" he asked.

The hostility in his voice surprised me. "Sitting with you guys," I said. "Jules isn't here this week."

"And what makes you think you can?" he continued. "We don't see you for months because you spend all your time with her, and now you want to come crawling back to us?"

Hurt and feeling threatened, I went on the offensive. "Yeah, I sit with her. She's my girlfriend. That's what a guy is supposed to do, and you'd do the same—if you had a girlfriend. You're just jealous."

"Yeah, right," he said, but his tone confirmed my diagnosis. "As if I'd go out with that—"

Nicky, ever the peacemaker, stepped in before the situation got out of hand. "Okay, so you're both assholes," he said. "Did anyone watch *Happy Days* last night? Did you see what the Fonz did?"

Though the tension between Sean and I passed, it still ran like a subterranean river through our relationship. And while envy and feelings of inadequacy had fueled his words, there was an element of truth to them. He was right: I had neglected my friends. I learned too late that friendship is like a garden. You need to tend it.

At the time, though, I figured it was a good trade—a hot girl for three fun but not-so-hot guys who would always be my buddies. When Jules returned from holidays, I went back to sitting with her.

The two of us took up where we had left off. We celebrated one year together, the equivalent of a lifetime to a teenager, in the fall of '77. I had accumulated a small fortune from a summer of hay-hauling and spent it all on an anniversary gift. After trolling the Eaton's fall and winter catalogue for weeks, I sent the company a money order for one hundred dollars. In return, I got a gold-plated women's wristwatch with an ornate bezel that contained, according to the descriptor, two microscopic diamonds. I wanted to buy a ring, but Mom suggested that Jules and her parents might view it as a marriage proposal. I felt ready to make that commitment, but my mother, having wed young and suffered for it, was not keen to see me make the same mistake.

"Now's not the time for that," she said. "You've got college ahead."

"I know," I replied. "It's not like we're going to get married right away. But I want her to know I'm serious."

Mom won, and Jules got the watch. I presented my gift to her on the bus ride home from school. Much to my disappointment, she didn't cry or make a big fuss over it. She seemed excited and appreciative, yet never rendered a hundred dollars' worth of either emotion in my opinion. It left me feeling cheated and guilty at the same time.

The watch fiasco didn't stop us, or at least me, from making plans. We talked of going to university where I would enroll in a full slate of courses, and she'd take a few electives while working part-time. The subject of marriage was discussed, and we even speculated on the number of children our union might produce. The future seemed to be unfolding as it should.

And then I went on a band trip.

Because Grassy was a small school, our band included musicians from grades five through eleven. I hung out with Fergus, the classmate who first suggested I join. He had been in the program for several years and already knew the other musicians. His friends became mine by default. Within days, I was having long, intimate conversations with a saxophone player named Sam LeBourdais.

Sam was short for Samantha, and she was a pathological flirt.

I was flattered by the attention, but Fergus preached caution. "She's Kryptonite, man," he said. "Yeah, she's a bunny, but she's only playing around. It's all a game to her. She'll make you do something you shouldn't and then walk. Trust me, I know."

His warning went unheeded. "I can handle Sam," I replied. "You keep pounding your snare drum."

Sam handled me.

For eleven days, I walked the ridgeline between fidelity and deceit, basking in the glow of Sam's affection while keeping our relationship platonic. Then I slipped, and very publicly.

Half the band's brass section were my steady girlfriend's classmates, so reports of my bad behaviour soon reached her. The day after we arrived home, Jules refused to see me. The note she sent through a friend made her displeasure clear.

I cornered her in the hallway and tried to make amends. "I don't know what you've heard about Sam and me, but nothing happened. We held hands once, and that was all. It was her fault and a stupid mistake on my part. I'm sorry."

I knew it was a lie, and so did Jules. She wouldn't even look at me. "I can't see you right now," she said. There was a catch in her voice that tore at my insides.

"Come off it, Jules. Don't do this. I love you."

"Yeah, right," she said, pushing past me.

I couldn't understand her reaction. The fling with Sam meant nothing to me, so I figured it should also mean nothing to Jules. Emotional infidelity was a concept as alien to me as Einstein's Theory of Relativity.

For two weeks, Fergus acted as an intermediary between Jules and me. He backed my story and tried to repair the damage I had done.

He was, in part, successful. Just before the end of school, Jules agreed to see me.

We sat together again on the bus, though not as close as before. The distance between us wasn't just physical, and nothing I said could bridge it. The future was no longer a topic of conversation, only the past and present.

Her family moved to Burns Lake not long after school ended. About a week later, Jules and her mother showed up on my family's doorstep.

The adults went in for coffee. Jules and I looked at each other.

"Let's go for a walk," I suggested.

We slipped through a barbed wire fence into the adjacent field, then walked for a long time without speaking. The air around us felt oppressive. Grasshoppers, sensing danger, scattered from underfoot.

I stopped at a spot that provided a breathtaking glimpse of Ootsa Lake and the eroded face of Mount Wells. Both looked cold and foreboding despite the July heat.

"What's it like living in town?" I asked.

Jules shrugged. "It's okay. Way more things to do."

"I bet."

More silence.

"How are you?"

"I'm fine. Why?"

"You just seem . . . different today. Well, not just today. You have for a while."

I pulled her close. She resisted at first, then relaxed and buried her face in my shoulder. Both arms wrapped around me the way they had before the band trip, and we held each other. Her hair felt soft against my cheek, and I caught a hint of lavender perfume.

"You know I love you, right?" I whispered in her ear.

She nodded her head but did not speak.

We stood like that for a long time. The wind murmured an apology as it disturbed the tall grass around us, and unseen insects conversed with buzzes and clicks.

A distant call broke the spell. Jules pulled away and rubbed a sleeve across her nose. I realized with a start that she had been crying.

"You all right?" I asked.

"Yeah. I've got to go. Mom's calling."

We walked back. I felt farther away from her the closer we got to home.

"I can come to see you this weekend," I said. "We're going to town on Saturday."

Jules plowed onward, head down. "I don't know," she said without looking at me. "We're pretty busy right now with the move and everything."

"Yeah, I guess. How about I call? Diggs has a phone I can borrow, or I can use the one at Lizzie's house."

"We don't have one yet. It's not hooked up."

I felt a growing sense of desperation. "Oh. Okay. Well, I'll write. I'll send you a letter every week. What's your address?"

She swatted at a bug with annoyance. "Jesus, Mike, I don't know. We just moved."

"Yeah, sorry. I'll just send them to general delivery. How about that?"

"Sure. Fine. Whatever."

We got to the barbed wire fence, and I spread the middle strands apart for her. Jules climbed through and kept going. She went straight to the car and got in. Her mother was already there and had the vehicle's motor running. After saying a polite but hasty goodbye, they drove away.

That was the last time I saw Jules. I wrote her almost every day for two weeks but never received a reply.

Diggs, Sean, Nicky, and I found summer employment with the Wistaria Recreation Commission. One morning in late July, while we were taking a break, Sean asked me if I had heard from Jules.

"No," I replied. "Nothing."

Sean smirked. "Yeah, I guess that's because she's riding around town in Jimmy Hudson's Trans Am. I heard they're going out, and he's already banged her."

Jimmy Hudson was a few years older than me and famously overweight. He had a face like a Gloucestershire hog and waddled when he walked.

The shock and hurt that appeared on my face brought a smile to Sean's. He revelled in my pain for a few seconds before continuing.

"Oh, sorry, man," he said with false regret as my world crumbled. "I thought you knew. Guess it's a real bummer to know she left you for the fattest guy in town, eh?"

He laughed when I got up and walked away.

Sean was right: Jules's betrayal stung. A lot.

How can this be happening? We made plans. We were going to be together forever. Why are you wrecking things, Jules?

In retrospect, our breakup should not have come as a surprise. The writing may not have been on the wall after my infidelity, but it was in my high school yearbook.

"No matter what happens," Jules wrote on the last page a few days before school ended, "I will always love you. I'm sorry for everything, and I hope you are always happy. I hope I will get to know you better in the future, but I know I will always remember you. Best of luck, Jules."

Somehow, her final note and its intimation got lost among all the banal inscriptions from other classmates. I discovered both last year while going through a box of keepsakes from my childhood and realize now that Jules was lost to me long before the end of school. Her last visit in July, and the embrace we shared in the meadow near my home, were the final movements in a dance that started twenty months earlier beneath a spray of stars outside Wistaria Hall. I thought the music was still playing; she knew it wasn't.

I haven't seen Jules in forty years. The torch I carried for her at sixteen was extinguished long ago. I found my soulmate, that kindred spirit with whom anything can be shared. But I haven't forgotten the sensitive girl with the pixie face and bright smile. I wonder what became of her. Did she discover her niche in the world, meet someone, have children, find happiness? Or is the dance still underway?

Where the Rubber
Meets the Road

All my Southside friends were driving by the time they reached double-digit birthdays. I was not so fortunate. My parents did not own a farm or a logging show—or much of anything, really—so there was no urgency to teach me driving skills. Olavi was our designated driver, and he kept a firm grip on the car keys.

Diggs taught me to drive. If not for him, I might still be commuting by bicycle, which can be unpleasant when there's a foot of snow on the ground.

My friend was at his wit's end after the ten-speed bicycle he had been riding suffered catastrophic failure. He appealed to his Uncle Jem for a new one, but the old farmer wouldn't hear it. I suspect Jem knew of Diggory's two-wheeled exploits and felt that he would be responsible for his nephew's untimely demise by purchasing a replacement bicycle. Faced with a choice, Jem elected to "go big or go home." He one-upped every parent in the community and got Diggs something better: a truck.

Diggory's new ride was a Willys Jeep from the Korean War. While the four-wheel-drive's fluorescent red body had more holes than a cheese grater, and the front windshield was a spiderweb of cracks, its cast-iron four-cylinder remained as reliable as the sun. Diggs was prohibited from driving on the main road, but that was not much of a restriction because there were so many abandoned skid trails on the Southside that he could still find his way to almost any destination. If the trip took a little longer, so be it. He had all the time in the world, or so it seemed. When you're fourteen, you have no sense of your mortality, and the years do not weigh on you like they do when you are forty.

The Willys was tired and slow; its top speed was thirty-five miles per hour, attainable only with the assistance of gravity. Yet even with bald tires and stale gasoline, it could go anywhere. Diggs drove it through mudholes that would have mired a water buffalo. When faced with a world-class bit of muck, he used the Jeep as a bulldozer and made a path around the obstacle, knocking down small trees like matchsticks.

We spent hours puttering through the meadows along Ootsa Lake in Diggory's Jeep. It was transportation, recreation, and a mobile hunting platform all in one—and because I was his best friend, he taught me how to drive it.

He gave me my first lesson in the field near his house.

"Okay, push in the clutch. Not that pedal; that's the brake. The one on the far left. Now put it in gear."

I complied, gripping the stick shift's worn black knob and pushing it forward. After some loud grinding and a moan or two, the transmission slipped into first gear.

"Sorry about that," I apologized, knowing how much my friend loved his Jeep.

"That's okay. Just push the clutch in farther next time, right to the floor if you have to, and don't rev the motor so much." He had to shout because the Jeep's muffler had long since surrendered to the elements. "Now, release the pedal under your left foot easy, and use your right to give it some gas."

Never good with instructions, I eased off on the accelerator and popped the clutch. The old truck lurched forward and stalled.

"Push in the clutch again," Diggs said. When I complied, he reached over and pulled the starter. The red beast roared to life.

"Slower this time. Just relax."

I let the clutch out about a millimetre per second and gave the engine too much throttle. The Willys had a series of convulsions and then reeled across the hayfield.

"Let . . . off . . . the . . . gas," Diggs said as we bounced along.

I complied, and the herky-jerky motion ceased. Feeling more comfortable, I pushed down harder on the gas pedal. The engine noise went from loud to deafening and blue exhaust rolled into the cab through gaping holes in the floor pan.

"Time to shift," Diggs yelled over the din. "Push the clutch in, grab the stick in the middle, and pull it toward you."

Glancing down, I found the applicable pedal and applied some pressure but did not let up on the throttle. The old motor howled in protest, prompting a frantic search for second gear. By the time I found it, third seemed more appropriate, so I shifted again and applied even more throttle. The Willys leaped forward as if fired from a cannon. We were bounding through the field and headed directly toward the weathered picket fence surrounding Diggory's house when I looked up.

"You might want to miss that," my friend suggested.

I threw the helm hard to starboard. The sloppy steering mechanism was slow to respond, but we cleared the last fence post with at least six inches to spare. There was no time for celebration because now the truck's blunt nose was on a collision course with my friend's outhouse.

"Slow down," Diggs said with a bit more feeling.

I panicked and stamped hard on the middle pedal with my left foot. Nothing happened, probably because the truck's brakes were terrible, and my right foot was still crushing the accelerator. The outhouse loomed through the cracked windscreen.

My friend lost his cool. "Holy shit!" he said, reaching over and turning off the key.

The motor died, and we came to a juddering halt with the truck's bumper resting against the shitter. The collision caused the facility's occupant at the time, Diggory's mother, to exit with her slacks down around her ankles. It was embarrassing for everyone involved.

Despite this near calamity, Diggs never gave up on me. The lessons continued, and under his patient tutelage, I learned to drive. It was the highlight of my summer and made me feel so grown up.

I drove a little in the years that followed, but only vehicles belonging to people other than my parents. Olavi never offered to help me, and I never asked him to. Teaching someone to drive is a difficult task that requires a deep well of patience, and my stepfather had none when it came to me. This deficit, combined with our mutual dislike for one another, guaranteed the experience would be disagreeable, if not disastrous.

Farmers often hired me during haying season, which allowed me to practice with farm machinery. Yet driving a tractor is one thing, piloting an automobile another. While their operating procedures are similar, they are very different animals. Because they are built tougher and go slower, tractors are more forgiving of operator error. The same cannot be said of automobiles.

A person who can drive a car can learn to operate a tractor but, as I soon learned, the reverse is not always true. Guiding Buford Atkinson's John Deere through an empty hayfield did not prepare me for driving an automobile on a narrow road used by other motorists, some of whom were little better at it than me. Neither did the Cullen Driving School for the Mechanically Inept, which honed basic driving skills like turning, accelerating, and shifting, but provided almost no instruction in braking and stopping. In Diggory's Jeep, the latter was often achieved by running into a quasi-immoveable object, e.g., a sapling or anthill, and then letting friction do the rest.

As my eighteenth birthday loomed, I was desperate to get a license. Unlike my friends, I did not yet have an operable motor vehicle, which was an impediment. I owned one for a time, a 1970 Plymouth Fury with four doors, a perfect body, and an automatic transmission; to my displeasure, the car also boasted a V-8 motor with a cracked block, a feature the seller failed to mention. It ran just long enough to get me home, after which it became one automotive lawn ornament among many. Needing another car, I appealed to my parents for temporary use of the family sedan.

We owned five vehicles at the time, two of which ran, but Olavi was unwilling to give me the keys to either of them. I was, however, able to negotiate a lend-lease deal with my mother. She granted me access to her Volkswagen Beetle, an oxidized relic about the same age and colour as the Berlin Wall, and offered to teach me the road rules.

While eager to drive the Bug, I was not keen to have my mother instruct me. By her admission, she was a terrible driver who should have been prohibited from operating anything more complex than a tricycle. The fact that she was authorized to do so by the Province of British Columbia was a testament to the licensing system's inadequacy back in the day. She was a hazard to herself and everyone else on the highway, and I feared her involvement would only guarantee me failure. But with no other options, I took her on as a co-pilot.

We practiced in the hayfield near our home. Thanks to Diggs, I was somewhat proficient by that time and soon graduated to short trips on Wistaria Boat Landing Road. After several weeks of trial and error, Mom felt comfortable enough to let me drive her to events on the Southside.

She had to break me of some bad habits, though. Diggs had stressed the importance of always taking the shortest route to any destination, which I later determined was not good advice when applied to left turns on narrow gravel roads frequented by logging trucks. Mom also told me that drifting, i.e., intentionally oversteering to cause the automobile's back end to lose traction on tight turns, was inappropriate and likely to result in misfortune. I wasn't so sure. The technique seemed to work fine for Nicky, the kid who taught me the skill, but I agreed to refrain from doing it whenever my mother was aboard.

I got my learner's license just before winter set in, leaving me with no time for further study. We also lacked a vehicle that would pass a safety inspection, so I relinquished the car keys and postponed my assault on the motor vehicle branch.

Mom and Olavi found me a car at an auction sale the following spring. My new ride was a 1975 Dodge Monaco that had started life as a police interceptor, and the government auctioneer in charge of the proceedings said it was roadworthy. Based on this statement and a cursory visual inspection, my parents bid $250 for a car no one else wanted, thus earning the right to drive it home.

Equipped with a 440-cubic-inch engine and a four-barrel Holley carburetor, "Purple Ugly" went like a bat out of Hell and consistently got six miles to the gallon. The car had its problems, though, and they included a crumpled right fender that gave it a quizzical expression. It also tended to drift right at high speed due to a pronounced S-bend in its frame—something Olavi's investigation failed to detect—and the rear doors would not open from the inside because the previous owners felt uncontrolled egress from the back seat would be detrimental to public safety. But these defects were, at least in my parents' opinion, minor ones. I agreed and took possession of my first reliable motor vehicle.

I drove the car around Wistaria for several months on an expired temporary permit, which allowed me to hone my driving skills to a blunt point while saving money. I also stopped cutting corners, though not for safety reasons. There was no need to take shortcuts of this ilk because the old Dodge was low-slung and hard-sprung and stuck to the road like Krazy Glue. After several weeks of good behaviour, I convinced my mother she no longer needed to accompany me.

As soon as she was out of sight, I started working on a new set of bad habits, one of which was speeding.

Purple Ugly was a monster. Even though the car's tired motor had about a million miles on it and smoked like a dumpster fire, it had horsepower to spare. I refrained from doing burnouts because the health of its three-speed automatic transmission was questionable—only God and the RCMP knew how many times sudden acceleration had been necessary in its previous life—but I had no qualms about putting the hammer down in a controlled manner.

As I soon learned, there was a prompt and very gratifying response whenever Purple Ugly's gas pedal was depressed. Push it halfway to the floor, and the speedometer would go from thirty miles per hour to sixty in about three heartbeats; apply a little more pressure, and the trees visible through the side window became a delicious blur. But the real thrill occurred when the accelerator was suddenly matted, causing the carburetor's two additional fuel jets to open wide and say, "aah." When they did, that big, beautiful collection of pistons and valves and worn-out camshafts under the dented purple hood bellowed like an angry bear and launched itself down the road so fast that gravitational forces pushed me back into the threadbare bench seat. It was a joyous experience, like being Han Solo after the hyperspace lever in the *Millennium Falcon* had been pulled. I half expected Chewbacca to trill his approval from the right side of the cockpit.

Yet, for every action, there is an equal and opposite reaction. As soon as the speedometer shot to the right, the needle in the fuel gauge started going in the opposite direction at an alarming rate. You could do the speed limit at an idle in Purple Ugly, but as soon as you gave the old girl her head, gasoline and oil consumption went through the roof. Gas jockeys in Burns Lake still blame me for the 1979 energy crisis. I started picking up hitchhikers so someone could me give me status reports during liftoff.

"How's my fuel looking?" I asked one terrified passenger as the four-barrel kicked in, and we screamed past a long line of cars headed for the ferry.

"Uh, you're okay," he said nervously. "Still three-quarters of a . . . half a . . . a third of a tank and going down faster than a stone thrown into deep water. Maybe you should slow down, kid, before you're out of gas or we're both dead."

"Okay," I said, easing off the throttle.

We made it to town, but not before stopping at Southbank for more rocket fuel.

I managed to avoid killing myself or anyone else that summer. But the clock was ticking, and by August, I could no longer put off the inevitable.

I had to take my road test.

Examinations frighten me. It doesn't matter how much I study for them or how well I know the subject matter. Even skill-testing questions on contest entry forms cause me to break out in a sweat. I would rather remove my toenails with needle-nosed pliers than face ten questions on a sheet of foolscap and a time limit for answering them.

Dr. Hastings once told me that my testophobia was caused by fear of failure. I thanked him for stating the obvious and asked what could be done about it.

"Not much," he said with a shrug. "You could take more tests. It's called exposure therapy. You do something more often to get over your anxiety about it. Drugs can also help, but they only treat the symptoms, not the cause."

I took the pills he offered and left. Taking more tests to alleviate my fear of them made about as much sense to me as turning into a skid. It might work, but there was a good chance the cure would be worse than the disease.

Mom booked me for a road test a month later. She told me I had one shot at passing it. "If you fail, you'll have to wait until next year because the examiner won't be back until you've gone off to school."

Thanks, Mom. That's just what I needed to hear.

I read the BC Driver's Handbook so many times that sections of it are still burned into my memory. Because parallel parking was deemed an essential skill, I lined all our wrecks nose to tail in the field and practiced backing the Dodge into a spot between two of them. The car was so long that I needed about an acre to make it work, but I kept at it. To improve my ability to start on a hill without rolling backward, I parked on the steep grade below Wistaria Hall, shut the car off, and started it again. Thanks to the automatic transmission, that part was easy, though it caused the little stick inside the oil pressure gauge to drop like a cardiac victim because all the engine lubricant had drained to the rear of the oil pan.

I got no sleep the night before the test. When it got light enough to see, I got up, took two of Dr. Hasting's wonder drugs, and headed for the ferry. My road test wasn't until 9:30 a.m., but there was no harm in getting there early, right? Besides, I figured I could use the time to familiarize myself with Burns Lake's six traffic signs.

The pills relaxed me. Partway to Ootsa Lake, I jammed a bootleg copy of the *Saturday Night Fever* soundtrack into Purple Ugly's new cassette player, cranked the volume, and did my best impression of Barry Gibb. If dogs barked, I didn't hear them. When it got warm inside the car, I rolled down my window and revelled in the breeze that blew through the opening. It smelled like warm aspen leaves, dry hayfields, and dirty motor oil burning on hot exhaust manifolds. It was great to be young and behind the wheel of a fast car.

Even the flat tire I suffered at the top of Chicken Creek Hill didn't cause me concern. I pulled over, replaced it with the spare, took another pill, and continued the journey.

That is when things started to unravel. Halfway between Jim Hurdle's place and the Takysie Lake junction, I noticed the Dodge's steering was sloppier than usual. The car always wandered the road like a freighter with a broken rudder, but this was different. A trickle of unease pushed through my drug-induced euphoria, and I pulled over for a look.

The problem was the left front tire, which was slowly going flat.

I looked at my watch, then the sky. It was seven-thirty in the morning, the ferry was scheduled to leave Southbank in a half-hour, and there wasn't another spare within ten miles.

The hole in the tire didn't seem catastrophic, so I pulled out the spark plug pump I had permanently borrowed from Olavi's toolbox and set to work.

For the uninitiated, a spark plug pump is a device for inflating tires. The forerunner of the portable electric compressor, it consists of a standard air nozzle connected to a long, thin hose, on the opposite end of which is a threaded metal pipe. To use this bit of mechanical wizardry, you remove one of your vehicle's spark plugs, insert the threaded pipe into the cavity, and connect the air nozzle to whatever needs blowing up. Then you start the car and let engine compression do the work.

It did not take me long to make the necessary connections. I pumped up the defective tire, replaced the spark plug, hopped in the car, and took off.

I had to repeat the process five miles down the road. To save time, I left the threaded piece of metal in place after the tire was reinflated and hit the road with seven-eighths of my previous engine capacity. I would have kept the air nozzle attached to the tire's valve stem too, but a short test run showed that the pump's rubber tubing became hopelessly snarled after a journey of fewer than one hundred feet.

The Dodge voiced its displeasure by backfiring like a brigade of Tiger tanks at the Battle of Kursk. Domestic animals within a mile of me that day still haven't stopped running.

Three stops and twenty-two minutes later, I reached Grassy Plains, but time was running out. With the Francois Lake ferry scheduled to leave Southbank in less than eight minutes, I pumped the left front tire up until it threatened to explode, coiled the air hose around the car's bent antenna, and took off like Apollo 13.

Even with seven cylinders, Purple Ugly had jam. It gobbled up the miles. I took my foot off the accelerator in Danskin, then reapplied it with greater force and let the Holley carburetor propel me to my destination. Despite weighing more than two and a half tonnes, the car was airborne much of the way.

I landed at Southbank and was the last car on the ferry.

I got to town with ten minutes to spare. There was no time to have the tire repaired, so I pumped it up and took another benzodiazepine instead. Then I bought another day permit for the car. There was no point in purchasing a year's insurance until I knew the results of my road test. The car still had a quarter tank of gasoline, which I hoped would be enough for a half-hour of city driving.

It would have been nice to return the spark plug to its rightful place in the engine, but that crucial chunk of metal and porcelain had gone walkabout somewhere between Grassy Plains and Southbank. It was last seen atop the carburetor, but that had been light years earlier, so the air pump remained tethered to the cylinder head. It was better to vent unburnt fuel into the atmosphere through a quarter-inch rubber tube than spew it into a confined space containing a lot of loose electrical cables. The driver's handbook was silent on the matter, but I assumed that sparking a catastrophic engine fire while transporting a representative of Her Majesty's Government would not be in my best interest.

The examiner, a fat guy in a three-piece suit, came out of the building with a sheaf of papers, took a long, hard look at my car, and winced. Then he climbed in behind me and started the interrogation.

"License and registration," he demanded.

I dug out both documents and handed them to him.

"This says you bought a temporary permit today. Is that true?"

"Yeah, the other one was going to expire. That's okay, right?"

He shrugged. "I guess. Where is your accompanying parent?"

"You mean my mom?" I said, looking at him in the rear-view mirror. "I dropped her at the grocery store so she could get some stuff. I'll pick her up when we're done."

He looked skeptical and gestured toward the front of the car. "What's that rubber thing wrapped around the antenna?"

The flow of lies continued. "Oh, that? Don't know. I thought it was a hood ornament. Came with the car. Probably some new kind of pollution control device."

"Hmph," he said. "And that sound I hear . . . Is air leaking from somewhere?"

"Yeah, it's from the spare tire in the trunk behind you. Had to change it on the way here."

"What about those pills on the dash? They yours?"

"No, they belong to my mom. She's excitable."

The guy shook his head sadly. "You're from the Southside, aren't you?"

"Yup," I said. "How'd you guess?"

He didn't bother answering.

Samuel L. Clemens, the famous American humorist better known as Mark Twain, once said that he lived through some terrible experiences, a few of which happened. His comment is an accurate description of my road test.

I stressed myself out for nothing. The examiner had me drive around Burns Lake for ten minutes before parking in front of the arena. The fact that it was summer and there were no other vehicles within a block of the place did not seem to matter to him. He never asked me to start on a hill, use hand signals, or change lanes. There were no trick questions. It was laughably easy.

"Okay," he said as we chugged along Francois Lake Drive. "You can head back now."

I pulled in front of the government building, slapped the transmission into park, and turned off the ignition. The sound of escaping air was loud in the silence that followed.

"Well, you passed," he said after a moment. "Come inside, and we'll do the paperwork."

His door lever clicked several times without effect, and there were some thumping noises behind me as he tried to exit the vehicle. After a moment of suspense, he asked, "My door seems to be stuck. Can you let me out?"

I did, and the rest, as they say, is history. My walking days were over. I celebrated this rite of passage by purchasing another spark plug and a year's worth of liability insurance.

Purple Ugly served me well for years. I sold it to a kid who wanted to compete in the Telkwa Demolition Derby. I did not witness the car's demise, but those who did say it acquitted itself admirably and sent many lesser vehicles to the boneyard before running out of gas.

My love affair with the automobile, which has outlasted one marriage and more vehicles than I admit, continues. It drives my wife crazy.

Crossroads

It was just after eight on a cloudless Saturday in late August. The sun had heaved itself over the rolling hills east of our house almost two hours earlier and was already hinting at another day of heat. But for now, at least, the morning was cool and perfect for walking.

I trekked alone down O'Brian Road with a faded green backpack slung over my thin shoulders. I held a fishing pole in one hand while the other clutched the handle of a battered metal tackle box. It had not rained in more than a month; my scuffed high-top running shoes were already powdered to the ankle with a fine dust that rose in grey puffs with each unhurried step, and the air was redolent with the subtle tang of desiccated pine needles. Insects droned in the shallow weed-filled ditch six feet to my right, black-capped chickadees tittered in the nearby willows, and a scruffy brown rabbit bounded across the ribbon of gravel ahead of me before disappearing into a grove of immature spruce.

My objective was the intersection of three old logging roads at the base of Bald Hill, a weedy hump of glacial till that had been cleared years earlier for hay production. It was there that I expected to meet Diggs, Sean, and Nicky, my best friends and fishing partners, for a weekend trip to Mumford Lake.

Mumford was an amoeba-shaped body of water bordered by swamp and wooded ridges. Despite being small and shallow—Diggs assured us it was only twelve feet deep—the lake was loaded with rainbow trout. The fish didn't grow very large, but there were lots of them, and they took almost any lure.

It was agreed weeks earlier that my friends and I would mount an expedition to the lake as soon as haying season was over. We had not seen much of each other since school let out. After hauling bales in the hot sun, a weekend at Mumford would be a great way to recuperate before heading back to class.

After another fifteen minutes of walking, I left the main road and headed southeast along an old skid trail. Little more than two dried ruts in the mud separated by a mat of dead grass, it skirted the foot of Bald Hill and crested a slight rise before rushing toward its confluence with two similar tracks that ran south and east.

The guys were waiting for me in a small clearing where the three roads met.

"Took you long enough," Diggs said as I approached. He sat on a stump, his long legs stretched out, his large, bony hands folded around an ancient spinning reel. He'd let his hair grow since I had last seen him, and it now hung almost to his shoulders in a rough facsimile of a mullet.

"How long have you been here?"

"About an hour," he answered, focusing again on the reel.

"He's bullshitting you. We just got here," Nicky said with a grin. The younger boy stood on the far side of the clearing. He had attached a heavy lead sinker to the end of his fishing line and was trying to cast it into a dusty Stetson that lay upside down in the grass twenty feet away. He finished retrieving his line as I watched, raised the rod tip, and flicked it forward again. The lead weight flashed dully in the sunlight before landing inside the hat.

"Good cast," I said. "Where's Sean?"

"Taking a dump," Diggs answered without looking up. He'd pulled a wad of fishing line off the reel and was trying to untangle it. "Second time since we left. Must have eaten something rotten."

"Technically, I was leaving a dump, but it's still there if *you* want to take it, Cullen." Sean emerged from the brush, fingers tugging at the zipper of his faded jeans. He was wearing a new ball cap with a bronze military badge attached to its bill. His long blond hair sprouted in all directions from beneath it. "And I didn't eat anything rotten, just a bunch of muffins. They always make me go."

He saw me and nodded.

"Nice hat," I said. "What's the metal thing on it?"

Sean finished buttoning his jeans and waddled over. He took the cap off and handed it to me. "It's my dad's unit insignia. He was a tanker during the war. Drove a Sherman at Normandy."

I admired the object before handing it back. "Cool. What's happening?"

"Nothing," he said, sliding the cap back onto his head. "Same old, same old. You?"

"Zip. Jude O'Brian didn't pay me again."

"You're shitting me," he said. "How much did the Crypt Keeper stiff you?"

"About a hundred. Worked most of the summer." I sniffed, then added, "Olavi got paid some, but not everything he was owed. She said we used too much gas."

Sean gave me a look of commiseration. "That blows, man. What you going to do?"

I shrugged. "I don't know. Nothing, I guess."

"Don't be a pansy. Find something of hers you like and take it. How about—"

"What he should do," said Diggs, pausing in his work, "is quit working for the old biddy. I told you before: she never pays anyone."

"Or burn her house down," Nicky suggested with a chuckle. He punctuated the statement with another long cast that fell about a yard beyond its intended target.

"No, that would bring the fuzz out," I said.

"Probably not. She likely hasn't paid them either," replied Diggs. He had his fishing reel in one hand; the other held a rat's nest of eight-pound test line. He surveyed the mess in front of him, then added, "Christ, this is a fucking disaster."

"I've got extra line. Why don't you bucket that jumble and start over?" Without waiting for an answer, I placed my tackle box on the ground, opened it, and dug inside for a fresh spool of nylon filament.

"Here," I said, tossing it in his direction. "Take as much as you need."

He freed up one paw and deftly caught the roll. "Thanks." Raising the reel to his mouth, the big kid bit his old line off close to the spindle, then started tying on fresh stuff.

Sean made a show of checking his wristwatch. "We going to blow this Popsicle stand? It's nearly nine."

"Give me a minute, for Christ's sake. I want to get this fixed," Diggs said, cranking the reel's handle like an organ grinder in a hurry. The small spool of line danced at his feet.

"Okay, okay," Sean replied. "Don't freak out on me."

We waited. Nicky kept casting, the weight landing in the flattened grass with a soft thump every few seconds. Sean extracted an apple from his pack, polished it on his plaid work shirt, and took a bite. A hawk cut lazy circles in the sky above us as it hunted for field mice.

At length, Diggs finished his repairs. "Okay," he said, throwing the burlap grain sack containing his camping gear over one shoulder. "Let's book 'er."

We headed east along the old skid road. The way was straight and flat and bordered on both sides by slender white-trunked aspens for the first mile, easy travelling and wide enough to accommodate the four of us walking abreast. The sunlight felt good on my face, like a warm caress. It was a great day to be sixteen and in the company of friends.

"So, you hear we're getting a new bus driver?" Nicky said. "Bob's packing it in."

The news came as a shock. Bob had been driving the Wistaria bus for as long as anyone could remember—so long that he seemed as much a part of the vehicle as its engine and transmission.

"No kidding?" asked Sean.

"Nope. Told me himself. Going to retire."

"That's what I heard, too," confirmed Diggs. "Harvey Stapleton is supposedly taking over."

"Be weird having someone else as a bus driver," I said. "Wonder what Harvey's going to be like."

We gave the matter some thought. Bob was a dinosaur, and driving the school bus for two decades had left him deaf to anything short of a nuclear blast. The previous year, Ralph set off a firecracker while seated in row ten. Bob hadn't batted an eye. The old man was also lax when enforcing bus rules, even allowing kids to change seats while the vehicle was in motion.

The need to break in a new driver was unsettling. After years of travelling with Bob, we had arrived at an understanding, if not a relationship. No one knew much about Harvey.

"Harv will probably be okay," Nicky said after a moment, though his comment lacked conviction. "He won't take shit like Bob did, though. No more spitball fights."

The prospect of holstering our spitball shooters was disappointing. We'd had some terrific battles in the past.

"For fuck's sake," Diggs said at last. "Why the hell are we talking about this? School doesn't start for another week."

Diggs loathed school. He had never liked it much, but his disdain had developed into hatred during the last few years. He had difficulty with everything but math and physical education. Numbers and sports were his things, words his nemesis. He just wanted to finish the unpleasant task and get on with life.

He was right, though. Today we were on our way to Mumford Lake.

"Hope the fish are biting," I said.

Diggs snorted. "At Mumford, they're always biting."

We walked in companionable silence for a time, each content to savour his thoughts. Mine revolved around food. Though it was only a little after nine, the prospect of eating fresh rainbow trout fried in butter was tantalizing. My stomach rumbled its agreement.

"Man, I'm hungry already," I said.

Nicky laughed. "You're always hungry."

Our quartet rounded a turn and saw a ruffed grouse crossing the dirt track ahead. The stocky bird advanced cautiously, its delicate head bobbing with each halting step.

"Fool hen!" said Diggs.

The big boy dropped his sack and looked for something to throw. The abrupt movement caused the grouse to take flight. It left the ground in a blur of stubby wings but, with the stupidity typical of the species, went only a short distance before settling on the lower branch of a juvenile pine. It squinted down at us and peeped with alarm.

We followed our friend's lead and pried stones from the cracked mud. The air was soon filled with missiles designed to knock the bird from its perch. None found their mark. The hen bobbed and weaved like a prizefighter.

Sean swore. "Bugger won't sit still," he said as his latest toss flew wide. "It's harder to hit than Ali doing the rope-a-dope."

"Do you blame it?" I laughed as my last rock disappeared into the forest beyond. "We're like a bunch of hungry savages."

"Spoken like a real Turkki," he replied.

Diggs muscled his way to the front. "Move, girls," he said. He licked the rough stone in his hand for good luck, took careful aim, and let fly.

His rock struck the grouse in the chest. It fell from the tree with a choking cry of alarm and lay flapping on the ground.

Diggs ran forward, scooped the bird up, and wrung its neck with a hunter's callousness. The casual violence made me gulp.

"Great throw," said Nicky.

"Eat it now or later?" Diggs asked, the bird dangling lifelessly in his hand.

"Now," said Sean before anyone else could answer. "They're better fresh."

Nicky and Sean started a fire with paper matches and dry twigs while Diggs field-dressed the grouse. The bigger boy placed a foot on each wing and pulled on the bird's spindly legs. Nothing happened for a second, then there was a sickening crackle of connecting tissues as most of the skin and feathers came away in one smooth motion. After that, he only had to remove the head and entrails.

"There we go," he said, placing the tiny carcass on a skewer over the flames.

We sat around the fire and watched the lean red meat cook. Despite the bird's violent demise, the smell of it roasting made my mouth water. My friend turned the spit a few times each minute to ensure even cooking. When the bird was done, he divided it into four equal portions.

I devoured mine and murmured in appreciation. It tasted delicious, strong but not too gamey, with an undertone of ripe sweetness.

"Man, nothing like a fool hen that has been eating berries all summer. Wish we had three each," Sean said after swallowing the last morsel. He reached over and absently wiped his greasy fingers on Nicky's shirt. The dark-haired boy looked indignant and leaned away while sucking the last vestiges of flavour from one of the bird's tiny thigh bones.

"Might be a few more around," Diggs said, hauling himself erect. "Let's get going."

We doused the fire by peeing on it and resumed our journey. Word of the grouse's murder must have spread like wildfire through the forest because we saw no more game.

It was almost eleven o'clock when the four of us emerged from the tunnel of pines into a broad expanse of saw grass and stunted black spruce. The track we had followed from Bald Hill deteriorated until it was nothing more than a trail that meandered toward a stand of evergreens a hundred yards away. We could not see the lake, but a loon's forlorn cry told us it was near.

Diggs pointed to the high ground in the distance. "That's where we're going. The raft's supposed to be around there." He started across the swamp, and the rest of us followed single file, hopscotching around the wettest areas. The area smelled of green willows, stagnant water, and black mire rich with decaying vegetation.

The raft was where Diggs said it would be. It wasn't much, a half-dozen knobby logs held together with nails and scraps of lumber from an abandoned bush mill, but it appeared seaworthy.

"Where are the paddles?" I asked.

"Don't need 'em," replied Diggs. "The water's so shallow you can push the raft around with those." He pointed to several long poles lying in the grass. I picked one up and trooped aboard.

We pushed off, staying close to shore for fear the lake might be deeper than expected. Though it was midday, fish rose exuberantly around us, creating glittering rings on the water's surface as they fed on larvae and winged insects. Nicky wanted to start casting right away, but Sean suggested we find a camping spot first. Diggs agreed.

"Let's set up over there," he said, gesturing toward a rocky headland that rose perhaps a dozen feet above the lake's eastern shore.

It seemed as good a spot as any, so we adjusted course. When the shoreline was close enough, Sean tossed our motley collection of bags and backpacks onto a slip of sandy beach. Nicky freaked out when his stuff rolled into the water, but Diggs recovered it before anything got too wet.

With all the non-essentials ashore, we poled out as far as our sticks would allow and started fishing.

I found a bright yellow spinner and attached it to the swivel on my eight-pound test line. Then, I sent the lure flashing over the water with a flick of my wrist.

It landed with a soft plop about twenty-five feet away, and I immediately felt a sharp tug on the line.

"Got one," I said as the rod leaped and bounced in my hand.

"Me too," Sean and Nicky said a half-second later. Diggs, still fumbling with a lure, laughed and tried to hurry.

I cranked the reel's stubby handle, and the translucent line zigzagged crazily through the water as whatever had taken my lure tried to free itself. It fought with increased urgency as the distance between us shortened, and my fiberglass rod bent in homage.

I saw the fish as it emerged from the depths. It was a green-backed trout, pan-sized, with dark, mottled fins and iridescent sides that refracted sunlight. Diggs offered his dip net, but I skipped that step and hoisted my wriggling catch out of the water with the rod. It landed on the worn planking where it drummed in protest.

I reached down, grabbed the fish, and rapped its blunt head several times on the grey decking. The taut body went limp as the life ebbed out of it, and I laid it down almost apologetically before retrieving my hook.

Sean and Nicky landed their catches in quick succession. Diggs secured his lure and quickly added to the haul.

"This is nuts," noted Sean after catching his third trout in as many minutes. "The fish aren't big, but they're crazy hungry. You don't even need bait."

"Told you so," Diggs said as he made another long cast into deep water.

We fished for hours, pausing now and then to scoop a drink of water from the lake. We practiced catch and release when we had enough trout for supper, removing our barbed hooks with care from each pearly mouth before returning the fish to its habitat.

The hours slipped by, and it was late afternoon when we poled back to shore. Sean and Nicky used pocketknives to clean the trout, wiping the grimy blades on their jeans before tossing the offal back into the lake. Diggs and I hauled everyone's gear up the short, steep incline.

There was a flat, grassy spot at the top. Someone had camped there in the past, leaving behind an uneven circle of fire-blackened stones and a crude lean-to between two firs.

We lit a fire and cooked the fish in a cast-iron pan until the skin was crisp and brown and the pink flesh flaked away from the bones. Diggs opened two cans of baked beans and set them amongst the glowing coals. When the fish was cooked and the beans warm, we divided them and feasted until our stomachs protruded like oil drums.

"I'm so full," said Nicky when we were done.

"Me, too. You guys want to fish some more?"

We poled the raft to a small bay on the south side of the lake where we had casting competitions and a fishing derby. Nicky caught the largest trout, a spunky rainbow fourteen inches long, and Sean landed the most fish. Diggs tossed a homemade flasher the size of a hubcap almost fifty feet.

The sun sank behind a curtain of pines, and the air was colder when we were done. Diggs and I took positions at the front of the raft and started poling toward camp. Nicky, a hard-core angler, stood between us and kept casting. Sean sat on a stump in the stern.

"Do you smell smoke?" I asked as we neared the lake's deepest point.

Diggs tilted his head and sniffed the air like a bloodhound. "Yeah," he said, peering through the gloom toward our camp. "Hope the fire didn't get away."

Sean snickered behind us. "Uh, guys," he asked, "can we turn this thing around and put my end first?"

Three heads swivelled in his direction. Nicky shrieked in alarm.

Sean had pried up a few loose boards and used them to light a fire on the raft. Fueled by the breeze created by our passage, it licked eagerly at the dry decking in front of him.

"Jesus," said Diggs, retrieving his push pole from the dark water. "Put it out."

"I can't," Sean said with a nervous laugh as he backed away from the heat. "There's nothing to bail with. Turn around."

Nicky dropped his rod, cupped his hands, and tried to throw water on the blaze. It did little good.

I joined Diggs on the port side. Together we sunk our poles into the lake's muddy bottom and pushed outwards, but the twenty-four inches of smooth pine we held gave us no leverage.

We pried the poles free and tried again. As awkward as a loaded oil tanker, the raft started a slow turn to starboard. Behind us, the fire crackled and threw off a curtain of sparks, its flames reflecting dully on the delicate ripples in our wake.

Sean was no longer amused. "For God's sake, hurry," he said.

Nicky stopped pretending to be a firefighter and added his pole to ours. The raft pivoted, and the flames forced Sean even farther back. The rubber toe caps of his high-topped running shoes were smoking, and his heels were dangling over the fantail.

He removed his plaid shirt and tossed it over the inferno. It landed at my feet.

"What are you doing, man?" I asked with a titter of amusement.

"I don't want to get my clothes wet," Sean replied, fingers working feverishly at the button of his jeans. "Shut up and push!"

By the time we got S.S. *Ample Tinder* headed in the right direction, our friend's clothing lay in a pile amidships, and he was floating in the lake. He worked his way down the starboard side of the raft as soon as we got up to cruising speed and called for assistance in a voice that made his unhappiness clear. Nicky stopped poling long enough to pull him aboard.

"So cold," Sean whispered through lips that were turning blue. Hugging himself against the chill, he turned toward his mound of clothing and gasped.

It was smoking.

"Shit," he yelled. "My st . . . st . . . stuff's burning."

The fire had reversed direction and was headed toward us. While Sean struggled to retrieve his smoldering underwear, I glanced toward camp and tried to gauge our chances of reaching it before Diggs gave the order to abandon ship. The prognosis was not good.

Water was my least favourite element, far behind earth, air, and fire. Burning was preferable to drowning any day of the week. "We've got a bloody long way to go," I muttered.

Diggs heard me. "Don't worry about it," he said. His eyes were red from smoke, and he was panting with exertion. "Just keep pushing. We'll make it."

Sean decided nudity was acceptable under the circumstances and looked around for a pole. The flames had already consumed his, so he fought Nicky for the remaining pine shaft.

"Let go, Sean," the younger boy said. "This one's mine."

Sean cast a fearful glance over his shoulder at the advancing wall of flame and redoubled his efforts. "Give it to me. I'm stronger than you, and I can use it better."

Nicky complied, which was something the blond kid had not expected. The stick, slimy from use, slipped from his numb hands and plunged over the side.

He wailed in frustration. "Look what you've done, you dumb fuck. Now we'll all burn up."

But we didn't. The advancing fire hit a piece of rotten decking and slowed. Sean and Nicky emptied their bladders on it, making it manageable. The stench of urine and half-cooked fish was appalling.

We spun the raft again upon reaching shore and went in stern first. Diggs found a lard pail and tossed water on the flames. I grabbed his frying pan and helped. The burnt decking hissed and belched dense clouds of acrid steam.

Sean snatched his clothing and ran past us toward camp. He was already dressed and putting kindling on the campfire when we caught up to him.

These flames were welcoming, and three of us stood with palms extended toward the warmth. Sean, his clothing charred from the shipboard blaze, rotated like a chicken in a toaster oven so he could soak up the heat evenly. When the chill had been driven from our bones, we sat in a circle around the dancing flames.

Nicky was the first to speak. "Why did you spaz out like that?"

Sean stared into the glowing coals before answering. His voice was soft and low and filled with emotion when he spoke.

"We had a house fire when I was little," he said. "My brothers and I were asleep upstairs when it started. When we woke up, the doorknob was too hot to touch, and the room was filled with smoke. Dad had to get a ladder and break the window to get us out. By then, the door was burning."

We considered the matter.

"That's freaky," said Nicky.

"It was," Sean replied. "I don't think I'll ever forget it. It's, like, branded into my brain." He paused and then looked across the fire at me. "You laughed at me, Mike."

His words oozed resentment, and I tried to make amends. "Sorry. I didn't know about the fire when you were a kid."

"You knew," he said, his tone accusatory. "I told you at Ootsa when the tree fort burned."

This was getting out of hand. "Well, I must have forgotten. Chill out, man. I'm sorry for laughing, but you've got to admit that seeing the raft on fire was funny—at least at the start. Like, who lights a fire on a wooden raft?"

The other guys chuckled, but not Sean. He picked up a short branch and poked the fire like it was a caged animal. "Maybe it was funny for you," he said quietly, watching his handiwork. "But not for me."

An awkward silence followed. The campfire popped and tossed sparks into the night sky.

"Watching you poke the fire gives me an idea," said Diggs. He left the circle of firelight for a moment and came back with a bag of marshmallows. After opening it with his teeth, he sat down again and threaded one of the puffy treats onto a long, thin stick. "Anyone else want some?" he asked, proffering the bag.

The prospect of eating something gave Sean an excuse to abandon his ill humour. "Yeah, I do," he said, extending one hand toward Diggs. "Hand them over."

We found some willow sticks left by previous campers and were soon gorging ourselves on toasted mallows. Each of us prepared them differently. Diggs liked his blue rare. Sean cooked them until the insides were runny and the exteriors a golden brown. I ate mine every way but burned.

Nicky was the odd man out. He preferred his well-done.

I watched as he pulled his latest mallow from the fire. It was burning like a torch, and he let the destruction continue until the outer layer was black and the flame began to wane. Then he blew it out and used his fingers to transfer the burnt offering from the stick to his mouth. He chewed, his eyes closed in silent rapture.

"How can you eat them like that?" I asked when he was done.

"Best way," he replied, licking caramelized sugar from his fingers. "Like the man says, 'Try it, you'll like it.'"

"Ugh. It's like eating charcoal. And the commercial is for Alka-Seltzer, dude."

We quit when the bag was empty. The sticky sweetness made us thirsty, so Nicky cracked the cap on a large cola bottle and passed it around. We chugalugged the warm soda and burped with satisfaction.

"This is the life," said Sean, his earlier anger forgotten. He tossed more wood on the fire and leaned back as it crackled to life. An owl hooted three times, and I knew that somewhere in the darkness, small, furry creatures cowered in fear against the cold earth.

"It didn't call my name," I said a second later. "Did it call yours?"

Diggs tilted his shaggy head and looked at me quizzically from across the fire.

"It's from *I Heard the Owl Call My Name*," I explained. "You know, that book we had to read last year about the priest who goes to the Indian village and learns that if you hear the owl call your name, it means you're going to die soon."

"I remember now," Diggs said. "I liked Ralph's title better."

I laughed. After hearing me prattle on about the book, Ralph referred to it as *I Heard the Turkki Call My Name*. "It wasn't bad for a schoolbook. Scary in places."

"You know what's really scary?" asked Nicky. He took another hit from the soda bottle before continuing. "Sasquatches."

Diggs snorted. "There's no such thing as sasquatches."

"Sure, there is," Nicky said with conviction. "People have seen them. Some have found footprints, and that guy in the States filmed one walking through the bush."

The big boy shook his head in disbelief. "Probably a bear or some jerk in a gorilla suit. Stuff like that's not real."

Sean looked at me across the fire, and our eyes met. "Tell the story," he said.

I picked up a piece of bark and tossed it into the hot coals where it smoked and then burst into flame. "I don't know, man. They won't believe it anyway."

Nicky, on my left, turned toward me. "What story?"

"Just something that happened to my parents," I replied.

"Tell it, Mike," Sean repeated.

"Okay."

I paused, took a deep breath, and launched into it. "Before I was born, my mom and dad lived way up north around Dawson Creek. My dad was a mechanic, and my mom used to go with him when he worked on stuff. If it broke down in the middle of the night, the company sent him to fix it no matter where it was.

"This was in the '50s when the Alaska Highway went through miles and miles of nothing. I guess it still does, but the only things living up there back then were animals and crazy people."

My voice cracked. Nicky handed me the cola, and I took a drink before continuing.

"One night around Christmas time, my parents were driving back from a job way up the Alaska Highway. It was about eight at night, pitch black, and they were miles from anywhere. Far back in the sticks with no houses for about fifty miles and no one else on the road.

"It was snowing heavily, not quite a blizzard but coming down hard, and there was quite a bit on the road. The car didn't have good tires, and my parents couldn't see very far ahead, so they weren't doing more than about twenty miles an hour.

"They came around a corner in the middle of nowhere, and my mom spots something up ahead at the side of the road. They get closer, and it's this thing standing in the snowbank. It has two hairy legs like a deer, but it's not wearing any pants, just a red jack shirt, and a toque, and it's slowly rolling a snowball. The thing was looking away from them when they first saw it, but when the headlights hit it full-on, it turned to look at them. Its eyes glowed just like an animal's.

"They passed it real slow and kept driving. They didn't say a thing for about two miles, then my dad turned to my mom and asked, 'Did you see that?' She says, 'Yeah, I did.' They were quiet for maybe another mile, then my dad asked, 'Should we turn around and go back for another look?' 'No bloody way,' said my mom. 'Keep driving.'"

I paused, took another gulp of pop, and tried not to look into the bush beyond the fire.

"They didn't talk about it for days. Then they told a few people what they saw. Most folks laughed and said they were crazier than shithouse rats. The only ones who didn't were long-haul truckers who drove the same stretch of deserted highway. They just looked at my parents and said, 'We believe you. We've seen some weird stuff up there, too.'

"My parents didn't stick around Dawson Creek long after that. They moved back to Vancouver as soon as they could. But Mom still gets goosebumps every time she tells the story."

Everyone was silent for a while. The darkness beyond the campfire crept toward us.

"Scary story, eh?" I asked at length.

"Yeah," said Nicky in a voice that betrayed his unease. "It is true?"

"Yup. I know a few more, too. Want to hear about Headless Valley? It's up the Nahanni River, and—"

Sean had heard enough. "Got anything else to eat?" he asked in a blatant attempt to change the subject.

We shared a can of Alpha-Getti and spoke of other things until our fear abated, then spread our sleeping bags in a line abreast inside the lean-to and crawled into them. None of us were tired, but it was getting colder, and we knew the sun would come up in a few hours.

I lay on my back and looked at the night sky. There was only a slip of moon; low in the west, it shed little light and couldn't compete with the stars that glittered overhead like diamonds tossed across a polished sheet of Ashford marble. The Milky Way was visible on the southern skyline, a narrow stain of luminescence that leaked upwards from the jagged band of darker forest. Meteors left brief but bright trails across the heavens.

The darkness, no longer menacing, loosened our inhibitions. Beside me, Sean sighed deeply.

"What do you want to be when you grow up?" he asked.

Diggs, two bodies to my left, spoke first. "A hockey player," he said as if it were something we didn't know. "I'm going to play for Boston and set all kinds of records. Nothing will stop me."

"Yeah, me too," replied Sean. "And when I retire, I'll move to L.A. and start a refrigeration company."

The two career paths seemed oddly dissonant. "Refrigeration?" I asked.

"Yeah," he explained. "It's super hot there, and everyone wants air conditioning. I'll make a fortune."

"Huh." It didn't sound like fun to me.

"How about you, Nicky?" Sean asked.

The younger boy didn't answer right away. When he spoke, the melancholic resignation in his voice nearly broke my heart. "I don't know," he said. "Probably end up like my old man."

Nicky's father was a logger who drank too much and spent most of his free time in inebriated self-pity. None of us wanted to think our young friend's destiny also lay at the bottom of a glass.

"No, you won't," Sean said. "You'll play pro hockey too, and then you'll come to California with me. With your looks, you'll probably become the next Henry Winkler, and I'll end up washing your cars."

"Aaayyy," said Nicky, doing his best imitation of Arthur Fonzarelli. "I'd like that."

"Then again, you both could end up robbing convenience stores, going to jail, and becoming some bad man's boyfriends," I suggested.

Everyone laughed.

"What about you, Turkki?" asked Nicky.

I hesitated. How could I tell them that the dream of NHL stardom was dead for me? I would never be a professional hockey player. I just wasn't good enough and, to be honest, neither were they. None of us would set foot inside the Montreal Forum or Boston Garden unless we paid for the privilege. Yet to say as much, to admit that my future lay along a divergent path from theirs, would be to deny the validity of our dreams.

"A hockey player for sure," I said. "But if that doesn't work out, I think I'd like to be a writer."

"You mean like your mom and put stuff in the local rag?" asked Nicky.

"No, more like Peter Kent, that guy on the CBC. I'd like to be a foreign correspondent, go to other countries and report on wars and plagues and natural disasters, and then write books about my experiences. But only," I added to mollify my friends, "after my long and glorious career with the Habs is over."

The night was quiet as they considered the matter. It was Diggs who finally rendered judgment.

"I don't know about you guys," he said in his deep growl, "but everything except the hockey part sounds fucking awful. And even I wouldn't play for the Flying Frogs."

Sean and Nicky laughed, and I couldn't help but join them.

At length, the conversation petered out. The sky was already lightening in the east when we fell asleep.

Sean woke me a few hours later by pouring cold water in my ear. "Rise and shine, you lazy bum."

The sudden shock disoriented me. "What the hell?" I asked, sticking a finger in my ear and trying to plunge the water out. "Why did you do that?"

He snickered. "Because it's time to get up. The fish are biting."

I pulled on my tennis shoes and joined the others around the fire. Diggs had scrambled a dozen eggs and was eating them out of the frying pan, pausing every so often to take a loud slurp of steaming coffee from a white enamel cup. Beside him, Nicky sat on his haunches and shovelled baked beans into his mouth straight from the can, the bent spoon rising and falling with the regularity of an oil derrick. Sean had deployed a folding camp stool and was separating a banana from its peel.

Seeing the others at breakfast, I returned to the lean-to and rooted in my pack for something to eat. There wasn't much—most of it had been consumed the night before—but I found a couple of items and took them back to the fire.

I sat on a chunk of firewood and contemplated my meal options. In addition to a sleeve of soda crackers, I had a mystery can that had held down the middle shelf in our pantry for eons. Its label had gone missing, which explained why it had not been opened years earlier.

"What you got there?" Nicky asked with interest. He had finished his beans and was gnawing like a rat on a withered heel of cheddar cheese.

I turned the tin over in my hand. "No bloody idea. The label is gone."

Nicky reached over and took it from me. Holding the can up to his ear, he gave it a shake.

"What do you think?" I asked.

"Hmmm . . ." he said, his handsome face screwed in concentration. "I hear something smushing around in there. Could be beans. Definitely not soup, though. Can is not right."

He handed the can to Sean, who gave it another jiggle and listened for clues.

"Then again, it could be lima beans," the blond boy said, giving it a speculative look. "Been around a while because it's got rust around the rim. What are you going to do?"

I made a face and shrugged. "Guess I'll open it and find out what's inside."

Diggs spoke up. He had finished his eggs and moved on to peanut butter and bread. "Throw it in the fire," he suggested. "Sealed cans explode when they get hot. It's far out."

"No, I'm hungry." I motioned for Sean to return the can. "Hand it over."

He clutched it to his chest. "No way. I want to see it blow up."

"Come off it, man. That's my breakfast," I said, getting off the stump and moving toward him.

He backed away. "But you don't know what's in it. What if it's dog food? You going to eat that?"

I found myself getting annoyed. "We don't have the money for canned dog food, so it's got to be something else. Give it back."

Sean grinned and held out the tin. When I reached for it, he pulled it back and laughed.

"Don't be an asshole, Sean," I said, taking another step toward him. "This isn't funny."

The smile disappeared from his face. "Sure, it is, Turkki-shit," he said while moving to his right. "It's just as funny as me on a burning raft."

So that's what this is all about, I thought. "Come on. I said I was sorry, so give me the can. You're starting to piss me off."

Nicky tried to intervene. "Give it to him, Sean. It's his, and I want to see what's in it."

Instead of complying, Sean threw the can over my head. Diggs, still munching on a sandwich, caught it with one hand.

"Ah, come on, guys," I pleaded. "Enough is enough. I'm hungry."

The tall Wistaria boy was on the verge of granting my request when Sean spoke up. "Oh, pass it back to me. I'll give it to the crybaby."

Diggs, thinking Sean wanted to make amends, complied.

"Okay, you've had your fun," I said, turning back to my tormentor. "Give me the can so we can open it and find out what's inside."

"You sure?" he asked with a sneer.

"Yeah, I'm sure," I said. "Look, if it's anything good, you can have some. Now toss it."

Sean's eyes glinted from under the bill of his new ball cap. "Okay," he said with feigned resignation, "you asked for it."

He took a quick step forward and threw my can into the heart of the fire.

Everyone scattered but me. Grabbing two pieces of kindling, I tried to roll the squat tin out of the glowing coals.

"Get out of there, dude," Diggs yelled. He had taken refuge behind a fallen log about ten feet away and was peering over its bark-covered edge.

My eyes were watering from the smoke, and the flesh of both hands felt like it was melting off the bone. I stepped back, took a breath of fresh air, and tried again to corral the can with my sticks, but only turned it upright. The lid bulged ominously, a sign that detonation was imminent.

"Oh, shit." I dropped the kindling, took two long steps toward Diggs, and dived for cover.

The can exploded, sending flaming debris and super-heated liquid skyward. Both rained down over a wide area.

I lay still for a second and then sat up. There was a long smear of brown goo on my left shoulder.

Diggs scooped it off with a finger and placed it in his mouth.

"Beef stew, I think," he said, smacking his lips. "Not bad."

We both started to giggle.

The four of us ran around and put out spot fires. When we were done, Diggs gave me his jar of peanut butter, and I spread copious amounts of it on my remaining crackers. Nicky donated an orange to hunger relief, and I ate that too.

Sean didn't offer anything and kept his distance.

When breakfast was over, Nicky announced he was going fishing. Sean and I elected to join him, but Diggs was sick of trout and wanted to look for more grouse. He was filling his pockets with rocks when the three of us, fishing poles and tackle boxes in hand, walked away.

We paused at the lakeshore to survey what was left of the raft. While its decking was blackened and burned in several places, the big spruce logs that provided most of the floatation appeared undamaged.

"The fire cooked it pretty good," I said.

Sean tugged the ball cap with its ornate military badge down on his head. "So what?" he asked, shoving me out of the way and stepping aboard. "It still floats."

Nicky and I grabbed push sticks and followed. We poled out as far as we could and started fishing.

Disaster struck five minutes later. Wanting to send a bright lure into deeper water, I extended the tip of my rod as far behind me as possible before casting. When I whipped it forward, the sharp hook snagged on something for a second before tearing itself free and continuing onward.

The weight felt wrong. As my line flashed overhead, I realized there was something large attached to it.

The mess landed with a dull slap a short distance away.

A cry of shock and pain erupted behind me. I looked over my shoulder and saw Sean staring into space. There was a laceration on his forehead just below the hairline, and it oozed a thin trickle of blood that gravity pulled toward one sandy eyebrow.

His hand flew to the wound. He withdrew it, looked at the blood on his fingers, and then felt for his hat.

It had disappeared, and I instantly knew what I had done.

"Shit," I said, turning toward Sean. "Sorry, man."

My friend went berserk. Anger coursed through his youthful features, transforming them into a mask of hatred. He threw down his rod and moved toward me.

"You bastard," he said. Strings of spital flew from his lips and landed on my cheap coat. "You almost took my fucking eye out. And my hat's gone."

His enmity hit like a blast wave and caused me to retreat.

"Jeez, Sean, I'm sorry." I glanced at his hat floating in the lake and started working my reel. After a moment's hesitation, my hook and its catch started toward me.

"No, you're not," he shouted and took another step forward. His face was now within a foot of mine, and I leaned away from the onslaught. "You did that on purpose because I threw your stupid can of stew in the fire."

The absurdity of his suggestion elicited a nervous giggle from me. "No, I didn't. It was an accident, honest. And see, your hat is hooked on my lure." I pointed the gyrating rod tip at his wet headgear.

"Gimme that," he said and snatched the rod from my hands. The sudden movement must have dislodged my Mepps spinner because Sean's ball cap stopped its forward progress. Weighed down by the heavy military badge on its brim, the hat sank faster than a tramp steamer hit by three torpedoes.

The blond boy with a cut on his face uttered a sob of anger and frustration. He tried to snag his hat again with a quick cast, but the hook fell short. The cap disappeared beneath the waves, leaving no ripples.

Sean screamed in rage and hurled my rod into the lake.

"Hey, that's mine," I said.

"Yeah? Well, why don't you go get it?" He placed both hands against my chest and gave me a hard shove.

His sudden violence was unexpected. I stumbled backward and lost my balance, fought to regain it, and almost succeeded before one foot slipped into a gap between the raft's burnt decking. Arms windmilling, I fell into the lake.

The frigid water closed over me and forced the air from my lungs. I thrashed my way to the surface and tried to stay there with a frantic dog paddle, but my legs felt like cement and pulled me under.

I came up a second time, managed a gulp of air and a strangled cry for help. The last thing I saw before going down again was Sean. He was standing at the raft's edge, and he was smiling.

Don't panic, I thought as the water closed over my head a third time. *Do what Mom says and just relax and swim. The water's not that deep.*

I tried to fight the rising panic but could not. Though my face broke the surface once more, it only stayed there long enough to give me a hazy glimpse of Sean. The boy who was my friend had turned his back on me. I experienced a moment of outrage, sucked in a bunch of water, and felt myself go under again. This time I went deep, filled my lungs with the suffocating coldness of it, and felt exhaustion setting in. Suddenly, drawing a breath didn't seem important. My terror ebbed away and was replaced by a strange feeling of tranquility.

This is weird, I thought just before blacking out.

Diggs was looking down at me when I came to. His dark eyes were concerned, and his long brown hair was plastered like mud to his bumpy skull. I heard him say something as if from a great distance, but then I felt sick and turned my head away. A tidal wave of vomit and water poured out of me.

"He's awake," Diggs said as he gripped my shoulder. "Help me roll him over."

I felt a second set of hands, these smaller, grab my jacket. "Will he be okay?" I heard Nicky ask.

"I think so," replied Diggs. "Just give him a bit."

I lay there coughing and puking and shaking for a while, the raft's charred decking rough against my cheek. Beyond lay a glittering expanse of water. I saw a fish jump. The sun felt good on my skin.

When all the excess liquid had been expelled from my body and breathing was easier, I rolled over. Diggs was on one side of me, Nicky on the other. Their heads were so close they almost touched.

"You all right now?" asked Diggs.

"Yeah," I said. "Sort of."

Nicky looked relieved. "Man, you damn near bought it," he said. "Diggs swam from shore and pulled you out."

Sean's face entered my field of vision. He was standing behind my friends against a backdrop of blue sky. "That was crazy, man," he said with a grin. "You really scared us."

The memory of him standing at the edge of the raft returned. "You pushed me in," I said, my tone accusatory. "And then you wouldn't help."

Diggs turned and stared at Sean.

The younger boy backpedaled as fast as he could. "That's a load of crap. I didn't know the fucker couldn't swim. Besides, he lost my hat with the war medal."

My anger flared again. "I almost died, you asshole."

"Sorry," Sean said with a smug grin. Then he walked to the end of the raft.

Diggs's eyes returned to mine. I knew he was looking for signs of deceit. "Is that true? Did you lose his dad's pin?"

"No. I mean, yes, I lost his hat, but he threw my fishing rod in the lake and then dumped me in too. He was going to let me drown. Ask Nicky." I looked to the younger boy for confirmation, but he wouldn't meet my gaze.

Diggs stared at me for a moment and then pushed himself erect. "Stop whining. He apologized, and you aren't dead."

We trolled the lake for hours in search of Sean's hat and my fishing rod. It was late afternoon when Nicky finally snagged my gear and pulled it in. Diggs peeled off his clothing and went diving for the ball cap with the military badge, but he could not locate it.

The sun was already well down in the August sky when we poled the raft to shore and broke camp. The hike back along the old skid trail was a somber affair. We walked together, but there were gaps in the line. No one felt much like talking.

A breeze kicked up and brought clouds and cooler air that foreshadowed rain. When we reached the crossroads, I turned north into the wind. They went south and seemed to draw closer together.

The trip proved to be the turning point in our relationship. Though we remained friends, there was never the same camaraderie between us. Before Mumford Lake, it had always been us, but after, it seemed to be them and me.

It was our last camping trip together.

The Last Hurrah

If you grew up at Ootsa Lake in the 1970s, there was a good chance your formal education ended without fanfare in junior high. Grassy Plains school, the area's esteemed institution of longer if not higher learning, did not offer classes beyond Grade Ten. The closest senior secondary was ninety minutes away in Burns Lake, which—thanks to the broad expanse of Francois Lake—might as well have been on the moon.

Not that there was a huge demand on the Southside for more instruction in the three Rs. By the time they reached the age of sixteen, most children had experienced enough of that nonsense and were eager to enter the workforce. Many parents felt the same way. There were more jobs in the resource sector than people to fill them, and almost anyone could make a good living mowing down old-growth timber or pushing dirt around with a bulldozer. Why stay in school when you could earn more than your teachers pushing buttons and pulling levers? For most kids, it made no sense.

Southside residents who felt their progeny should get a high school diploma had two alternatives: send the kids to school in town or enroll them in correspondence courses.

Then my parents and a few others decided there should be a third option.

My mother felt that sixteen was too young an age to leave home. She was also not a strong proponent of distance learning, having served as headmaster at the prestigious Turkki Home School for Mentally Deficient Boys Named Mike our first winter after leaving Vancouver. She railed against the school board's policy of offering no more than Grade Ten on the Southside and enlisted the support of others in her cause. After several refusals and at least one turbulent public meeting, District 55 agreed to establish Grade Eleven at Grassy as a "pilot project." The course offerings were minimal and did not include science or French. Still, anyone who wanted to get closer to graduation could do so without moving to town or becoming a walking advertisement for the Ministry of Education's correspondence branch.

Sadly, only a handful of families cared enough to take advantage of the opportunity. When classes started in the fall of 1977, Grassy's inaugural Grade Eleven class had but a half-dozen students: Diggs, Fergus, two girls, a cheerful lad named Danny who had been out of the system for a year, and me. Our homeroom was a cubicle adjacent to the library.

Our group may not have been large, nor did it enjoy the school district's full support, but it did have one thing going for it: a great teacher.

Some people become teachers because they like hanging out with children. Others enter the profession because they love a specific subject and want to share their passion with others. A tiny minority choose the classroom as a workplace because they can think of nothing better to do, and an even smaller number view it as a stepping stone to more lucrative endeavours like telemarketing and assassination for hire.

To everyone's good fortune, some members of each category have the innate ability to communicate knowledge in a manner that ensures its retention, if not future use. Then there is the rare bird, the gifted empath who can not only teach the dullest topic to the most obtuse student but do so in a manner that makes the information seem relevant and the recipient of it feel blessed. The latter were scarce on the Southside, and they seldom stayed.

Mrs. Devoue was the *rara avis* of Grassy school. A tall woman with a moon face framed by straight black hair cut unfashionably short, she was committed to her calling and felt genuine affection for the young adults in her care. She had a great sense of humour, tried to connect with her students, and often went beyond the call of duty. During that final turbulent year at Grassy, our last in public school, she became a friend and ally.

And, Lordy, the woman had patience. Bucket loads of it, more than anyone else in the country. Which was good because she needed it.

Our first morning back, the school's principal—a lanky, unpleasant organism named Mr. Hetherington who was trying to retain his shitty job in a crappy school until he could collect his offal pension—interrupted our orientation with an unscheduled visit. He made it clear by his message and tone that no one was happy to see our sorry carcasses again, then stated he expected us to act like adults during what the entire faculty ardently hoped would be our last ten months at Grassy Plains school.

"I think I speak for everyone, including the board of trustees, when I say that as school seniors, you are to set a good example for the younger pupils," he said with his usual pomposity. "If you do not, there will be consequences, both for you and others who may wish to attend Grade Eleven here in the future. Do I make myself clear?"

Hetherington, a British import who had earned the nickname "Templeton" because of his freakish resemblance to the nefarious rodent in *Charlotte's Web*, had the gall to expect a response. When it became apparent none was forthcoming, he shot us a look of disgust and scurried away.

I suspect his performance was designed to frighten us into compliance. If so, it was a poor one, and the audience was not receptive. Most of us hated the man, so we resolved to be as horrid as possible.

Except with Mrs. Devoue. We spared her the indignities reserved for others.

We were all enrolled in core subjects like English, Social Studies, and Physical Education. Electives were few and ranged from the benign (Home Economics) to the dangerously malignant (Algebra). Because there were so few of us and Grade Eleven was an afterthought, we were often required to share a classroom with younger students. Diggs, Fergus, Danny, and I felt this was unbecoming of our status as Grassy's elder statesmen and vowed to take only those courses that kept us segregated from the underlings.

First block was something called Applied Business Technologies (ABT). Given the name, I thought it might prove useful, but Diggs wasn't so sure.

"Maybe for you," he said after taking a seat behind one of the school's massive Smith-Corona typewriters. "What am I going to do with one of these on the farm?" He gave the machine's "D" key an exploratory poke and was surprised when the metal typehead rose like a spectre from the grave and assaulted the black rubber cylinder in front of it. The sound was so pleasant that he repeated the action several more times.

"Stop that, Diggory," said the instructor, a nervous thirty-year-old who had not yet learned the '60s were over. She still wore her auburn hair in a towering beehive and arrived each day in a staid business suit of grey tweed.

My tall friend no longer enjoyed school and was eager to escape the institution that had imprisoned him for so long. A month before classes resumed, he was offered a full-time job driving skidder for a local man who had won at timber sale roulette. He begged his mother to let him accept the position, but she thought the timing was wrong and instead signed him up for another ten-month sentence at Grassy. He considered the exercise a complete waste of time, and his displeasure translated into general surliness with the guards.

"Why not?" Diggs asked the teacher.

His challenge made Mrs. It-Can't-Be-The-'70s uncomfortable, but she held firm. "Because you'll damage the surface of the platen."

"The what?"

"The platen," she repeated as if speaking to an idiot. "The round thing that holds the paper. You shouldn't strike the keys unless there's paper in it. You could damage the machine or leave ink on the platen."

Diggs leaned forward and peered into the machine's inner workings.

"I doubt that," he said. "Looks pretty solid to me." To prove the point, he pounded the "D" key several more times, then put all his fingers atop the buttons and pushed them down simultaneously. The result was an eight-key pileup at the type guide.

"Whoa," he said in amazement. "Didn't see that coming. Looks like I broke it. Better use another one."

He relocated to another typewriter and stared at the teacher with one hand poised over the keyboard like a bird of prey.

"Don't you dare," she said through clenched teeth, "or I will call Mr. Hetherington."

"Templeton?" Diggs asked with a snort of derision. "Go ahead. I don't sweat him."

Fergus tried to prevent the confrontation from escalating. "Here, Cullen," he said, offering our classmate a sheet of foolscap. "Put this in her first."

Diggs ignored him and used the keyboard to pound out the opening notes of *A Fifth of Beethoven*. The staccato sound of metal striking hardened rubber filled the classroom. I decided the Big Apple Band's version was better.

His actions elicited the desired response.

"The principal's office," the teacher said, pointing toward the door. "Now."

Having achieved his purpose, Diggs got up and sauntered out of the room. The teacher followed him, and they marched off in the direction of Hetherington's nest.

I groaned and looked at Fergus. This wasn't a good start.

To no one's surprise, Diggs did poorly in ABT, and it was not the only course that gave him problems. He struggled with social studies and was horrible at English. If the class involved a lot of reading and writing, or the instructor was a poor lecturer, you could bet he would never post a grade above C+.

It wasn't a question of intelligence. Diggs was as smart as anyone in the school and often proved it by mastering concepts that stumped the rest of us. If the teacher could orally communicate what needed to be known, my friend would learn it. But he was forever at war with the written word.

In retrospect, I believe Diggs had acute dyslexia. After listening to him read aloud in elementary school, an excruciating experience for him and everyone within earshot, I asked why he found the task so troublesome.

Embarrassed by his inability to read, he at first refused to answer. But I pressed him on it, and later, when we were eating lunch alone on the school's front steps, he explained his dilemma.

"The letters jump around on me," he said, "and the harder I try to make them stop, the worse it is. Sometimes I almost figure a word out, it's so close, and then the bouncing starts again, and I have to start all over." He paused as if trying to decide something, then shrugged. "I don't know. I guess I'm just dumber than you and everybody else."

The sadness and resignation in his voice made my chest ache.

"Don't say that," I said. "You're not dumb, Diggs. Look at how good you are at math. I'm terrible at it, and no matter how many times I stare at a problem, I just can't figure it out. It's all Chinese to me, but it's easy for you, like scoring goals in hockey. The math teacher sends the puck your way, and no matter how bad her pass is, you pound it into the net, the red light goes on, and everybody else sits there looking stunned because you're so damn good. God, if it weren't for you, I'd still struggle with Grade Six fractions."

"Yeah, I guess," he said, but I could tell from his tone that he didn't believe me.

What I said was true. Diggs might have had trouble with words, but he had a genius for numbers. He could add and subtract long strings of them with ease, do multiplication and long division in his sleep. The most complex algebraic formulas were child's play for him. When Mrs. It-Can't-Be-The-'70s brought one of the first pocket calculators to ABT class, Diggs refused to use it. She tried to prove the device's value by challenging him to a math competition.

"If you can add these up faster with a pencil than I can with my calculator," she said, pointing to six three-digit numbers she had arranged in a neat row on the blackboard, "you can have the rest of this class off."

"No," said Diggs, who was aware of his dismal performance in ABT. "If I win, you have to give me a pass this term."

The teacher was so convinced of the power of modern technology and my friend's stupidity that she didn't hesitate.

"You're on."

Diggs finished three seconds ahead of her, and his answer was correct while hers was wrong. We gave him a standing ovation.

It may have been the only time in school that he felt special.

The class that followed ABT on our timetable was a new one called Basic Commerce. School district officials, desperate to fill the Grade Eleven calendar with low-cost offerings that wouldn't strain the budget, had created this one just for us. We didn't know what it was, but Mrs. Devoue ended the mystery.

"I am going to teach you entrepreneurship," she said.

"What is entre . . . puny . . . er, whatever you said?" asked Danny, who was also suspicious of words containing more than three syllables.

"Business skills," explained Mrs. Devoue. "You will learn how to set up and operate your own company."

It sounded like institutionalized boredom to me, but Diggs stopped drawing hockey plays on the cover of his notebook.

"You mean, like a farm or logging show?" he asked.

"Yes, though not on that scale. But the principles are the same."

Diggs gave a noncommittal grunt as he wrapped his mind around the idea. "Huh. Might be okay."

"It will be more than okay," said Mrs. Devoue enthusiastically. "It will be cool because we will create our own business: a school canteen."

Fergus was unimpressed. "No one here needs a canteen. There are plenty of water fountains."

One of our female classmates, a dark-haired girl named Nora who lived in Danskin, rolled her eyes. "No, you moron. She means a small store."

"You got it," said Mrs. Devoue. "We'll buy things like pop and chocolate bars wholesale and then retail them to the other students. No one will have to leave the school grounds for stuff."

This was not good news. For the past few years, a shady underworld figure known as the BIC had made good money forging permission notes for students who needed a sugar fix from the Grassy Plains Store. Selling candy at school would reduce the need for my—I mean, his—services.

"I don't know if this is such a good idea," I said, shaking my head. "Parents might not like that stuff being around. Too easy for kids to get hooked on it."

Mrs. Devoue put both hands on her well-rounded hips and gave me a long, hard look. "For crying out loud, Drumstick," she said, using the nickname I had earned the previous year. "We're talking about selling candy, not heroin."

Everyone laughed but me.

"I think it's a great idea," said Nora.

"Me too, but how are we going to do it?" asked Cindy. Her family ran the country store at Southbank, so she knew something about retail. "We don't have any start-up money."

"Easy," said the teacher. "If you each put in a few dollars, say five or ten, we will have enough to purchase stock. Then, when we sell it, we can use the profit to buy more."

I remained unconvinced. We were talking big money here, and my parents didn't have much.

"What if we don't have five bucks?" I asked.

"Again, no problem," she said. "I will lend you the money at a low interest rate, which you will have to calculate as part of your homework and then pay back."

Diggs was now fully engaged. "Easy as pie," he said. "I can do that."

Mrs. Devoue smiled. "And you know what the best part is?"

Her question hung in the air for a moment like the smell of Christmas pudding. She had us on the edge of our seats.

"What?" asked Nora when the anticipation grew too great.

"As an investor in the company, you will be entitled to a share of its profits," said Ms. Devoue with a wide grin. "I am confident that if you work hard, you will learn something and make a few extra dollars. Everybody wins."

Smiles and nods all around. She now had our attention.

"Cool," said Diggs. He pulled a chain drive wallet from the back pocket of his faded jeans and laid it on the table. "Where do I sign up?"

We got to work at once. Mrs. Devoue made the business plan a class project and gave everyone a job. Nora interviewed students and staff to determine their snack needs and how much they thought they might spend on candy each month if it were readily available. Cindy got the address of an established wholesaler from her parents and obtained the company's price list. Danny, who had a gift for sales and could talk penguins into buying refrigerators, sold the canteen idea to Hetherington and developed the bones of a marketing plan. Diggs and Fergus used everyone's information to calculate our anticipated income and expenses, then found retail space in a broom closet down the hall.

I did what I was good at: writing stuff that sounded wonderful but didn't mean much.

"Whoa," Diggs said after running the numbers. They were encouraging, judging from the energetic way he was gnawing his mechanical pencil.

Fergus looked over the bigger boy's shoulder at a page of calculations. The chicken scratch would have meant nothing to me, but our classmate gasped. "No way. That can't be right, dude."

Diggs managed to look excited and offended at the same time. "It is," he said. "I've checked everything three times."

Having just inspected the broom closet, I was eager for some good news. "What's up?"

Fergus turned to me. "What's up," he said with a wink, "is that we are going to make a tonne of money."

We shared the news with our classmates. Mrs. Devoue was surprised by the projected return on investment but knew better than to question our resident math expert.

"Good work," she said. "What's next?"

Danny made his pitch. "Well, based on everyone's information, we need about thirty dollars to purchase our first shipment of candy and pop. That should last us a couple of weeks, and then we'll have to buy more."

"Okay," said the teacher. "How about this? Each of you put in five dollars. In return, you will get one of six shares in the company."

Everyone was good with the idea except Diggs, who saw the canteen as his ticket to freedom. I could see the cogs turning in his head as he did the calculations. "That's only a 16.7 percent share of the profits. I was going to put in ten dollars because I want to make enough to blow this Popsicle stand."

The rest of us snickered. There was no way he would make enough in eight months to bribe his mother. Then again, he was smart enough to cook the store's books.

"All right," Mrs. Devoue said. "You put in ten, and everyone else will invest five. That will entitle you to two-sevenths of the profit, and the rest will be split equally."

"Hmmm . . ." he said, giving himself time to do the math. "That's almost 28.6 percent, which equates to seventy-five dollars and . . . Yeah, that'll work."

The deal was struck. Cindy ordered a boatload of candy and soft drinks from Kelly Douglas & Co., promising cash on delivery, and we prepared for the grand opening. Danny offered George the Janitor free soda for a week if he would cut a hole in the broom closet and install a counter, a deal the affable man accepted in the blink of an eye. It proved to be our only lousy business decision. George, we learned too late, had a Coke dependency the size of New York City and could make the stuff disappear faster than Keith Richards on a Rolling Stones tour. He consumed two dozen bottles of the syrupy beverage in our first five days of business, then had to take two weeks off work to get his diabetes under control. We sent him a get-well card even though his misfortune saved us from financial ruin.

Our store was an instant hit. Kids were lined up at recess and lunch hour, and they seemed to have an endless supply of pocket change. We learned later that most were embezzling from their parents, but we were born-again capitalists and didn't care where the money came from as long as it ended up in the cash box.

We sold out in a week and had to buy more junk food from Cindy's parents at higher prices. It made no difference. We marked everything up one hundred percent, and it still sold like there was no tomorrow. Product was flying off the shelves faster than we could unpack it. We sold enough Pixy Stix to sink the *Bismarck*, more potato chips and chocolate bars per capita than the Redwood Food Store in Burns Lake. Kelly Douglas & Co. started calling us every Thursday to make sure we were happy with the service. It was amazing.

The money poured in. There was so much of it that we had to buy a safe and hire two bible-thumping ninth graders to accompany Nora to the credit union when she made deposits. They were the only kids at Grassy who could be trusted not to steal from us because, in addition to being afraid of what we might do to them in this life if the money went missing, they were terrified of facing God's wrath in the next.

We diversified our operations, moving into the field of publishing. Nora was good with a camera, and I could write anything, so we decided to put out a school yearbook. When Danny had sold enough advertising to cover our costs, we had a hundred copies printed and peddled them to students and staff for three dollars each. It, too, was a money-maker.

When Diggs handed out our first-quarter financial statement, it was evident that Grassy's Grade Eleven class had more money than it knew what to do with. I suggested we start a bank and lend money to students at exorbitant interest rates. My argument was simple and, I thought, persuasive: any money borrowed by our classmates, all of whom were by now hopelessly addicted to sweets, would flow back into the canteen and our pockets. Fergus was eager to serve as debt collector and had even found three bullies willing to help for nothing more than job satisfaction, but Mrs. Devoue gave the idea a resounding "no." The scheme, she said, amounted to something called loansharking and would result in expulsion if not jail time for all involved.

We found other uses for the cash and even gave some to the student council for a Valentine's Day dance. Our philanthropy did, of course, have a purpose. We set up a concession stand and made back twice the amount donated.

Diggs was a willing participant in all these activities, and his outlook on education changed. Mrs. Devoue praised his bookkeeping skills and encouraged him to pursue a career in accounting. While he still insisted his time in school would be short, he did not oppose it with his usual vigor. Once, when he thought no one was looking, I caught him in the library reading a syllabus from the British Columbia Institute of Technology. His brow furrowed, and his lips moved silently as he tried to decipher each troublesome word.

Then someone decided we were becoming too successful.

The school board didn't want us to do well. If we did, educators might have no option but to make Grade Eleven—and, perhaps, Grade Twelve—a permanent fixture on the Southside. For financial reasons, the pilot project at Grassy needed to crash and burn, and Hetherington was more than willing to help.

I was making my way back to class after a washroom break when I saw him talking in the office with Mrs. Devoue. Their conversation sounded heated, so I went into spy mode and found reason to dawdle.

"You can't be serious," I heard our teacher say.

"I am," said Hetherington. "This school does not exist for the financial enrichment of your students, and their efforts are not only impoverishing the other children but creating a litter problem. I am prepared to allow this retail establishment to continue in the short term because it fills a need and keeps them occupied. But any profits derived from its operation must revert to the school."

"But the kids are doing so well," said Mrs. Devoue. The desperation in her voice was uncharacteristic. "Some of them, even Diggory, are now thinking about staying in school until they graduate."

She meant well, but it was the wrong thing to say. Hetherington wanted nothing to do with a plan that might keep us in the system for another year.

"That is, in addition to being debatable, extremely unlikely," he said with distaste. "I have seen their report cards, Mrs. Devoue. Your students have limited potential and little interest in achieving it. Young Turkki might one day graduate and enter college, and perhaps Miss Bradley, but the others never will. Nor should they because they have neither the intelligence nor determination to finish the job. One or two might make decent tradesmen but, for the most part, they are best suited to marrying and creating a new generation of pupils for us to teach. And as for Master Cullen, well, I expect he will end up in prison."

His words were like sledgehammers, and there was a sharp intake of breath from Mrs. Devoue as they hit home.

"I disagree," she said. "All of them could graduate with a little encouragement, and Diggory has changed. He now—"

Hetherington didn't let her finish. "You are entitled to your opinion, Mrs. Devoue, and I applaud your optimism even though it is baseless. But this is not a debate, nor is Grassy school a democracy. I am the principal here, and my mind is made up. Henceforth, all monies from the canteen will be given to me for safekeeping. Do I make myself clear?"

Fearing apprehension and possible execution for espionage, I booked it back to class. I was about to tell the others what had transpired when Mrs. Devoue returned and beat me to it.

Hetherington had so little intestinal fortitude that he made her deliver the edict. She was partway through her narrative when our resident math wizard put two and two together and came up with forfeiture.

"We have to give everything to the school?" asked Diggs.

Mrs. Devoue nodded.

"You've got to be fucking kidding," he said. "You told us we could keep whatever we made. We trusted you. I gave you ten bucks."

Mrs. Devoue tried to diffuse the situation. "I know," she said, both hands held out in supplication. "And I'll see that you all get your money back. This is not what I intended."

Diggs guessed the source of our misfortune. "Templeton is making you do this, isn't he?"

Her silence spoke volumes.

"That prick!" said Diggs. "I'm going to kill him."

He threw his pencil down, slammed his chair back, and headed in the direction of Hetherington's office.

"Oh, shit," said Fergus and took off after him. We followed.

Hetherington was still seated behind his desk when the Grade Eleven crisis management team arrived, but he was leaning as far back as his oak office chair would allow. The heat-seeking missile called Diggory Cullen was trying to get both hands around the principal's scrawny neck. There was too much real estate between him and his target, so my friend attempted to make up the deficit by climbing over the desk.

Fergus grabbed a handful of the big kid's wide leather belt and pulled him back.

"Don't, Cullen," he said. "He's not worth it."

"Lemme go!" Diggs said. He was so angry that white foam had formed in the corners of his mouth. "I'm going to strangle this useless bastard."

Danny, showing admirable courage, placed himself between our berserk classmate and the principal. "Nope. We're not going to let you do that."

I walked over and put a hand on my irate friend's shoulder. His breathing sounded like the panting of a steam engine under heavy load, and so much adrenalin was coursing through his lean, muscular body that he was shaking.

"Come on, Diggs," I said. "You don't want to do this."

He shrugged my hand away and glared at me. "Yeah, I do. Someone's got to teach this rat a lesson. Get out of the way so I can do it."

"No, Diggs," I said. "Don't you get it? He wants you to thump him so he can kick you out of school. Look at him."

It was true. Our intervention had allowed Hetherington to regain his composure and reflect on the situation. With grave personal injury no longer imminent, he relaxed and watched the proceedings with keen interest.

Diggs saw that I was right. The madness leaked out of him like water from a punctured bucket.

"You're lucky, Templeton," he said as we eased him toward the hallway. "But I'm going to get you for taking our money, I swear."

His final threat, lobbed like a hand grenade over Fergus' shoulder, had no visible effect on the evil creature behind the desk.

"Perhaps," said Hetherington with a smirk, "but not immediately. As per district policy, you are hereby suspended for two weeks, and I will strongly recommend that the board of trustees make your expulsion permanent. My secretary will inform your mother and arrange for your removal from the premises. Goodbye and farewell."

Upon hearing these words, Diggs tried to return to the scene of his crime and finish it, but Danny again barred the way. "Come on, Cullen," he said. Then, in a voice so low that only the four of us could hear it, he added, "We'll figure out a way to fix Templeton's little red wagon."

And we did. While Diggs was gone, Grade Eleven's three remaining male students came up with a plan so brilliant it hurt the eyes.

Diggs served his suspension. Much to his disappointment and Hetherington's, the school board declined to extend it, thanks in large part to the efforts of my mother and Mrs. Devoue. Both women appeared at the Wistaria boy's parole hearing and spoke eloquently on his behalf. Diggs was not thrilled by this display of solidarity and left the room without comment when the decision was rendered. At that point, I believe he would have preferred life behind bars to more schooling.

When he returned to class in late February, we implemented Operation Insolvency.

The canteen's profits plunged. By mid-March, return on investment was down fifty percent. A month later, what had once been a going concern was just meeting expenses.

Mrs. Devoue and the girls could not account for the sudden change. When Hetherington noticed the sharp decline in profits and came looking for an explanation, they could not give him one.

"Demand for candy has remained steady," Cindy told him. "We had more than five hundred dollars in sales last month, but we barely broke even after buying more stock."

"Has someone absconded with the funds?" Hetherington asked, casting a suspicious glance in my direction.

Mrs. Devoue came to my defense. "No," she said. "The students record everything sold each day, and the money in our cash box reconciles with it. Surely you've seen that?"

"Of course I have," said Hetherington with a healthy dose of condescension. "Well, I expect you to do better. I have plans . . . I mean, the school has plans for that money. Many things are needed at Grassy, and the board is counting on Basic Commerce 11 to provide the necessary funds. Diagnose the problem and fix it forthwith. Perhaps another price increase is in order."

As usual, I could not keep my mouth shut. "I thought you said we were charging too much and impoverishing the students?"

Hetherington shot me a look of surprise. "How did you—"

Fergus cut him off mid-question. "We'll do our best, sir," he said, raising a hand in mock salute. "You can count on us to do our duty."

Hetherington thought he was serious. "Bravo, Mr. Wilson. That's the spirit. Well, I must be off. Other matters to attend to. Always things to do at the top."

"Right oh," Danny said in fake Oxford English when Hetherington was gone. "Got some other kids to bugger, what?"

The rest of us laughed.

"Okay, that's enough," said Mrs. Devoue. The smile on her face belied the censure in her voice. "Let's find where the money is going and fix the leak."

Four of us already knew why selling candy was no longer lucrative, and we had no intention of sharing the information. We had found a way to deplete the canteen's retained earnings without declaring a dividend. The money, per se, wasn't going anywhere; business was good, and every penny that went into the register made its way uninterrupted to Hetherington's office. Cash security wasn't the problem. It was inventory control.

Profits were down because we were eating them.

It had never been necessary to keep track of the canteen's stock. Everything Cindy ordered went out as fast as it arrived, so Mrs. Devoue decided there was little point in implementing this critical accounting measure.

We took full advantage of the weakness. Whenever Mrs. Devoue was absent from school—which, by February, was often because the strain of teaching us had taken its toll—we locked ourselves in the canteen and sampled the merchandise.

Cases of potato chips and chocolate bars disappeared overnight, and our female classmates were unwitting participants in this larceny. They should have known something was amiss because there was an explosion of generosity on our part after Diggs returned to school.

"Hi, Cindy," I said to my pretty classmate for the third time that week. It was late April, and Operation Insolvency was going as planned. "Danny and I just finished our shift in the concession, and I thought you might like something. You're partial to Coca-Cola and Old Dutch barbecue chips, aren't you?"

"Ah, that's sweet, Mike," she said with feeling, "and yes, they're my faves."

Not to be outdone, Danny dropped an Oh Henry bar on the open financial statements in front of Nora, who was still trying to follow a money trail we knew did not exist.

"Here you go," he said. "I know you like these."

"Thanks," said the recipient of his generosity. "Gee, you guys have been so nice since Hetherington threw a fit."

It's easy to be charitable with other people's money, I thought.

By May, the canteen was one feast away from bankruptcy, and our female classmates thought we were the best thing to come along since Mr. Wrigley invented chewing gum.

But all good things must come to an end, and our program of asset liquidation was no exception.

Mrs. Devoue had taken another sick day when our plan went out the window. It was the first period after lunch, and we had locked ourselves in the canteen for dessert. To reduce the risk of apprehension, we left the lights off and groped for what we wanted. It did not slow us down.

We were munching away in the darkness, as happy as trenchermen at an all-you-can-eat buffet. Then someone knocked on the door.

"Hello? Are you boys in there?" asked the luckless substitute who had the task of teaching us in Mrs. Devoue's absence.

"No," said Danny through a mouthful of what smelled like salt and vinegar chips. "There's no one in here. Go away."

The woman was neither deaf nor stupid. "I hear you," she said. "You come out right now, or I'm getting the principal."

When the response to her threat was discreet giggling, she left.

Fergus felt for the light switch and turned it on. "Well," he said with a sigh, "I guess we better get back to class before Hetherington arrives."

"Fuck 'em. You guys go ahead. I'm staying here and getting my money's worth," said Diggs. He used his large incisors to tear open another chocolate bar, then spat the bright yellow wrapper on the floor at his feet, where it joined an impressive pile of cellophane. From the look of things, the big kid had laid waste to three Coffee Crisps, two Jersey Milks, and a jumbo package of Twizzlers in ten minutes. He laughed when I told him he'd be a walking zit by the end of the week.

We were discussing the pros and cons of having one last snack for the road when footsteps approached. There was a faint metallic jingle outside the door. Then someone inserted a key into the lock and turned it.

It was Hetherington. We had been caught red-handed.

"What are you boys doing in here?" he asked.

"Having a party," said Diggs. "You're not invited. Close the door."

"Out," the principal said. "You will retire to the office immediately. I will join you after speaking with Mrs. Smeagol."

We had no choice but to comply.

Hetherington's lair was crowded with the four of us in it. None of us intended to be there long, so we made the best of the situation. Diggs, Fergus, and Danny took up positions on the window ledge while I occupied the leather chair reserved for honoured guests.

Our judge and jury rode a wave of righteous indignation into the office. I waited for him to ask if we pleaded guilty to the charges, but he skipped that formality.

"Failure to attend class is a serious offense in my school," Hetherington said. "I have one question before communicating your punishment. Did you pay for the items you ate?"

Lying was easy for a hardened criminal like me. "No," I said. "But we were going to."

The statement sounded convincing because it was half true. Hetherington stared at me for several seconds. I met his gaze even though it made my skin crawl.

"Very well," he said. "You will make restitution immediately upon leaving this office."

We rose as one and started for the door.

"Where are you going?" he asked in a high-pitched squeal that reminded us again of the rat in *Charlotte's Web*.

"Leaving," said Fergus. "You said we could go."

"I did not!" Hetherington said.

His tone made it clear he would brook no further insolence. The verdict no longer in doubt, we lined up with the sullen resignation of condemned prisoners.

Sentencing didn't take long. For Danny, Fergus, and I, the punishment was light. Because these were our first offenses—or, more accurately, the only ones we had been caught committing—we were given a month's detention and ordered to pay two dollars in reparations.

The fourth member of the Cullen Gang was not so fortunate. Diggs got kicked out of school again, this time for a month. But that was not the worst part of his sentence. He was also required to write a four-hundred-word apology to the school and read it at an assembly held solely for that purpose.

It was cruel and unusual punishment, even by Hetherington's standards. Diggs could have appealed the decision, yet he chose not to. His mother didn't force him back to class, either. By this time, she also saw education as an evil best avoided.

Diggs never again set foot in Grassy school. He found employment at Eurocan's Andrew Bay logging camp and spent his wages on a car and alcoholic beverages. The combination was a recipe for disaster, and it was not long coming. Four months after leaving school, he was involved in an automobile accident that left him with a permanent limp and no way of getting to work. He lost his job and, like many other adults with learning disabilities, slipped into despair and addiction.

He is better now. Today, the student who showed promise in Basic Commerce 11 runs the family farm and supplements his income by driving a truck. There is nothing wrong with his career choices, but I can't help wondering if he was meant to do more. With a little encouragement and a few more sympathetic teachers, Diggs might have taken another career path. Did Hetherington's sadism rob Canada of a homegrown Steve Jobs? Would Diggs, if given a chance, have revolutionized NHL player scouting with hockey's version of sabermetrics? How many others like my friend never achieved their full potential because they attended rural schools with limited resources and fewer champions?

I try not to dwell on these questions because I suspect their answers would shake my faith in public education.

As for the rest of us, Grade Eleven was our last hurrah. We finished the year, but it was interminable without Diggs. Mrs. Devoue must have felt the same way because she left the district and was never seen again. Someone told me a few years ago that she quit teaching and became a psychiatrist. If so, I'm sure she has plenty of work thanks to people like Hetherington.

Although secondary students can now take online courses at Grassy, comprehensive in-person learning has never been offered in its entirety. Some people blame us, but it's probably just a question of numbers. Diggs could give you a straight answer. He is better with numbers than I am.

Leaving Ootsa Lake

My final year of high school was an unhappy one. In retrospect, it was the winter of my discontent, but it felt like one of the other seasons. Unlike the protagonist in Shakespeare's *Richard III*, I had little cause for optimism. There was no sun of York to give me hope, no victorious battle to celebrate, no sense that brighter days were just around the corner. My first serious love interest had decided her prospects looked better elsewhere, and I was out of step with my childhood friends. I felt as bereft and defective as the play's namesake.

I spent the summer working for a local farmer, which proved a welcome diversion from my misfortunes. But my angst increased as a new school year approached. While everyone who mattered felt my education should continue, no one—not my parents, the school board, or the Ministry of Education—had a plan to ensure it did.

There was no chance of returning to Grassy school full-time. In the opinion of most teachers and trustees, Grade Eleven had been an unmitigated disaster, and they had no intention of giving the same group of miscreants another kick at the education can. Going to town for my final year of high school was an option the school district encouraged, but my mother was not keen to see me leave home at age seventeen. Her justification for not sending me to Burns Lake with the other bookish types was financial. She told anyone who asked that our family could not afford to pay for my room and board. She was right, of course; just putting food on the table and keeping a roof over our heads was often problematic for her. But I believe she had another reason.

She just did not want me to go.

I think Mom hated to depend on my stepfather for anything. If I remained in residence, at least one male in the household could be counted on to do his duty. Besides, who would listen to what she had written each week if not me? Laina was too young to appreciate my mother's literary endeavours, and Kelly preferred the works of Carolyn Keene. Olavi only cared about the stuff if it sold.

She got no argument from me because I didn't want to take Grade Twelve in town at that point. While the world beyond Burns Lake had an allure, the dirty little village that was our source of resupply did not. There were, or so I thought, no great mysteries there, no unexplored rivers to cross or mountains of adventure to climb. And having lived so long in a place where four-legged creatures outnumbered two-legged ones by a wide margin, meeting new people was difficult for me. I already had enough bipedal friends and had no immediate desire to make new ones.

Besides, my former girlfriend went to high school there, and the thought of seeing her with someone else felt like the emotional equivalent of castration.

Mom registered me with the Ministry of Education's correspondence branch in September. I never thought to pave the road to graduation with courses like Basket Weaving 12 and Music Appreciation for Dummies. Instead, I signed up for difficult ones that my mail-order counsellor said were college prerequisites. Arithmetic, which had been my nemesis for eleven years, was compulsory. I had enough sense to enroll in General Math, the academic equivalent of the common cold, rather than one of the more virulent offerings like Algebra or Calculus.

The biology course had a laboratory component involving dissection. While tricksters in the correspondence branch suggested the work could be completed at home with little more than a sharp stick and a strong stomach, they recommended taking the pickled specimens to a nearby school or hospital for further examination. Government institutions, they assured me, were not averse to providing mature students with temporary access to their facilities.

I signed up for Biology 12 in a heartbeat, but not because the course would be easy or get me into university. I had my sights set much lower.

Biology was going to be my readmission ticket to Grassy school. Under the guise of education, I could socialize with kids I already knew and maybe find a replacement girlfriend. The possibilities, while not endless, were better than those associated with home study.

My parents asked the district to let me attend Grassy one day per week. While they waited for an answer, I wrote to Fergus, the former classmate who had become my best friend. Like me, he had chosen not to attend school in town, and I thought he might also be eager to return to the scene of our most infamous crimes.

The grey clouds around me parted for the first time in months, and I felt something approaching optimism. Life as I knew it might not be over.

Fergus sent his response home with Kelly.

"Dear Mike," he wrote in a childlike scrawl at the bottom of my original letter. "Good to hear from you and about school. Go ahead and try it for yourself, but not for me. I can never go back. My parents have me working in the sawmill now, and I doubt they will ever let me go. Best of luck. Your friend always, Fergus."

His words betrayed a sense of misery and hopelessness more profound than mine. I was crushed. Nevertheless, when the school board approved my request to use the laboratory at Grassy Plains, I welcomed the opportunity.

My return was less than triumphant. I had expected Sean and Nicky, who were still in school, to greet me with open arms. They did not. When I boarded the bus at Wistaria and dropped unannounced into the seat in front of them, they stared at me as if I were a rare fungus that grew only on dung.

The reception at school was no warmer. As soon as I got there, I wanted to go home. Grassy seemed different, its long, central hallway narrower and more congested, the classrooms smaller and shabbier. The facility's inmates were not overtly unkind to me, nor did they act as though I were the ghost of a student past. Their treatment of me was far worse.

They ignored me.

It took me a half day to diagnose the problem. *I don't fit in,* I realized with a start. *Everyone has moved on except me.*

The kid who was once popular was no longer relevant.

It was such a humiliating experience that I never went back. The specimens, frogs and eyeballs and something that was supposed to be a piglet but looked like a shrunken head, stayed in their jars. I left Biology to the pointy heads with scalpels. I didn't want to be a doctor anyway.

Winter arrived in late November with a blast of frigid air and a foot of snow. I sat at a table in the living room and tried to teach myself Math, Social Studies, and Geography, feeling like life was a bullet train with no room for me. As the drifts piled up outside and the days rolled by like flickering images in a bad silent film, my sense of isolation grew. It was most acute in the evenings when Olavi turned on the twelve-volt car radio he had adapted for home use. His contraption brought disc jockeys like Wolfman Jack into our home, and their breathless excitement served as daily reminders of the world beyond Ootsa Lake.

School was a struggle, and I soon learned that the education provided by District 55 was far below provincial standards. Even Creative Writing, which had been my strength, gave me fits. I cursed the day I had agreed to take Grade Twelve by correspondence.

I resented the hand that life had dealt me and tried to rid myself of the feeling by giving it to others. I tormented Laina, picked fights with Kelly over trivial matters, engaged in verbal sparring matches with Olavi at every opportunity. Even Mom became a target of my resentment, and I criticized everything she tried to do for me. The travel trailer became a prison cell, the pine forest beyond an unscalable wall topped with viridescent spikes. Wistaria no longer felt like home. For the first time since we moved to the Southside, I saw it not as a place of safety beyond the iniquitous reach of civilization but as a backwater community fifty miles from a one-horse town located in a region that was of little consequence to the rest of humanity. It would be years before I saw it as anything else.

Adding to my misery was the sudden and unexpected appearance of acne. For reasons unknown, my face—which, while not handsome, had until then been unblemished—erupted in a mass of angry red zits. I tried to stem the crimson tide with astringent, but it only compounded the problem. By Easter, my forehead looked like the surface of Mars as seen through a powerful telescope, a wasteland of mounds and craters and ridges with a couple of barren vermilion plains thrown in for good measure. My self-confidence, already at a low ebb, took another hit.

With two months left in the school year, I was on track to complete four of the six courses needed for graduation, three of them with passing grades. I had been at odds with my English teacher because she questioned my skill as a writer. She said my poetry indicated I had no understanding of iambic pentameter, and my short stories were verbose and somewhat dark. I admit that both were bleak and not very good, but they expressed how I felt at the time and should have been worth at least a "C." She disagreed and flunked me.

"Though you comprehend the material, your mastery of it is unsatisfactory," she wrote upon reviewing my last assignment. "Perhaps you will do better next time."

There would be no "next time." I would not enroll in the course if Miss I-Can't-Do-So-I-Teach remained involved. Someone told me that instructors employed by the correspondence branch were assigned students based on the latter's last name. Perhaps, if I abandoned Turkki in favour of the name on my birth certificate—which started with a letter lower in the alphabet and was not half as derisible—I might have better luck. It was too late in the year to test the theory, so I cut my losses and mailed the teacher some moose turds disguised as chocolate-covered almonds.

Math was also a write-off, and my biology quizzes had never felt the pressure of a ballpoint pen. The chance of being accepted by a reputable university seemed remote, so I started checking out the schools that advertised in Olavi's comic books. One looked promising, so I clipped a coupon next to an ad for Sea-Monkeys and wrote away for more information. The response I received was encouraging. The company claimed anyone could earn a diploma while living at home and studying part-time. Was it true? If so, why would anyone attend university? Six easy payments of $19.99 seemed a reasonable price to pay for lifetime employment in the field of my choice. I would have forked over the money if not for the fact that I was torn between small engine repair and a fine arts degree.

Then, during a random visit to the Burns Lake Public Library, I found a syllabus from the regional college in Prince George. It was torn, well-thumbed, and a year out of date, but I stole it anyway—and entered a world of possibilities.

It was like being a kid in a candy store. There were dozens of courses on topics ranging from film appreciation to political science. Instead of just one history class, there were ten, all of them different, and there was even something new called Introduction to Personal Computing. I wasn't interested in Personal Computing if it had anything to do with the punch cards that Mrs.

Raymond made us complete in Grade Nine. The technology, I figured, was just a fad that would last a few years before disappearing into the annals of time like hula hoops and poodle skirts.

The institution's biggest selling point was that it had no second language requirement. Two years of high school French had given me just enough fluency to decipher the ingredients on a box of instant oatmeal, and I was yet to find a university that considered pig Latin a reasonable substitute.

According to the English poet Alexander Pope, "Hope springs eternal in the human breast." At that moment, it did in mine, so I filled out the college's admission form. My mother provided a letter attesting that the applicant was enrolled in Grade Twelve and expected to graduate with a C+ average. The crucial word here was "expected," which did not, I felt, bind the applicant in any way. This may have been a matter of semantics, but it was important because the applicant did not share his mother's optimism. He decided to keep his mouth shut and pen sheathed.

We mailed the documents away and waited for a response.

I heard nothing for months. Despondent, I abandoned my attempts to finish high school and started looking for a job. If it was my destiny to remain at home another year, I might as well try to make some money.

Buford Atkinson wanted to hire me again, but I found work with the Wistaria Recreation Commission. The group wanted to refinish the floor in the community hall and hired Diggs, Sean, Nicky, and me to do it. Because we only had a belt sander and some paintbrushes, a job that should have taken a couple of weeks lasted the entire summer.

The work was as physically demanding as it was boring. One of us would get down on his hands and knees and grind away at the ancient planking in a cloud of wood dust while another swept up the leavings and tried to remain conscious. This left two employees free for administrative and supervisory tasks, but because there were none, the wastrels played grass hockey in the parking lot until their co-workers needed a rest. It was perfect for anyone planning a career in the civil service.

I took the job partly because it allowed me to hang out with the guys. Over the years, as the shared passions that had once bound us together disappeared or took a back seat to other interests, we drifted inexorably apart like a handful of smooth pebbles dropped on the verge of a shallow lake. Gravity and slight imperfections had caused each to find his path to the bottom, and while still near the others, we knew the first big wave might scatter us forever. What had once been a band of brothers now felt more like them and me. I missed their companionship and felt like d'Artagnan in Alexander Dumas' classic novel *The Three Musketeers*: a participant in something great and noble yet not quite an accredited member. If anything, my pain was greater than that of the book's hero because I had once been a musketeer and knew how it felt to be part of something larger than myself.

I still hoped for reconciliation, though, and felt a summer working together might cure what ailed us. Perhaps, just as the belt sander was peeling away layers of damage and neglect inside the Wistaria Hall, working together would remove our differences and renew what had been a bright and shining friendship for six years. I still believed our group's whole was greater than the sum of its parts.

It did not happen. The experience emphasized the differences between us, the greatest of which was our plans after high school. My friends could not understand why I wanted to keep learning if my goal was the same as theirs.

"You want to make money, right?" Diggs asked me one afternoon as we drank lukewarm Coca-Cola in the shade cast by the hall's grey-shingled east wall.

"Of course," I said. "Tonnes of it. As much as I can."

"Well, why not get a job driving truck or running a chainsaw?" he asked. "You'll make more in the bush than you ever will in an office."

I doubted this was true but did not wish to argue. "Yeah, maybe. But what if I don't want to drive a truck or run a chainsaw?"

Sean joined the discussion, and his tone was antagonistic. Two years earlier, when I chose to spend time with a girl rather than him, he had decided I was no longer worthy of his friendship. Since then, the boy who was once my best friend had campaigned tirelessly for my expulsion from the brotherhood.

"Why? Is there something wrong with those jobs? My dad's a logger, and so is Nicky's."

Sensing a trap, I proceeded with caution. "No, but I suck at both of them. If Diggs hadn't taught me to drive, I'd still be riding a bicycle."

"You are still riding a bicycle," corrected Nicky.

I laughed. "Yeah, but I can drive a car now. Sort of."

Sean was like a dog with a bone and would not let the matter go. "So, what are you going to do? Be a professional student?"

He was trying my patience. "No," I said. "I don't know what I want to do. I don't even know what I'm good at."

Nicky made an obscene pumping gesture with his fist. "I know what you're good at, but I'm not sure you can make any money doing it."

"Ha ha," I said. "Very funny."

Diggs guffawed. "It is pretty funny. But seriously, why keep going to school? It's a waste of time."

I felt besieged, and my response reflected it. "Not for me, it isn't."

It was the wrong thing to say, and it left me exposed to Sean's next thrust. "Are you saying it would be a waste of time for us?"

I felt like a bomb disposal expert. One false move and everything would blow up in my face. "No, I don't mean that. You guys could go to school too, and you should. You're all smart."

"Right," said Sean. "And it's because we're smart that we're not going to college. College is for assholes who can't do a real day's work." He drained his cola in disgust and tossed the bottle at a nearby litter barrel. It broke on the receptacle's steel rim, sending shards of glass flying like shrapnel into the stubble below.

He got up and walked away. The others followed.

If I needed further proof of the widening gap between us, I got it a few weeks later.

Diggs had a driver's license and used his first two pay cheques to buy a second-hand Camaro from a guy down the road. The muscle car had left GM's Norwood plant ermine white, but after twelve years and 150,000 hard miles, most of them on the Southside, it was so bagged out and rusty that it looked like a wedge of overripe Roquefort cheese. But it was still a Camaro and a symbol of my friend's newfound independence, and I believe he loved it more than his mother.

The car was equipped with an 8-track tape player, and we took our breaks inside the cockpit surrounded by the pounding rhythms of Nazareth and Bob Seger. One morning, I spotted three rainbow trout on the corroded rear floor pan as I climbed into the car. My friend must have caught the fish before coming to work because they were already dry and stiff.

Needing to make room for my feet, I tossed the trout on the Camaro's stained rear seat.

Diggs went berserk. "What the fuck are you doing?"

"Moving the fish," I said.

"Don't put them on the fucking seat, you asshole." He shoved me out of the way, grabbed the dehydrated trout, and walked them toward the garbage can.

"I'm sorry, Diggs."

He turned on me and snarled like a junkyard dog. "You're lucky I don't kick the shit out of you. And my name's not Diggs. It's Diggory."

The animosity on his lean face was astounding, and his words felt like daggers. It was the first time he had spoken harshly to me since elementary school. All I could do was stammer a second apology.

Diggs returned after bucketing the trout and gave me another hard push before getting into the car. Nicky and Sean followed him. They slammed and locked both doors, leaving me on the outside looking in.

"Come on, man," I said to Sean.

He sneered at me. "Don't just stand there, dink. Fuck off."

It was my turn to get angry. He had left the side window down about four inches, so I reached in, grabbed a handful of his faded Van Halen T-shirt, and tried to drag him through the narrow gap.

My violence surprised him. He experienced a moment of panic before realizing I couldn't do him any harm.

"Let go of me, Mike," he said.

I did not because my mind was filled with thoughts of murder. "No way. I'm going to kill you, you obnoxious little prick."

By this time, I had him half out of his seat, and the cotton shirt he had on was stretched to the breaking point.

He rolled the window up as far as it would go and repeated his request. When I refused to relinquish my grip, he reached into the pocket of his jeans and pulled out a disposable lighter.

"If you don't," he said, holding the lighter so I could see it, "I'm going to burn you."

I didn't think Sean had the stones to do it, but he did. After giving me a chance to comply, he flicked the lighter's tiny wheel and sent a cascade of sparks onto the wick. A small tongue of flame sprang to life in his hand, and he applied it without hesitation to the underside of my wrist.

A few seconds elapsed before the heat pierced the adrenalin in my bloodstream and sent a searing jolt of pain up my arm. Then reflex took over, and I released my grip on Sean's T-shirt.

"You fucker," I said, now madder than ever.

Sean laughed, rolled up his window, and gave me the finger. He handed the lighter to Diggs, who used it to set fire to a doobie he had rolled during the conflict. The big guy took a long hit from the joint, then handed it to Nicky, who cranked the car stereo so none of them had to listen to me swear.

I paced around the car like an enraged bear before going back into the hall. My wrist felt like someone had poured molten lead on it, and the skin was already blistering. With no bandages available, I tore a strip from the bottom of my shirt, poured water on it from Sean's canteen, and wrapped the burn.

The anger inside me boiled away, leaving in its place the stewed remains of our friendship and a profound feeling of sadness.

When coffee break was over, the guys got out of the car and came inside. Diggs walked past me without saying a word, knelt beside the electric sander, and resumed work on the floor. Nicky, also mute, picked up a broom and started sweeping. Sean found something of interest at the far end of the hall and had enough sense to stay there for an hour.

We finished the job two weeks later. While there were still moments of goodwill between us, they were fleeting. The earlier disagreement had been the tsunami that separated us forever. Our estrangement did not seem to bother Sean, Nicky, and Diggs—they hung out together and partied as if nothing had happened—but it troubled me. Fergus, my remaining friend, lived thirty miles away in Cheslatta, so I had no one who could help me through it.

The situation at home was no better. Olavi felt my temporary employment entitled him to rent and tried to requisition fifty dollars a month from me. I appealed to Mom, and she agreed the money would be better spent on tuition if any institution accepted me. My stepfather relented, but he was not pleased and made his feelings known.

"If he's not going to school, he should be paying room and board," he complained. "He's an adult now."

And there was still no word on my application. Time, I knew, was running out. People with experience told my parents that affordable housing was difficult to find in Prince George. Anything still available this late in the year, they said, would be the urban equivalent of a pig pen.

Despondency enveloped me, and with it came the same breathless panic I had experienced years earlier after falling into Mumford Lake. I could not take another winter at home. I tried to relax and figuratively tread water, but it did no good. The depths, cold and viscous, pulled at me, and I knew, just as I had at Mumford, that it was only a matter of time before I drowned.

Just before I went under for the last time, the college registrar's office threw me a lifeline in the form of an acceptance letter. It was like getting word that a relative you thought dead was, in fact, alive. I was ecstatic because escape was imminent.

The momentous day arrived. Olavi loaded us into the van with two suitcases full of things I thought might be helpful in the months ahead. We drove to Prince George. The sun was shining in an Indian summer sky dotted with fluffy white cumulus, and Canada geese were standing in the stubbled fields beside the road. Like me, they were headed elsewhere.

There was a momentary hitch at the registration desk when I could not produce my Grade Twelve transcript. Mom told a bald-faced lie and said it was in the mail. The overworked registrar took one look at the growing lineup behind me and decided proof of graduation was not immediately required. She took my cheque and handed me a receipt.

And with that, I was a student again. By the time college officials discovered they had been duped, I had changed my name and disappeared into the education woodwork like a bark beetle among mature pines.

We spent the night in a fleabag motel on Second Avenue while Mom and Olavi sifted through advertisements for rental accommodations. They found me a place to stay, a dingy bedroom in a home owned by a raging alcoholic who had never heard of the Twelve Steps, and booked it sight unseen over the telephone.

The following day after breakfast, my parents drove me to the place that would be my home for the next eight months. A cool wind had sprung up overnight, bringing with it dark clouds. The air smelled like rain and dry lightning.

Mom and Laina started crying the moment we pulled up to the curb. Even Kelly, who had said earlier that she would be glad to see me go, looked distressed. I hugged them all, said goodbye, and got out. Olavi pulled my heavy suitcases from the van and set them on the sidewalk. If my departure troubled him, he never showed it.

I lifted my baggage and struggled toward the house. Mom said something as I passed her, but with both hands full, all I could do was nod and keep going.

Five steps later, my burdens felt less weighty, and the morning seemed brighter. My pace quickened, and a door opened in front of me. I moved toward it eagerly and felt a tingle of excitement. It was like starting a book I had wanted to read for a long time.

I turned the page and never looked back.

Afterward

It has been more than four decades since I lived on the Southside, and the place is different now.

The big changes started in 1982 when the area's primary employer, Eurocan Pulp & Paper, closed the Andrew Bay logging camp and moved its operations to East Ootsa. The company held a giant auction sale at the old site, and Southside residents watched as structures that had been part of their lives for nearly two decades sold to the highest bidder.

Closure of the Andrew Bay camp marked the end of an era on the Southside, and you could see that knowledge written on the faces of those who witnessed it.

When Eurocan left, so did most of the people. Loggers who had worked for the company packed their belongings into pickup trucks and moved away. The trailer park on Tim Blakely's property became a ghost town of abandoned cement pads and derelict automobiles.

Only the area's original settlers, and a few newcomers who had fallen in love with the place, stayed and tried to make new lives. The exodus continued in the years that followed, as evidenced by declining enrolment at Ootsa Lake Elementary, which dropped from almost fifty in 1972 to a baker's dozen in 1988. District 55 closed the school not long after and, like Eurocan, sold the buildings.

Logging did not end with the big company's departure. Timber harvesting continues, but the industry has a new face. Government policies favouring larger companies forced the small ones out of business. Today, none of the mom-and-pop mills remain in operation, and tie-cutting, once a thriving industry, has all but disappeared south of Francois Lake. While the trees keep falling, most of them go to giant computerized mills along Highway 16 where they become forest products destined for unknown points.

People weren't the only inhabitants affected by these changes. Moose, plentiful when I was a child, are now scarce, and the caribou that Tim Blakely hunted in Tweedsmuir Park are almost extinct. Even some of the lakes we fished as kids are now barren. From an airplane, the country looks like a patchwork quilt that gets a little more threadbare each year. Talk has it that all the merchantable timber and most of the wildlife will be gone within a decade. No one likes to think about what will happen then.

And what became of the people in this book? Time, as we know, waits for no one, and many familiar faces are gone. Diggs's Uncle Jem died in his sleep one winter in the mid-1980s, the victim of an aneurism, and Granny Keighley passed away a few years later of pneumonia. She maintained her hermit-like existence, refusing to seek medical attention in Burns Lake, a town filled with "so many people."

The Blakelys outlived their trailer court and remained on the family homestead until moving to town a few years ago. Tim is now a spry centenarian. His wife Mindy doesn't plant trees anymore, but she looks just as she did when I was a boy.

Even my parents are gone. Their house, its asphalt roof bowed like the spine of a swayback horse, was abandoned when Mom's failing health made it impossible for them to stay. They moved south, first to Salt Spring Island and then to Sooke, where my mother struggled to earn a living as a freelance writer while my stepfather did as little as possible for as long as practicable.

Sometimes, for reasons that escape me, I go out to the old place. It's eerie inside, as if my parents left yesterday. Books still stand on the shelves, the pantry cupboards are full of canned goods with no labels, and tarnished knives and forks lie like forgotten soldiers in a drawer beside the kitchen sink. There are even a few articles of clothing in the bureau drawers and closets, including Mom's familiar down-filled coat, which has hung on a hook near the back door for so long that it's once again in fashion. It's as if my parents have gone on an extended camping trip with Brody and will be back soon. They will not, of course; Mom lost her battle with emphysema in 1994, and Olavi—after a brief remarriage—now lives alone somewhere on Vancouver Island. I have not seen him in twenty-five years and have no desire to.

My heart aches when I see my childhood home and the barren logging blocks along Ootsa-Nadina Road, but not all that made the area special is gone. The Wistaria Community Hall, its shingled roof and walls now clad in blue aluminum, still stands like an aged sentinel atop the high bench over-looking Ootsa Lake. The tiny church at the bottom of the hill is still upright too, and I hear that services are held there now.

Some of the people I knew as a child have remained. Brody, his hair and beard now a dignified silver, never left. He lives near Wistaria and drives around the Southside in whichever of his many vehicles happens to run the best, sometimes with valid insurance. He is old enough to qualify for a pension, and it has given him a steady income for the first time in his life. I hope he makes the most of it.

Our old bus driver, Bob, keeps house near his family's farm, and when I return to the Southside on day trips, Mona still greets me at the door of her cabin with that familiar shy smile. She has not changed a bit in forty years and is just as quick to offer a cup of coffee and a plate of cookies as she used to be. Her dog Shep, like Rusty, died a long time ago, and she now has a cranky blue heeler by the name of Tip. He defends the farm with vigor equal to his predecessor's, but I ignore all the yapping and snarling. It would take more than an ill-tempered mutt to stop me from visiting Mona because time spent with her is good for the soul. The woman's honesty and kindness, two qualities that seem in short supply these days, are as refreshing as a draught of water from one of the many streams that flow down Mount Wells. I drink from that watercourse as often as I can.

And despite all the changes on the Southside, something about the place still beckons. It's the original pioneer spirit, that sense of independence and unadulterated goodness that sustained the early settlers through two world wars, the Great Depression, and countless forest fires. Those who remained after the big logging companies left have stayed true to the place. The community's leaders are no longer the Blakelys, Lawsons, and Atkinsons, though. Now, the movers and shakers are people with last names like Cullen and Alcott.

That's right. The spell that draws me back to the Southside has worked its magic on my childhood friends. Diggs, the rebel, is now Diggory, the recreation commission president. He is married and has three teenage boys who look just like him. Seeing them is like stepping into a time machine; suddenly, I'm twelve again and about to embark on the great quest called life. And while my old friend finds different things to occupy his time, he still lives on the family farm and dreams of putting it into big-time production just as his Uncle Jem did.

Sean is back, too. After working in California and sampling life in several other states, he returned to the land his parents bought when he was seven. In the 1980s, he realized his boyhood dream of owning a new Jeep Cherokee. The pride on his face when he showed it to me almost brought tears to my eyes.

Nicky left but did not go far. He owns a moving company in Burns Lake and drives a school bus part-time. He is still handsome and, just as everyone predicted, married the prettiest girl in town.

Despite all that has happened over the years, the old saying "the more things change, the more they stay the same" applies to the Southside, the land of my youth. Kids still play hockey there. The names of their heroes may have changed from Lafleur, Esposito, and Cheevers to Crosby, McDavid, and Price, but they play the game with the same frenetic energy we did. And while residents dismantled the ice rink at Grassy Plains long ago, they have built a new one near Danskin.

If you drive south from the ferry landing on a cold winter night, you may see men and boys playing shinny under the rink's flickering electric lights. Dressed in everything from toques and parkas to the latest hockey gear, they will pass the puck to open wingers, fight for space in front of the net, and make spectacular end-to-end rushes that leave their opponents dumbstruck. From a distance, the ragtag group might look like we did almost five decades ago—and for good reason.

Because, hell, it might even be us.